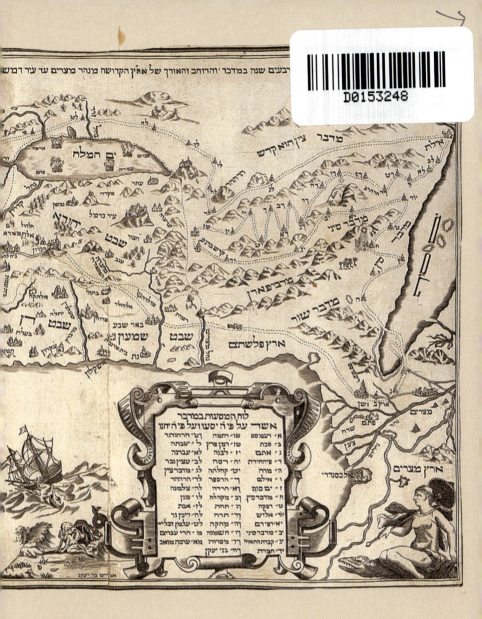

D0153248

909.049
B

Trenton Veterans Memorial Library
2790 Westfield Road
Trenton, MI 48183
734-676-9777

3 9082 11642 8858

√ OCT 2 8 2010

WITHDRAWN

A Short History
of the **JEWS**

A Short History
of the **JEWS**

Michael Brenner
Translated by Jeremiah Riemer

PRINCETON UNIVERSITY PRESS
PRINCETON AND OXFORD

English translation copyright © 2010 by Princeton University Press
This is a translation of *Kleine Jüdische Geschichte* by Michael Brenner,
© Verlag C.H. Beck oHG, München 2008

Requests for permission to reproduce material from this work
should be sent to Permissions, Princeton University Press

Published by Princeton University Press, 41 William Street,
Princeton, New Jersey 08540
In the United Kingdom: Princeton University Press, 6 Oxford Street,
Woodstock, Oxfordshire OX20 1TW
All Rights Reserved

Library of Congress Cataloging-in-Publication Data

Brenner, Michael, 1964–
[Kleine jüdische Geschichte. English]
A short history of the Jews / Michael Brenner ; translated by Jeremiah Riemer.
p. cm.
Includes bibliographical references and index.
ISBN 978-0-691-14351-4 (hardcover : alk. paper) 1. Jews—History. I. Title.
DS117.B7213 2010
909'.04924—dc22
2009046777

British Library Cataloging-in-Publication Data is available

The translation of this work was funded by Geisteswissenschaften
International–Translation Funding for Humanities and Social Sciences
from Germany, a joint initiative of the Fritz Thyssen Foundation,
the German Federal Foreign Office, the collecting society VG WORT
and the German Publishers & Booksellers Association.

This book has been composed in Adobe Jenson Pro

Printed on acid-free paper. ∞

press.princeton.edu

Printed in China
Book design by Marcella Engel Roberts

1 3 5 7 9 10 8 6 4 2

3 9082 11642 8858

TO MY MICHELLE

Contents

Foreword

THE HISTORY OF THE JEWS has been told in different versions ever since the end of the seventeenth century. The first historian who composed a comprehensive post-Biblical history of the Jews was a French Huguenot living in exile in the Netherlands. Jacques Basnage and many other Christian authors after him wanted to show that the Exile was divine punishment for the Jews' failure to recognize the True Faith, namely Christianity. In their interpretation, Jewish history was part of a Christian plan for salvation. Modern Jewish historians, in turn, who since the beginning of the nineteenth century devoted their careers to studying Jewish history using scholarly methods, wrote with other motives in mind. Many German-Jewish scholars of the early nineteenth century wanted to prove that their contemporary fellow Jews deserved emancipation. Therefore they told Jewish history as the story of a religious minority that adapted to the states in which they lived and contributed to their well-being. Later Jewish historians in Eastern Europe, by contrast, depicted the Jews as an independent nation among other nations—a nation, however, that had no territory of its own and also needed none, and whose political autonomy was expressed in the institution of the Jewish community. Zionist historians, finally, placed the land of Israel center stage. For them, the dispersion of the Jews among other nations was merely an interim phase. Wherever they lived, according to the Zionist historians, Jews have awaited return to their ancestral homeland, Israel.

In the face of such different interpretations of Jewish history, it would be presumptuous to attempt now, at long last, to write a "true" history of the Jews. Every historian today knows that one cannot, as Leopold Ranke believed in the nineteenth century, tell history "as it actually was." Historians, like all human beings, are products of their time, their background, their teachers, their environment, and their political convictions. They may regard one source as more reliable than another. It is important that they consider the questions that generations before them have posed, and also consider those sources that contradict their own interpretations, that they are self-critical enough to recognize where their own perspective on history threatens to serve political or religious interests.

Telling the history of the Jews is not easy, because people in almost every corner of the world have not only heard something about the Jews, but also have opinions about them. For a group that never made up more than one percent of the world's population, this may be no small honor. The perspective of distance that is essential to the historian's craft, however, is hampered when one encounters talk about the Jews as "God's Chosen People" or as "deicidal," when "Jewish intelligence" is invoked or "international Jewish finance" is pilloried, when Israel is praised as a bastion of civilization in the midst of barbarism or condemned as a brutal regime in the midst of a peace-loving world.

For many Jews, Christians, and Muslims, the Bible—and therewith the origin of the Jews—is the Word of God and cannot be doubted. Many nonreligious people who grew up in the Jewish, Christian, or Muslim worlds also know stories and sayings from the Bible—frequently in a secularized form detached from their original religious content—and have thus also acquired a certain picture of the Jews' early history. The later history of the Jews, especially in light of the Holocaust, is often perceived as an unbroken sequence of persecutions in which the Jews were always victims. The genocide perpetrated against the Jews in the twentieth century thus appears as the logical outcome of a precursory antisemitism. Finally, today the nature of the media's focus on Israel overshadows all other perspectives on the Jews. They are frequently viewed above all else as players in the Middle East conflict, and their history is then often understood as the cause behind the escalation of this conflict.

A history of the Jews must broaden the horizon so that it reaches beyond these themes. Within the given framework of this book, however, some chapters of the larger three thousand-year history can only be touched upon tentatively, while others must remain completely unmentioned. The golden thread that runs throughout this book is migration. Jews were not always wandering, but wandering has characterized Jewish history across all epochs and continents. Thus, every chapter is introduced with a story about some relocation. At the very beginning of each chapter there is an illustration from a Passover Haggadah. That often richly illustrated collection of Biblical passages, legends, and prayers is read in family circles on the evening of the Seder, the beginning of the Passover festival that recalls the Exodus from Egypt. Every era and every region has found and continues to find its own images for this story. The selected illustrations can thus stand for the many-sidedness of Jewish history.

No historian today, in light of the copious literature, can claim to be an expert on all periods and geographic regions of Jewish history. So I am especially grateful to a number of colleagues who took the time to provide critical reviews of some chapters in this book. My special thanks goes out to Eli Bar-Chen, John Efron, Jörg Frey, Eva Haverkamp, Matthias Lehmann, Christoph Levin, Jürgen Matthäus, Michael A. Meyer, Ken Moss, Marcus Pyka, Jonathan Sarna, Daniel Schwartz, Avinoam Shalem, Stephen Whitfield, and Israel Yuval. At Princeton University Press I enjoyed the support of Brigitta van Rheinberg from the first to the last minute. Clara Platter was an excellent editor, Terri O'Prey a most careful production editor. Jeremiah Riemer has been more than a wonderful translator. The English edition also profited from his valuable suggestions to improve the German original. I would like to thank the United States Holocaust Memorial Museum, where I was a Fellow during the academic year 2007/2008, for allowing me to take time off from teaching duties so that I could finish this book. My final thanks go to my wife Michelle who contributed the most valuable of all suggestions to make this a more appealing book.

A Short History
of the **JEWS**

לַעֲבֹדָתוֹ שֶׁנֶּאֱמַר וַיֹּאמֶר
יְהוֹשֻׁעַ אֶל כָּל הָעָם כֹּה
אָמַר יְיָ אֱלֹהֵי יִשְׂרָאֵל בְּעֵבֶר
הַנָּהָר יָשְׁבוּ אֲבוֹתֵיכֶם
מֵעוֹלָם תֶּרַח אֲבִי אַבְרָהָם
וַאֲבִי נָחוֹר וַיַּעַבְדוּ אֱלֹהִים
אֲחֵרִים

וָאֶקַּח אֶת אֲבִיכֶם
אֶת אַבְרָהָם מֵעֵבֶר הַנָּהָר
וָאוֹלֵךְ אוֹתוֹ בְּכָל אֶרֶץ
כְּנַעַן וָאַרְבֶּה אֶת זַרְעוֹ
וָאֶתֶּן לוֹ אֶת יִצְחָק וָאֶתֵּן

A Haggadah from Mantua (1560), alluding to a passage from Joshua 24:2 ("Your fathers dwelt of old time beyond the River"), shows Abraham crossing the river in a gondola. In this way, the picture alludes to the origins of the Patriarchs in Mesopotamia and to the long history of their wanderings.

1. From Ur to Canaan
A WANDERING PEOPLE

IN THE BEGINNING there were wanderings. The first human beings, Adam and Eve, are banished from *Gan Eden*, from Paradise.
The founder of monotheism, Abraham, follows God's command, *"Lech lecha"* ("Go forth"), and takes to wandering from
his home, Ur in Mesopotamia, eventually reaching the land of
Canaan, whence his great-grandson Joseph will, in turn, depart
for Egypt. Many generations later Moses leads the Jews back to
the homeland granted them, which henceforth will be given the
name "Israel," the second name of Abraham's grandson Jacob.

So at least we are told in the Hebrew Bible, certainly the most
successful and undoubtedly the most influential book in world
literature. Its success story is all the more astonishing when one
considers that this document was not composed by one of the
powerful nations of antiquity, such as the Egyptians or Assyrians, the Persians or Babylonians, the Greeks or Romans, but
by a tiny nation that at various times in the course of its history
was dominated by all of the above-mentioned peoples. And yet
it was precisely this legacy of the Jews that, with the spread of
Christianity and Islam, became the foundation for the literary
and religious inheritance of the greater part of humanity. By

this means, too, the legendary origins of the Jews told in the Bible attained worldwide renown.

The Hebrew Bible, which would later be called the Old Testament in Christian parlance, contains legislative precepts, wisdom literature, moral homilies, love songs, and mystical visions, but it also has books meant to instruct us about historical events. We are not dealing here, as a rule, with historically verifiable accounts. Nor was it the intention of the Bible's authors to describe historical events as authentically as possible. Rather, it was their theological interpretations that they placed center stage. Precisely when people began telling legends like those of the above-mentioned wanderings is as little known as the exact date when those legends were committed to writing. The core of the historical tradition handed down undoubtedly goes back to the time of the kingdoms of Israel and Judah, but the books of the Hebrew Bible first acquired their definitive form in the Persian and Hellenistic eras. The texts of these books give us more insight into the makeup of the Israelite and Judean population during those eras than during the earlier times they purport to describe, and so must be understood in the context of the Persian and Hellenistic periods. Only starting at that time can one accurately speak of a "history" of the Jews. If our account begins earlier, however, it is for one simple reason: The books of the Bible, quite independently of their historical truth content, shaped the consciousness of the Jews in so many different ways and for so many centuries that our familiarity with them is critically important for understanding Jewish history. This chapter, therefore, does not deal mainly with historically attested events, but rather with myths and legends the importance of which extends well beyond Judaism.

Mythic Beginnings

The Bible begins not with the history of Israel, but with the origins of humankind. Adam and Eve are not the first Jews, but the first human beings. In primeval times, according to the Biblical worldview, there were no different peoples. Only the sacrilegious effort to build the Tower of Babel (that act of extreme hubris whereby humans hoped they might ascend to God) led to divine intervention that split a heretofore united humanity into different nations with different languages. In Judaism, Christianity, and Islam, there is also the figure of Abram (Abraham after his transformation), who stands for the transition from polytheism to monotheism and, thereby, for what was perhaps the greatest revolution in the ancient world. From Abraham's family are also descended those peoples who became Israel's neighbors and enemies. Special mention must be made of his eldest son Ishmael, who (according to Islamic tradition) joined Abraham in building the Kaaba in Mecca.

It may be a reflection of the future Israel's own situation, frequently kicked around between the powerful Assyrians, Babylonians, and Egyptians, that the Bible routinely makes legitimate heirs out of younger sons. Isaac succeeded his elder half-brother Ishmael, Jacob his twin Esau, Jacob's son Joseph was the eleventh-born, and David the youngest of eight brothers. But the most important protagonist in the entire Biblical narrative is neither one of the above-mentioned heroes nor Moses, who liberated his people from Egyptian bondage, nor one of the prophets who, like Isaiah and Jeremiah, are undoubtedly among the Bible's most powerful voices. The lead character is first mentioned when Jacob wrestles with an angel. In the course of this wrestling match Jacob becomes "Israel," "he who strives with God." In contrast to the New Testament's Jesus and the Koran's Muhammad, at the center of the Biblical narratives we find a collective, the *people* of Israel. This is also what distinguishes the Bible from the contemporary Greek sagas that revolve around individual heroes like Aeneas or Odysseus.

Every culture has its own birth myths. In the case of Israel these are complex and manifold. The concepts that we would today term "religion" or "nation" are conceived as inextricably

According to the Biblical account, Jacob wrestled with an angel and became "he who strives with God"—as shown here in Rembrandt's representation from 1659.

linked with each other from the outset. This holds true in the consciousness of many Jews well into the modern era: To them the Bible serves both as an authoritative religious code of moral conduct and as a history book about their purported ancestors.

Abraham, who (according to Jewish tradition) broke with his father Terah's idol worship to revere a single, invisible God, is already the recipient of God's "national" promise: From his seed shall issue a great nation, chosen by God himself. In later Jewish self-conceptions, this election is not interpreted as a moral elevation over other nations; instead, it is above all understood to imply that special duties fall to the Jews, as elucidated in the religious law section of the Torah, the Five Books of Moses. That Biblical Moses, to whom God entrusted the tablets of the Law on Mount Sinai, stands at the beginning of a new understanding of religion. He is the central figure who

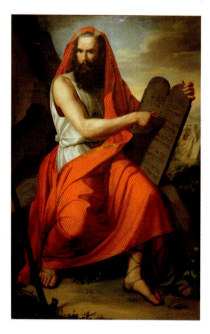

Moses served as the creative inspiration for legions of artists from Michelangelo through Rembrandt to Chagall. Jewish and Christian motifs thereby exerted a mutual influence on each other. Here is a nineteenth-century German-Jewish artist, Moritz Daniel Oppenheim, depicting Moses with the tablets of the Law.

not only leads the Hebrew slaves out of Egypt but also shapes them into a people.

The Exodus, for which (as with all of the historical events depicted in the Five Books of Moses) there is no extra-Biblical evidence, has entered the collective consciousness of successive generations as a decisive experience and, as it were, the "second birth" of the people of Israel and the Jewish religion. To this day Jews all over the world commemorate that wandering with holidays. During the Passover festival they eat unleavened bread, as if they were wandering through the desert, and on Succoth (the "Feast of Tabernacles") they build booths that are meant to recall how the Israelites camped out in tents during their wandering. Most impressive of all is the affirmation made on the evening of the Passover Seder in which all Jews declare that they should relate the experience of liberation from slavery to their own existence, as if they were conscious themselves of leaving Egypt and arriving in the land of Israel. Thus, over the course of centuries, the Biblical story became a paradigm for the historical sensibility of succeeding generations.

The Jewish yearly cycle contributes to this conception of history as oriented around Biblical events. Each spring Jews experience anew the departure from Egypt when they read out the story of the Exodus. Every winter they kindle the Chanukah candles that commemorate the rededication of the Temple in Jerusalem in the second century BCE. Each year they reenact the rescue of the Persian Jews as described in the Book of Esther. Even more important are the portions of the Torah recited in the synagogue on a weekly cycle. Since the same passage is recited within the same time frame in every synagogue all over the world, all Jews experience, so to speak, the creation of the world in autumn, the biographies of the patriarchs in the winter, and the wandering through the desert in the spring.

In the traditional Jewish conception of history, all the events from the centuries following Biblical times are of secondary importance. The next major event is relocated to the future: the coming of the messiah, who has been longingly anticipated for centuries and is expected to usher in an epoch where all people will live together in peace. By contrast, the time between Biblical prehistory and that messianic utopia is regarded as merely a lengthy interim whose events—save for a few exceptions like the destruction of the Second Temple in the year 70 CE—are hardly worth being recorded, much less collectively remembered.

Biblical history depicts a wandering people. These two terms—"people" and "wandering"—denote central elements of the Biblical conception of history that have shaped the Jewish self-image all the way through to modern times. Bible narrative revolves around themes of homeland and exile, as exemplified by the periodic destruction of Israel at the hands of the Assyrians and by the Babylonian exile of the Judeans. At the very least these themes afforded consolation and hope to Jews experiencing dislocation in later eras.

Although the land of Israel is promised to Abraham and his descendents in the Biblical account, fulfilling that promise is not so easy: Abraham left Mesopotamian Ur by way of the city of Haran for the land of Canaan, but then he moved on to Egypt and only later returned to the Promised Land. His grandson Jacob spent two decades with his father-in-law Laban in Aram, then returned home, but in old age followed his son Joseph to Egypt. Only four hundred years later did Moses and Aaron lead the now enslaved Hebrews back to the land of Israel. Yet by no means is this return a triumphal procession. Along the way the people of Israel constantly grumble and long for the fleshpots of Egypt. The land that is supposed to be flowing with milk and honey is a strange, inhospitable land in which there are giants and very few welcoming people. What had once been home has become foreign. Ten of the twelve spies sent out to scout the territory would rather return to the country from which Pharaoh had finally agreed to expel them following the ten plagues. Finally, under the leadership of Joshua, the Israelites conquer their unfamiliar homeland, yet neither Moses himself nor the generation of those who commenced that journey forty years before are allowed to cross the Jordan. Just as Odysseus returns home to Ithaca only after many tribulations, here too the homecoming resembles an obstacle course.

From Jacob to Israel

The dichotomous relationship between homeland and exile has continued to shape Jewish existence. There has always been an emotional relationship to the land of Israel, and yet even in Biblical times a large portion of the "children of Israel" lived in Egypt and Babylonia under Persian, Greek, and Roman rule. Many of the books of the Bible were shaped by the perspective of this Diaspora.

The term "Israel" has multiple meanings. Originally it was the self-designation of the northern kingdom of "Israel." If, however, one follows the Bible, it initially designates Jacob/Israel and his descendents, literally the "children of Israel." These include the twelve tribes who, according to Biblical tradition, divided up the land they conquered west and, to some extent, also east of the Jordan, and who then appointed judges and kings to lead them. After the death of King Solomon, thus the Bible continues, the country split into the northern kingdom of Israel and the southern kingdom of Judah around the capital city of Jerusalem. From then on the state of Israel represented only a portion of the "children of Israel." This northern kingdom of Israel, moreover, fell to Assyrian conquerors in the year 722 BCE, and its inhabitants were led into exile or enslaved. To this day numerous legends have circulated about the fate of these ten "lost tribes." Their descendents are supposed to have been spotted anywhere from East Asia to West Africa and South America. After the kingdom of Israel disappeared from the map, the southern kingdom of Judah appropriated its traditions and self-conception and defined itself as "Israel." The term "Israel" retained this usage even two and half millennia later, when a modern State of Israel was founded.

But at the same time that the southern kingdom of Judah was maintaining its provisional existence, the terms "Judeans" or "Jews" (Yehudim) took on added weight. Slowly the two terms began to fuse. In addition, we occasionally encounter the equally Biblical term "Hebrews" (Ivrim), after which the language of the people of Israel (or of the Jews) is named.

Similarly, a variety of terms are used to designate the territory of Israel. The original name was "Canaan." The Israelites called the country "Israel" or "Judah." The Assyrians turned the northern kingdom of Israel they had conquered into the province of "Samaria," named after its capital. After Judah was conquered by the Babylonian king Nebuchadnezzar and its capital

Jerusalem destroyed in 586 BCE, it became first the Babylonian and then the Persian province of "Yehud." Only in the Roman era did "Palestine" (after the Philistines) catch on, a term that was deliberately humiliating to the vanquished Jews. The formation of a people out of different tribal communities is always associated with the cutting off of that people from their surrounding environment; among the Jews this led to increasing isolation over the course of the centuries. Certainly the gravest difference distinguishing Jews from the other peoples of the ancient world was monotheism (with some exceptions, such as a brief period under the pharaoh Akhenaton in Egypt.) The notion of a single and (moreover) invisible God was the result of a long process of evolution. It only received its purest expression during the experience of exile and against incomprehension and frequently even robust rejection by the nations surrounding Israel. Other instances of the Israelites cutting themselves off from their surroundings that are described in the Bible may have taken place earlier and more rigorously. Among the numerous dietary laws, special mention should be made of the early taboo on pig's meat, which distinguished the Israelites from their neighboring peoples, in whose settlements archaeologist have found lots of pigs' bones. In later times, when other peoples also began adhering to monotheistic religions, everyday peculiarities like these helped Jews preserve their own identity. Already in the Bible there are multiple references to the special role of the Jews among the nations, most clearly in the Book of Numbers (23:9–10), in which the foreign seer Balaam calls Israel "a people that shall dwell alone, and shall not be reckoned among the nations."

The Bible itself (not least of all) played a decisive role in the formation of the Jewish people's tradition. Belief in the story of the Exodus out of Egypt and passage into the Promised Land, of the violent conquest of Canaan under Joshua, and of a powerful united kingdom under David, solidified into the myth of a past "Golden Age" to which the Jews might some day return. This Biblical narrative became their common historical legacy, a legacy that would shape not only their consciousness, but also the way they were perceived by those surrounding them, for centuries. For the first time a religion (or a people) would define itself by way of texts, through a holy scripture. In the course of time, the Biblical story became the paradigmatic narrative for a wide variety of cultures. Whether it was the subjects of the Ottoman Sultan Sulaiman recognizing in him the wisdom of Solomon, the Puritan settlers in New England establishing their "New Canaan," or black slaves on Virginia plantations singing gospel songs about the Exodus from Egypt, the reception of the Hebrew Bible by Christianity and Islam turned the history of early Israel into the historical model for a large portion of humanity.

From Legend to History

What we know about the earliest beginnings of the people of Israel comes only from its own sources, which are Biblical. Documents of other peoples that mention Israel during the first few centuries of its existence are extremely rare, and from the Biblical material alone we cannot derive any claims of historicity. It is a different matter, though, when an event that occurs in a Biblical narrative is supported by external sources and archaeological finds. But what incredible irony there is in the very first extra-Biblical document mentioning Israel's existence! On the stele of the Pharaoh Merenptah from the thirteenth century BCE, the extermination of a people is mentioned whose millennia-long history is supposed to have just begun at that time. Exactly what was then understood by the term "Israel" remains something of a mystery, but this inscription testifies to the existence of a group of people in Canaan designated by that name. What might the origins of these people have looked like?

Archaeological finds discovered toward the end of the twentieth century give a prosaic picture of Israel's beginnings. The patriarchal narratives may point to origins in the Mesopotamian Fertile Crescent, but this could also be the product of wishful thinking on the part of a group anxious to claim origins in the renowned city of Ur. The sojourn in Egypt may be related to the constant immigration of Semitic peoples into the land along the Nile, where famines were comparatively rare. A connection has been suggested between this episode and the immigration of the Hyksos, who had also been coming out of Canaan since the eighteenth century BCE, attained dominance over Egypt, and were then expelled from the Nile Valley around 1570. The latest scholarly research is rather skeptical about any link between the Biblical Exodus and either the Hyksos or another people mentioned later in Egyptian documents, the *Apiru* (or *Habiru*—marginal groups in ancient Near Eastern society whose name bears a resemblance to that of the Hebrews). Whether the Exodus actually took place is questionable. There are, in any event, no archaeological findings of any kind pointing to a massive immigration into Canaan from Egypt in the thirteenth century BCE.

Scholarly research today does not usually proceed from the assumption of a violent conquest; instead, it assumes that the people of Israel took shape in Canaan itself. Individual groups may indeed have immigrated to or returned from Egypt. What we know from archaeology indicates that the first Israelites were shepherds and farmers, most of whom lived in broadly autarkic village communities around the turn of the millennium. Some Biblical tribes certainly go back to the kinds of extended family communities that took their names from geographic points in their immediate surroundings. What the Israelites of

On a stele dated from around 1230 BCE, Pharaoh Merenptah celebrates his victory over different peoples. In addition to the Hittites, Canaanites, and Hurrians, this is the first time where we find the name Israel mentioned in an extra-Biblical source: "Israel is wasted, its seed exists no more."

The Gezer Calendar from the tenth century BCE is the oldest lengthy Hebrew inscription we know. It records, month by month, the most important activities of farmers, such as sowing, harvest, and viticulture, and thus affords us our earliest look into the daily life of the population of Israel.

that period understood by religion must be envisaged as a far cry from the idealized monotheism of a later era.

The history of Israel up to the beginning of the first millennium BCE is largely unknown. The heroic deeds of the Judges, David's powerful kingdom, Solomon's resplendent temple—none of these can be supported either by archaeological excavations or extra-Biblical sources. There is not a shred of evidence even for the existence of a united kingdom of Israel and Judah in the tenth century BCE. Only in the ninth century does this murky past begin to be illuminated. Extra-Biblical sources point to a northern kingdom of Israel that was gaining strength but that increasingly came under pressure from Assyria in the

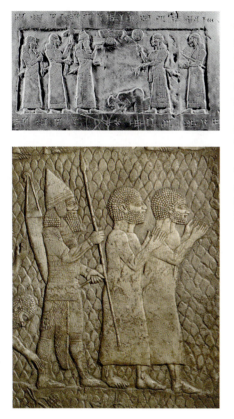

On the black obelisk from the ninth century BCE (above), some of the early military campaigns of the Assyrian King Shalmaneser III are depicted. In the second scene King Jehu of Israel surrenders and offers the Assyrians his tribute. The text underneath says: "Tribute of Jehu, son of Omri."

This mural relief from the palace of Sennacherib in Nineveh shows a family from the vanquished city of Lachish going barefoot into exile.

eighth century and was finally deprived of its sovereignty in 722. After this date all that remained was the southern kingdom of Judah, which up to this point had been a thinly settled and militarily insignificant state with few urban structures. Under King Hezekiah (727–698) Judah's population quadrupled and its capital Jerusalem became a major political and cultic center for the first time.

The political rise of Judah, however, was brutally interrupted by the military campaigns of the Assyrian King Sennacherib (705–681), who ravaged large parts of the country and demanded

King David as he lives on in legend: a powerful figure in a stately palace, with
the Book of Psalms attributed to him and the harp he was said to have played.
Appearing in a cloud are the words "ruach hakodesh" or holy spirit. The artist
who made this Haggadah in 1740 in what was then the Danish city of Altona
(near Hamburg) was Joseph ben David (originally from Leipnik in Moravia); he
produced a total of thirteen Haggadoth.

enormous tribute payments from Hezekiah and his successors.
The kings who followed him, especially Manasseh (698–642),
were obedient vassals of the Assyrian empire, and it was only
the latter's decline at the beginning of the seventh century that
restored to Judah a measure of political and religious room for
maneuver. Next the Egyptians assumed hegemony in the region
of Canaan, but they were mostly interested in the coastal region.

Under King Josiah (639–609) Judah rose to become a significant regional factor. Josiah attempted to consolidate Judah's power by concentrating official cult worship at Jerusalem. He declared that the once important rulers of the northern kingdom were responsible for its decline, since they had been venerating the God of Israel in rival "idolatrous" shrines of Beth El and Dan. Josiah aimed to turn the remnants of Israel spared exile and enslavement into adherents of the Jerusalem temple cult. One possible historical interpretation is that the transfigured past of a united kingdom would underscore Judah's predominance as the successor state to Israel. David, the legendary founder of the Judaic royal house and progenitor of the lineage leading to Josiah was supposed to have ruled over both kingdoms at the same time.

A long and rich history was attributed to the formerly insignificant site Jerusalem. The religious program conceived at that time was later, during the Second Temple era, turned into the foundation for a conception of history that focused on venerating the God of Israel in Jerusalem as the only and invisible god. The apostasy of the people of Israel—who had turned away from this God, worshiped the Golden Calf during their wanderings in the desert, and been idolaters under the last kings of Israel—had brought punishment in its train. By contrast, obedience to the God of Israel and his exclusive worship in Jerusalem always resulted in reward.

A section of the Second Book of Kings tells of Josiah's three religious reforms. In the eighteenth year of his reign, the year 622 BCE, a book of the Torah was reportedly found during a renovation of the Temple in Jerusalem, and this book served Josiah as the foundation for a new covenant concluded between God and his people (2 Kings 23:2–3). This "found" book is widely held to be an early version of Deuteronomy, the Fifth Book of Moses, containing the foundation for a form of Biblical monotheism (or Biblical "monolatry," worship of a single God while simultaneously recognizing other gods) that espoused the exclusive veneration of God in Jerusalem and established rules for Biblical festival days and numerous laws about social welfare as well as moral regulations. Whether it was the weekly day of rest or the injunction to free slaves after six years, whether love of one's neighbor or property law, many of the precepts laid down here became part of the modern world's legacy and the foundation for numerous other laws that are still in force to this day.

For reasons unknown, Josiah was killed in 609 BCE by Pharaoh Necho II in Megiddo. His four successors—three sons and a grandson—were unable to stop the advance of a menacing new power from the east, Babylonia. The Babylonian king Nebuchadnezzar II seized Jerusalem and established Judah as a Babylonian protectorate. King Jehoiachin was led into exile, along with the Judean elite, and his uncle Zedekiah was installed as a vassal king. Under the influence of the Egyptians, the Babylonians' enemies, Zedekiah attempted to break free from the empire. This ended in disaster. The prophet Jeremiah had warned against this self-destructive enterprise, which would end with the demise of the kingdom of Judah. In 586 Nebuchadnezzar laid siege to Jerusalem, leveled the flourishing center of Judah to the ground, and had the disloyal king Zedekiah's eyes put out. Like his predecessor Jehoiachin, Zedekiah was led into exile. When the governor of Judah, Gedaliah, became the victim of an assassination, numerous Judeans fled to Egypt, where they prepared themselves for a long stay. Jeremiah has something similar in mind when he writes to the Babylonian Jews (Jeremiah 29:5–6): "Build ye houses, and dwell in them, and plant gardens, and eat the fruit of them; take ye wives, and beget sons and daughters; and take wives for your sons, and give your daughters to husbands, that they may bear sons and daughters; and multiply ye there, and be not diminished."

Time and time again for centuries to come, Jeremiah's maxim served the Jewish communities of the Diaspora as encouragement to establish a foothold and plant roots outside their ancestral homeland. By contrast, another Biblical passage from Psalm 137 was understood, even by Jews in exile, as evidence of the Babylonian exiles' unalterable loyalty to their country of origin. It was later quoted by Zionists as a foundational text for the Jewish return to the Land of Israel: "By the rivers of Babylon, there we sat down, yea, we wept, when we remembered Zion." Over the next two and a half millennia, the better part of Jewish history would play out between these two poles, attachment to the old homeland and loyalty to the new one.

The Temple that was rebuilt under Persian rule served as the model for numerous illuminated manuscripts. In each case, it always reflected the architecture of the artist's immediate surroundings. In the Sarajevo Haggadah, which originated in Barcelona in 1350, the Temple recalls a medieval Spanish palace.

2. From Exile Back Home
PRIESTS AND PROPHETS

ON A CERTAIN DAY in the month of Nissan in the twentieth year of the reign of King Artaxerxes I, Nehemiah, one of the Judean exiles living in the Persian capital Susa who had risen to the rank of cupbearer in the royal court, took heart and addressed his king. As he poured him a glass of wine, he beseeched him: "If it please the king, and if your servant has found favor with you, send me to Judah, to the city of my ancestors' graves, to rebuild it." Not without first giving the queen a scrutinizing glance and also making sure that Nehemiah would later return to the Persian court, the king let his attendant depart. Protected by royal soldiers and supplied with letters of escort to the satraps governing the provinces beyond the Euphrates, Nehemiah set out on his journey. In the ruins of Jerusalem he immediately began rebuilding the city walls. It was around this time, too, that Ezra ended his exile and, after his return, decreed strict laws dissociating the Jewish from the non-Jewish population.

Restoration

The return to the Promised Land is the starting point for the two Biblical books of Ezra and Nehemiah (both mid-fifth century BCE). The Hebrew Bible's detailed and embellished accounts of the return may be consigned to the realm of legend, but a kernel of historical veracity seems to lie at their core. In contrast to Assyrian or Babylonian rulers, the region's new rulers, the kings of Persia, pursued a policy of freedom of worship and political pacification in the subjugated provinces. What is more, central sanctuaries like the Jerusalem Temple were to be fully restored in all their splendor within four years. According to the Biblical account, the Persian King Cyrus issued orders for the Temple's reconstruction as early as the first year of his reign (538) and also bore the costs. Finally, he was supposed to have issued an edict stipulating not only that the ritual objects used in the Temple be returned, but also that the exiled Judeans themselves be allowed to go back to their homeland.

Not all Judeans had been led into exile. Those who had remained behind in Judah had continued to conduct worship services in the ruins of the Temple. As they were later depicted by the returnees from exile, however, those who remained behind in Judea would eventually have assimilated to their surroundings if the leadership of the returned exile community had not placed the highest priority on the preservation of Jewish ethnic and religious peculiarities. It was in this spirit, too, that a new balance of power inside Judea would be established. The descendents of the northern kingdom were no longer viewed as part of one and the same people and ritual community. As "Samaritans" they had built their own sanctuary above the city of Samaria on Mount Gerizim, where, according to tradition, God had blessed the people of Israel (Deuteronomy 11:29). This conflict illustrates the Samaritans' claim (never fulfilled) to be regarded as part of the same people and the same cult as the Judeans in the south.

Things were different with the Jews of Egypt. To be sure, there had been a temple in the Jewish military colony in Elephantine since the sixth century BCE, yet the Jews there recognized the authority of the center in Jerusalem. Admittedly, as a letter from the year 408 shows, they also continued to view the Samaritans as co-religionists. And there were other ways in which they had adjusted to their environment. Their language was no longer Hebrew, but rather Aramaic, the lingua franca of the late Persian world. They recited a blessing for the God of Israel as well as for the Egyptian god Khnum. In contrast to the Jews of the Near East, and in keeping with their Egyptian environment, they prohibited polygamy and granted women the right to divorce. Spatial and cultural proximity to their Egyptian neighbors did not, however, save them from conflicts. These conflicts culminated in the year 411 with the destruction of the temple, which was never rebuilt. Nonetheless the Jewish military colony remained in Elephantine and was later taken over by Alexander the Great.

We do not know how many of the exiles returned from the different centers of the Diaspora, but a large number of them remained behind in the Persian empire or in Egypt, even after the Second Temple in Jerusalem was finished. Others, like Nehemiah himself, returned to Babylonia once their work was done. In Judea the new elite under Ezra took drastic measures to counter syncretic tendencies. In the Biblical account, Ezra is entrusted with the mission of implementing the "law of the God of heaven." In addition to the requirements to keep the dietary laws and observe the seventh day as a day of rest, separation from the rest of the population was the central demand. Circumcision, as a sign of belonging to the covenant with God, may have served to distinguish the inhabitants of Judah from some of the peoples in their environs, especially the Philistines. But even more important was Ezra's demand that all marriages between Judeans and members of other peoples had to be dissolved. The marriage of the high priest Joiada with the daughter of the Samaritan governor Sanballat showed how far this common practice had reached into the upper ranks of the people. Because of this marriage, Nehemiah had Joaida expelled from Jerusalem. It is doubtful, however, whether Ezra was able to prevail in implementing his rigorous demands.

In the Second Temple period nothing changed regarding the subordinate position of women vis-à-vis men. While women were also bound to obey the key laws, they did not share in the duties reserved for men, such as offering sacrifices, praying, and studying. Belonging to the covenant with God was primarily demonstrated by the sign of circumcision, reserved for men. This division of gender roles, one common to many cultures, did not prevent able women from assuming outstanding roles in this male-dominated world. Biblical heroines who saved their people through cunning or force were not uncommon. Consider the deeds of the judge Deborah and the stories of Esther and Ruth, after whom entire books of the Bible were named. Moreover, Judaism must have had a certain attraction for women (if not especially for them), since the sources indicate that the number of female converts to Judaism in subsequent centuries was relatively large.

The rebuilding of Jerusalem, associated with the mission of Nehemiah, and the implementation of laws concerned with segregating the inhabitants of Judah from their neighboring peoples, attributed to Ezra, were decisive steps in the reshaping of Israel. In contrast to many other vanquished nations, the Jews survived the catastrophes of their sanctuary's and their state's destruction not least of all by constructing an efficacious historical narrative. The Bible itself, large portions of which were written down under the impact of the catastrophe, formed an important foundation for this survival. Jews saw their own destiny reflected in earlier generations of Biblical heroes who had themselves experienced expulsion and exile. Just as these earlier generations had repeatedly returned to the Promised Land, the Jews themselves, with the help of Almighty God, would be able to rebuild their own state. Thus, as early as the period following the destruction of the First Temple, we already see the emergence of one of those strategies that would make it possible for Jews to survive catastrophes in later centuries as well.

A seal from the sixth century bears the inscription: "Belonging to Yehoyishma, daughter of Shamash-shar-usur." The female name assigns this to a woman with a name originating in the Babylonian exile: "The Lord will hear." Her father's name, of course, is a Babylonian one that means: "May [the god] Shamash protect the king." Conceivably, the father, who had already been given a Babylonian name as a result of acculturation, wanted to give his daughter a Hebrew name as part of a return to Jewish roots.

A New Self-image

Even in exile a new identity had taken shape, which also led to a new self-designation. Flavius Josephus was certainly not wrong when he remarked, a half millennium later, that those returning from the Babylonian exile should be called "Jews" (or "Judeans") and no longer Israelites (11.5.7.§173). This name change mirrored a far-reaching development in the people's self-image. The remnants of Judah, under the leadership of the returning elite and with the outwards signs of a community of blood, took shape as the new Israel. That new Israel, however, was actually characterized less by common ancestry than by the principle of a theocratic community with a canonical law now binding upon it. Being a "Jew" or a "Judean" did not just mean belonging to an ethnic group within a territory; it was now also a designation that included inhabitants scattered from Babylonia to Egypt who were all adherents of a specific cult—of a religion.

Even if post-exilic Jews had a self-image that consciously referred to continuities with pre-exilic Israel, the differences were considerable. Instead of kings in an independent state, priests under foreign sovereignty were now the decisive forces within society. If pre-exilic Israel had been a population into which one was born, the Jews of the post-exilic period developed mechanisms by which one could join the community or be forcibly excluded from it. Marriages with foreigners were now forbidden. To animal sacrifice at the Temple there was added—initially in the far-flung Diaspora—collective prayer in the synagogue. But individual prayer, meditation, and the study of Holy Scriptures also increased in importance. Judaism at the time of the Second Temple developed into a book religion; the process of canonizing the Holy Scriptures began. In addition, some of the future religion's fundamentals took shape, such as the idea of a future world after death, in which the just would receive their reward and evildoers their punishment.

Until the destruction of the Temple, the priests had been civil servants of the king. Now the high priests, who claimed descent from Moses' brother Aaron, were the highest religious dignitaries and simultaneously the most important representatives of a new theocracy. In their role as political representatives they sought good relations with surrounding states and nations, displaying at all times a tendency toward assimilation, which became especially apparent when they married non-Jewish women. In their religious function, by contrast, the high priests had to monitor the autonomy of Jewish ritual. There were thus tendencies toward assimilation to and dissociation from the surrounding world.

If the prophet Malachi is to be believed, enthusiasm and religious fervor soon abated and turned into neglect. The prophet criticizes the sacrifice of ritually unsuitable animals, "mixed marriages," and the practice of dissolving marriages with older women so that younger ones could be wed.

Prophets

Even for the period after the return from exile, we only have extremely scant extra-Biblical sources at our disposal. The greater part of our knowledge derives from the Bible itself, especially from historical writings like the books of Ezra and Nehemiah and the so-called Books of the Chronicles. They originated in the early post-exilic period, as did the prophetic books of Haggai, Zachariah, and Malachi. Portions from the prophetic literature are recited every week in synagogue following the Torah reading. Hence, the way that Jews have for centuries looked back at this post-exilic epoch has been substantially shaped by the prophets or the editors of the prophetic books.

To the prophets was attributed the gift of communicating the voice of God to human beings. There are similar figures to be found throughout ancient oriental literature, yet nowhere else do they exercise such a direct influence on political events. Miracles were attributed to some early prophets, like Elijah and Elisha; above all, they acted as admonishers of political rulers. Whereas Amos and Hosea were active in the northern kingdom of Israel before it was destroyed, Isaiah, perhaps the greatest of all prophets, emerged in the southern kingdom of Judah. As with Amos and Hosea, his central message was one of social justice. Ultimately, his name will always be linked with the vision of a coming time at the end of days, when "they shall beat their swords into plowshares" (2:4) and no nation shall learn war any more. From the house of David, according to this prophecy, a just king would then arise, under whom "the wolf will dwell with the lamb" (11:6). This was a radical expression of an ideal of world peace and universal justice.

With Jeremiah, a century later, self-criticism took center stage. The entire nation had sinned, and so it was God's plan to destroy Jerusalem. Resistance against Nebuchadnezzar was therefore of no avail. Only after a long exile would the people return in a purified state. Jeremiah himself remained in Jerusalem during the siege of the city, survived its seizure by the Babylonians, and was carried off to Egypt, where all traces of him vanished.

In the post-exilic prophetic books, on the other hand, we encounter yet other motives. Ezekiel consoles the people. The

Isaiah's vision of beating swords into plowshares has had an impact well beyond the Jewish world, serving as a universal symbol of world peace. This sculpture by the Russian artist Yevgeny Vuchetich was donated by the (atheist!) Soviet Union to the United Nations. It is located on the grounds of the UN building near the East River in New York.

children should not have to suffer because of the sins of their elders. Just as the dry bones will be gathered up and awakened to new life, so the people of Israel will return to its land and re-establish the Temple. Ezekiel's vision of the divine throne with the four cherubim, the dimensions of the throne-chariot, and the anthropomorphic depiction of God would later become the foundation for numerous exercises in Kabbalistic speculation.

The Emergence of a Canon

Not only did the Persian era give us the Hebrew block letters that are still in use today; this was also the period when the most important writings of the Hebrew Bible were canonized, a process that lasted well into the Hellenistic era. Canonization laid the foundations, both theological and legislative, for an autonomous Jewish community that knew how to disassociate itself from the surrounding culture and yet remain part of a superordinate social order.

The destruction of the Temple and the ensuing expulsion were, in contrast to similar events in other nations, not interpreted as a defeat for one's own god at the hand of other gods, but rather as the consequence of the Jews' apostasy before the only God. Unconditional belief in this invisible God, an article of faith already set down in the First Commandment, now became the point of departure for a religion shaped by the destruction of the polity. The experience of exile influenced the Torah. If one keeps this in mind, it becomes understandable why the Biblical narrative begins with the banishment from Paradise, continues with multiple expulsions from the Promised Land, and ends with the return to the land of Israel following slavery in Egypt. Just as Moses had died before he could return to the land for which he yearned, the establishment of a new polity remained a distant dream for those returning from the Babylonian exile.

The end of Persian rule saw a solidification of the writings that would go into the Hebrew Bible. They were divided into three parts, in order of importance: the *Torah* (the Five Books of Moses or "Pentateuch"), the *Prophets* (which includes such historical books as Judges, Samuel, and Kings), and then the remaining books, known simply as *Writings*. Based on the initial letters of the three Hebrew designations for these sections (*Torah, Nevi'im,* and *Ketuvim*), the Hebrew Bible is also called "*Tanakh.*"

With the formation of a Jewish Diaspora, it became especially important for the Jews to have a common scripture that would connect them with each other, now that there was no longer a common territorial tie. So, according to the Jewish reckoning, there emerged a work consisting of twenty-four books, a number which (in light of the doubling of the constantly recurring number "twelve") must certainly be interpreted as having a symbolic value. This number could only come about because the books of Samuel, Kings, and Chronicles were not

The caves of Qumran by the Dead Sea, where in 1947 the most important collection of ancient Biblical writings was found.

yet divided and the books Ezra plus Nehemiah, along with the twelve Minor Prophets, were conceived as a unit. There would be no further tampering with this unity.

Toward the end of the first century CE the canon of the Tanakh was definitively set. This meant that the two books of the Maccabees, the books Judith, Tobit, Sirach (Ben Sira), as well as other writings were no longer admitted to the Jewish Biblical canon, although they were accepted into the Greek and Latin collections that formed the foundations for various versions of the Christian canon. These writings, later characterized as "hidden" or "Apocryphal," often contain historically valuable information about the history of the Jews.

Additional Jewish sources, called pseudepigrapha, because they are named after their purported Biblical authors, such as Abraham, Moses, or Enoch, were passed down in some cases by the Eastern churches. Some had even disappeared without a trace only to be rediscovered in the nineteenth century. In the Eastern Orthodox churches the Septuagint (see Chapter 3) remained the basis for the canon, while in the Western churches it was the Vulgate, Hieronymus's Latin translation of the Bible, that provided the foundation. The Protestant Reformation returned to Hebrew textual sources. Hence, when people talk about the "Old Testament," they are not necessarily referring to the same corpus of texts.

For religious Jews, the Biblical text that was definitively set in the first century CE remains the word of God to this day, and therefore textual emendations of any kind are out of the question. The precise traditional text is based largely on the work of the "Masoretes," scholars who lived between the eighth and tenth centuries along Lake Kinneret (the Sea of Galilee), and who provided vowel and accent marks for an originally consonantal text. The two oldest extant manuscripts are the Codex Petropolitanus in St. Petersburg (previously known as the Codex Leningradensis), which was produced in Cairo in 1008, and the Codex of Aleppo (incomplete since 1948). The oldest handwritten Samaritan Torah goes back to the twelfth century. Another important source is the collection of texts discovered in 1947 in eleven caves at Qumran by the Dead Sea, which contains all the books of the Tanakh with the exception of Esther, most dating to the first two centuries BCE.

The Latin term *Biblia*, which comes to us via the Greek *biblion*, already implies that we are talking not just about a single book, but rather about a collection of books. The "Book of Books" is literally, in this sense, also a book that consists of a number of books.

וַהֲקֵבָה מְצַלוֹמְיֵנֵּי

זֵא לָמֶד מֵה

בִּקֵשׁ לָבָן הָאֲרַמִּי לַ

עֲשׂוֹת לְיַעֲקֹב אָבִינוּ

שֶׁפַּרְעֹה לֹא גָזַר אֶלָּ

עַל הַזְּכָרִים וְלָבָן בִּקֵשׁ

לַעֲקֹר אֶת הַכֹּל שֶׁנֶּ

אֱמַר אֲרַמִּי אֹבֵד אָבִי

"A wandering Aramean was my father, and he went down into Egypt" is recited by Jews every year at the Passover festival. In this Haggadah (the so-called First Cincinnati Haggadah), which was made at the end of the fifteenth century in Germany, the verse comes at the end of this page.

3. From Hebrew into Greek
DISDAIN AND ADMIRATION

The First Bible Translation

"A WANDERING ARAMEAN was my father, and he went down into Egypt," it says in the Book of Deuteronomy (26:5). In the Septuagint, the Greek version of the Torah, this is freely translated as: "My father abandoned Syria, and went down into Egypt." This first translation of the Hebrew Bible into a foreign language was made, according to Jewish legend, by seventy-two Jewish scholars working in Alexandria in the first half of the third century BCE at the initiative of King Ptolemy II. It was a political document as well as a religious text. Judea, like the rest of the Near East, had been conquered by Alexander the Great. After his death in 323 BCE, there were struggles for succession among his generals, leading in 301 to a tripartite division of the empire. In addition to the Macedonian part of the empire in Europe, the Middle East with its center in Syria was ruled by the Seleucids, while the Ptolemaic dynasty controlled northern Africa with Egypt at its center. The small, previously inconspicuous territory of Judea was now located in the middle of the conflict zone between these two parts of the empire—initially it was under Ptolemaic, and later (after 200) under Seleucid rule. When the Septuagint talks about how the forefathers of the Jews left Syria and went down into Egypt, its readers must have recognized this as an indication of the new supremacy of the Ptolemaic (Egyptian) over the Seleucid (Syrian) kingdom. In a similar vein, Jacob's devious stepfather Laban became a symbol of Syria, whereas Joseph (by contrast) found salvation in Egypt.

It was remarkable that the most important Jewish scripture, the Five Books of Moses, and soon thereafter additional Biblical books, were translated into Greek. We do not possess comparable translations of original religious texts from the ancient world. The Septuagint might be the very reason that the Jews were given the name "People of the Book"; it was through this translation that their books and therewith their religion became increasingly known among non-Jewish peoples.

But the translation of the Bible was no accident. In contrast to polytheistic cultures, monotheism is always about universal recognition. Peoples who themselves worship a variety of gods do not, as a rule, have any problem tolerating and respecting other peoples' gods. But it was different for the monotheistic Jews, as it would be later for Christians and Muslims: If only a single God exists, this must be the true God, who ideally should be recognized by people everywhere. The religion should be spread to other peoples, and the stranger could become a proselyte (someone who comes along). This idea of a universal religion was probably formulated for the first time in Isaiah 56:[1–]7: "[Thus saith the Lord: . . .] My house shall be called a house of prayer for all peoples." By contrast, most peoples in the ancient world, including the Athenians, reserved the cult of their gods for their own people. In the Bible itself, there is no one consistent position regarding aliens during the post-exilic era. Evidence can be found both for segregation and integration. The Biblical laws frequently stipulate that the stranger should be treated according to Judaism's own laws, like a part of the community, and that one should "love him as thyself" (Leviticus 19:34). While Ezra certainly espoused a strict policy of dissolving "mixed marriages" and maintaining an ethnically pure community, most of the prophetic books leave it in no doubt that non-Judeans could become Jews. But only the Talmud established a formal procedure for converting to Judaism.

Did monotheism, convinced as it was that it had recognized the truth of one invisible God, mean that those belonging to other nations and religions had no claim to God's grace? The Biblical book Jonah showed that this did not have to be the case. Here it is the sinful city of Nineveh that repents and is therefore forgiven by a merciful God. The book's Jewish author is critical of Jonah, who wants to have the iniquitous city destroyed, and (by way of contrast) the author also depicts a God who shows compassion even for those souls who do not offer Him sacrifices.

Early Separation

Tiny Judea and the Jewish religion were initially little noticed in the gigantic Greek dominion. Only with the expansion of the Jewish Diaspora and the translation of Jewish scriptures into Greek did interest intensify. As early as the first known writing by a Greek about the Jews, both positive and negative characteristics are mentioned. Hecataeus of Abdera, in a history of Egypt written at the turn from the fourth to the third century BCE, described the Jews as a people that educates its young to practice bravery. Moses is portrayed as a lawgiver distinguished for great wisdom and courage. But at the same time we find here accusations that are repeated later, especially by Tacitus, to the effect that the Jews separate themselves from their surroundings and lead a way of life that is hostile to foreigners. Hecataeus admits, to be sure, that this is a result of their bad experiences in Egypt, from which they had been expelled because they had been held responsible, along with other foreigners, for an outbreak of the plague. Here Hecataeus was probably mixing the Biblical Exodus tradition with an account of how the Semitic Hyksos were driven out of Egypt.

Later Hellenistic authors were less balanced in their depictions, and one may detect in their writings early traces of anti-Jewish polemic. Frequently, however, these authors' depictions have only been preserved because of the apologetics issued in response to them by Jewish authors of the Diaspora. Jewish apologists like Philo in Alexandria and Flavius Josephus in Rome felt called upon to react to these writings and publicly defend Judaism. All the same, a kind of counter-history to the Exodus narrative that was so critical for Jews everywhere was being disseminated in Greek literature. According to Josephus, the Egyptian priest Manetho who lived in Heliopolis described the Jews as leprous slaves, also afflicted with other diseases, who worked in the quarries until their leader Osarsiph (whom a subsequent glossator identified with Moses), broke all of Egypt's laws, and took arms against its king. Together with the Hyksos in Jerusalem, who had already been driven out of Egypt, they led a gruesome campaign against Egypt. Manetho, according to Josephus Flavius, was not the only Hellenistic Egyptian author to disseminate anti-Jewish polemics. Apion, a grammarian who lived in Alexandria in the first century CE, made numerous accusations against the Jews. He mocked the Jewish Sabbath, linking it to a disease of the groin (*sabbatosis*) that allegedly struck Jews after a six-day march and forced them to rest.

Some books of the Bible also told of anti-Jewish inclinations, most significantly the Book of Esther, which recounts how the Jews of the Persian empire were saved by the courageous intervention of the Jewish queen Esther and her cousin Mordecai. The ambitious official Haman is, according to this account, so incensed by Mordecai's failure to show him the respect due a king's advisor that he wants to have all the Jews killed. "And Haman said unto King Ahasuerus, 'There is a certain people scattered abroad and dispersed among the peoples in all the provinces of thy kingdom; and their laws are diverse from those of every people; neither keep they the king's laws; therefore it profiteth not the king to suffer them. If it please the king, let it be written that they be destroyed . . .'" (Esther 3:8–9).

It goes without saying that one cannot read the Book of Esther as an authentic historical source. It is noteworthy, to begin

The Esther story as told by Shahin of Shiraz in a manuscript from seventeenth-century Persia. In this scene, Arasir (corresponding to King Ahasuerus) convenes the most beautiful maidens in the land, among them Esther, in order to select a bride.

with, that the separation of the Jews from their surroundings emerges as a cause of persecution in this late text from the Hebrew Bible. It becomes even more interesting, however, when we look at the Greek translation of a nearby passage in the Septuagint. There the Jews, in the words of Haman, become a "hostile people" who disregard the laws of other peoples and commit the worst of misdeeds. And if one listens to Josephus' commentary on the Greek supplement to the Book of Esther, it becomes even clearer that the authors of the Septuagint were aware of these contemporary accusations against the Jews: In Josephus the talk is of a people that is the enemy of all humankind.

One should be careful and avoid making direct comparisons with modern antisemitism, which has a different context and needs to be treated separately. Yet even modern antisemitism did not arise out of a historical vacuum but had many roots, some of which go back quite far, perhaps even to pre-Christian traditions. These early elements include a rejection of the Jews as separatist and misanthropic. An explanation for such an accusation is not hard to find. If the Jews felt like Greeks, why then did they not revere the same gods as the Greeks? To revere an invisible god was regarded as incomprehensible in a polytheistic environment, special dietary laws were seen as superstitious, and treating the seventh day of the week as a day of rest seemed like a waste of valuable work time.

Two things should not be forgotten about the aversion to Jews that is documented in our sources. The Jews were not alone as objects of disdain. There were other peoples who also got a bad press in Roman and Greek literature, especially if they had been involved in tenacious combat with these two empires. At the same time, and partly for the same reasons that led to their rejection, the Jews were also accorded sympathy and respect. In some Greek texts they are esteemed as a nation of philosophers. The large number of Greeks and Romans who in subsequent centuries either converted to or sympathized with Judaism also testifies to a fascination that coexisted with repudiation.

Conversely, the Jews also appropriated the Hellenistic culture of their environment, both in the tiny territory of Judea and in the Diaspora. A Jewish author by the name of Ezekiel composed Greek dramas, while others wrote historical accounts modeled after Greek prototypes. Some later texts that found their way into the Biblical canon even testify to the influence of Greek thinking, such as the philosophical discourses in the Book of Ecclesiastes. The Letter of Aristeas, composed in the

Greek motifs on a Jewish burial chamber in Tel Maresha, a city in southern Judea, reveal the Hellenistic influence on Jewish culture during the era of the Second Temple.

second century CE and not included in the Biblical canon, is yet another illustration of the synthesis between Hellenism and Judaism. Aristeas tells the story of how the Septuagint came into being, and of how King Ptolemy II honored the Jewish scholars, who were equally well versed in Hebrew and Greek literature, by organizing a seven-day symposium with a sumptuous meal. At this banquet, Aristeas's Jewish scholars adeptly answer questions of a general nature, and their High Priest speaks much like a Greek philosopher even as he stresses how important it is to keep the Jewish dietary laws and to make sure that the Greek-speaking public becomes acquainted with the Hebrew Bible.

Not always, admittedly, would Jewish tradition and the Hellenistic lifestyle be bound together in such harmony. Philosophers and high priests, who were the spiritual, political, and also religious elite, had assimilated to Greek ways of life. But among the peasant population in the countryside, there was resistance to any type of Hellenization that went so far as to question native religious practices. And it was for this reason that social tensions exploded in the middle of the second century BCE.

יִבְנֶה בֵיתוֹ בְּקָרוֹב · בִּמְהֵרָה בִּמְהֵרָה בְּיָמֵינוּ ·
בְּקָרוֹב · אֵל בְּנֵה · אֵל בְּנֵה · בְּנֵה בֵיתְךָ בְּקָרוֹב ·
טָהוֹר הוּא · יָחִיד הוּא · כַּבִּיר הוּא · לָמוּד
הוּא · מֶלֶךְ הוּא · נָאוֹר הוּא · סַגִּיב הוּא ·
עִזּוּז הוּא · פּוֹדֶה הוּא · צַדִּיק הוּא · יִבְנֶה
בֵיתוֹ בְּקָרוֹב · בִּמְהֵרָה בִּמְהֵרָה בְּיָמֵינוּ בְּקָרוֹב ·
אֵל בְּנֵה · אֵל בְּנֵה · בְּנֵה בֵיתְךָ בְּקָרוֹב · קָדוֹשׁ

צוּרַת בֵּית הַמִּקְדָּשׁ וְעִיר יְרוּשָׁלַיִם תּוּבַב אֲכִיר

In one form or another, the Second Temple stood in Jerusalem for half a millennium, until it was destroyed by the Romans in the year 70 CE. Messianic expectations have been associated with its restoration, as in this Haggadah from Bohemia in 1728/29.

4. From Modiin to Jerusalem
A JEWISH STATE STANDS AND FALLS

IN THE WINTER OF 167/66 BCE, Syrian officials made their way to Judea in order to command the province's inhabitants to sacrifice at the altar of the god Zeus. When they arrived at Modiin, a small town on the slopes of the Judean hills, they ran into fierce resistance. One Mattathias, descended from a local priestly family, refused to obey the command, slew a collaborating priest, and destroyed the idolatrous altar. Together with his five sons and numerous followers, he started a resistance movement against the introduction of this alien cult that had come out of Jerusalem. Three years later, after a grueling guerilla war, Mattathias's son Judah, whose epithet was Maccabee ("the Hammer"), marched into Jerusalem in triumph and laid the cornerstone for political and religious rule by his family, the Hasmoneans, better known as the Maccabees.

The Hasmoneans

How did things get to this point, to this uprising that one side viewed as an act of political terrorism, the other as a struggle to free an oppressed people? In the year 167 BCE, the Seleucid king

Antiochus IV had issued a command that sacrifices be made to Greek gods in the Jerusalem Temple and simultaneously had revoked the law of Moses. Circumcision was made punishable by death, as was observing Sabbath rest. Outside Jerusalem, too, altars to the Greek gods were set up and pigs, which the Jews regarded as unclean, were introduced as sacrificial animals.

By no means did the Hasmonean initiative result in Judeans closing ranks in support of this act of resistance; instead, it ushered in a bitter civil war that pitted the rebels against factions that favored extensive assimilation to the ruling culture. These included the high priests, who, although they held to a few basic principles of the Jewish religion, had otherwise taken the lead in Hellenization. By paying a large sum of money to King Antiochus IV, Jason had gotten himself declared High Priest; in return for his appointment, he was prepared to transform Jerusalem into a *polis*, a Greek city-state. In the gymnasium of such a *polis*, athletic competitions in the nude were held in violation of Jewish law. Jason's rival Menelaus, an even more radical Hellenizer, bribed Antiochus with an even larger sum. In his eagerness to be appointed High Priest, he was not above plundering the Temple's treasury. In their assimilation to their environment, the radical Hellenizers went so far as to justify the laws enacted by Antiochus. If the highest Greek god was revered as Zeus of Olympus, why could one not also serve the Jewish God symbolically while using this name for the highest divinity? And why should a law that Moses had once ordained not be replaced by the law of an equally wise priest?

In parts of the population, there was major resistance stirring against such an interpretation of Judaism. Antiochus's unprecedented edict simply provided the final impetus to revolt. Preserving Judaism as an independent religion was the aim of the group around Mattathias and his five sons. After his death at the end of 166 or beginning of 165, he was succeeded by the third of his sons, Judah. Owing to a skillfully conducted guerilla war,

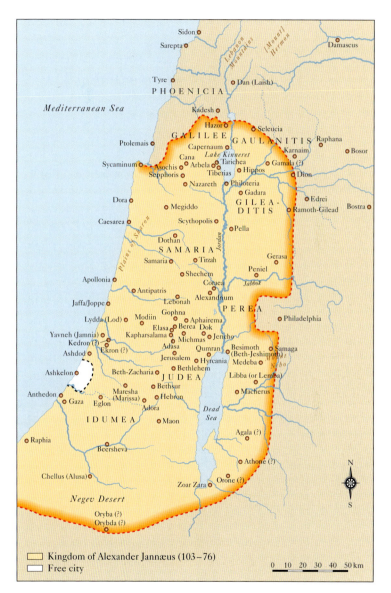

Palestine in the Maccabean era.

successful negotiations, and (not least of all) thanks to the lucky coincidence that there were other trouble spots in the Seleucid empire, Judah and his troops succeeded in retaking Jerusalem in 164 BCE and restoring the desecrated Temple. In the collective memory of the Jews, this act is preserved to this day in the eight-day festival of Chanukah ("Dedication").

What erupted in the events of the year 164 was essentially a conflict between particularistic and universalistic interests. If the Jews wanted to preserve their Judaism, they needed to defy a policy of the Seleucid state that demanded religious syncretism and the acceptance of universal Hellenistic culture as prerequisites for blending into a multinational state. For Antiochus, Judea's noncompliance represented an act of political and religious defiance. Apparently the Jews placed their one, invisible God above the Greek's highest god. In the second century CE the Roman historian Tacitus took the Seleucid side: "King Antiochus strove to destroy the national superstition, and to introduce Greek civilization, [with the aim of] improving this vilest of nations" (*Histories* V:8).

The frontlines were by no means as clearly drawn as the official sources would have us believe; for the resisters fighting excessive Hellenization were themselves unable to withdraw completely from the Hellenistic world in the midst of which they lived. In addition to waging military warfare, therefore, they simultaneously made arrangements that were fully in keeping with prevailing Hellenistic values. They concluded alliances with other states, like Rome and Sparta, that were actually potential enemies. In itself the fact that the Hasmoneans introduced the rededication of the Temple as a national holiday shows how complex the question of Hellenization was in that era. To this day the Chanukah festival is the only Jewish holiday that is not based on a book from the Hebrew Bible. What is more, the very act of commemorating a military victory in the context of a holiday is an imitation of similar Greek practices. Not even the rebuilding of the Second Temple under the Persians had found its way into the Jewish calendar of holidays.

After the High Priest Menelaus, branded as a traitor, had been executed, a moderate Hellenizer by the name of Alcimus was briefly installed as the new High Priest. The Hasmoneans were soon offering him resistance as well, and after his death in 159 they appointed one of their own as High Priest: Jonathan, the brother of Judah, who in the meantime had died on the battlefield. This brought the highest office in the land into the line of succession of a family that in fact had no legitimate claim to it.

Jonathan brought Judea its first major conquests in the northwest and northeast. He had come to power through an alliance with the Seleucids, but the very intrigues that had catapulted him into power brought him down again. He was captured and ultimately killed by opponents of his patron, the Seleucid king. Jonathan was followed by another brother, Simon, who succeeded in freeing Judea from having to make its remaining tribute payments. In 141 he had himself proclaimed Prince (or *Ethnarch*). Judea thereby became a sovereign monarchy again, for the first time since the destruction of the Temple in 586. The chronicler of the book First Maccabees quite consciously describes Simon's coronation in terms that recall the glory days of King Solomon.

After Simon was murdered by his own son-in-law, he was succeeded by his son Yohanan Hyrcanus. Under Hyrcanus' lengthy rule (134–104) Judea conquered major portions of bordering states. Now Samaria and Galilee in the north as well as Idumea in the south belonged the Judean kingdom. Following the brief reign of Aristobulus I (104–103), who was certainly the first to use the title of king, Alexander Jannæus (103–76) led Judea to its peak of military strength and its broadest territorial expansion.

By now, admittedly, very little was left of the Hasmoneans' original goal, purging Judea of Hellenistic tendencies. Even the names taken by this generation of Maccabees distinguished them from their fathers. In addition to their Hebrew names, each now also had a Greek name: Yohanan Hyrcanus, Judah Aristobolus, Alexander Jannæus (Jannæus or Yannai being a shortened form of Jonathan). Also telling are the coins minted by the Hasmoneans. They featured on one side nationalist inscriptions in an ancient script recalling the era of the Davidic kingdom, but on the other side displayed traditional Hellenistic symbols, from the wheel to the palm. Also contributing to the massive extent of Hellenization was the fact that a large proportion of the population in the expanding kingdom had only recently converted to Judaism. But in the era of the Hasmoneans certain central ideas of Judaism did take shape. The concept of *Ioudaismos* emerges for the first time ever in the Books of the Maccabees.

If we were to rely on the rabbinic tradition alone, we would have only scant knowledge about the history of the Jews in the Hasmonean period. The last book that found its way into the Hebrew Bible—a story that is apocalyptic even if no longer among the prophetic books—was the Book of Daniel, which was completed in 165 BCE. The two books of the Maccabees, which did not gain entry into the canon of the Hebrew Bible, are particularly interesting as historical sources, since they depict the events from different perspectives. First Maccabees, which was written in Hebrew, concentrates on the Hasmonean dynasty and displays a great deal of interest in details of the Temple cult and the geography of Palestine. Second Maccabees, by contrast, was composed in Greek in the Egyptian Diaspora and is preoccupied with the fate of the city and its legal system. While the first book, written from a national perspective, sees all non-Jewish rulers as bad, assumes that all other nations hate the Jews, and also describes intra-Jewish divisions, the cosmopolitan author of the Greek account puts the accent on benevolent rulers and good relations with the non-Jewish world, seeing the Jewish community as essentially a harmonious whole.

This coin from the reign of Alexander Jannæus (103–76) shows the Greek epigraph of the king next to an anchor on one side, and on the other side his name between the spokes of a wheel. The symbols and bilingualism testify to the influence of Hellenistic culture on the Maccabees.

Finally, the writings by the two most important Jewish authors of the first post-Biblical century, the historian Flavius Josephus and the philosopher Philo of Alexandria, have only been preserved for us (like the Apocrypha and pseudepigrapha mentioned in Chapter 2) in non-Jewish sources. Both biographies are intimately linked with the fate of first century Jews.

From Philo of Alexandria, one of the most important philosophers of his time, we learn details about the political situation of the Jews in Egypt. Philo himself belonged to a delegation that visited the Roman emperor Caligula after there had been a bloody conflict in Alexandria between the Jews and the Greek-speaking population in 38 CE. Ostensibly the issue was the legal status of the Jews of Alexandria; Greek-speaking Alexandrians felt that their preeminent position in the city was threatened. The actual causes of the bloody disturbances, however, went deeper. Philo describes not only the brutal massacre of Jews by the Greek-speaking citizens of the city, but also the profound hatred of the Egyptian population for the Jews. In the course of the disturbances Jewish property was plundered, synagogues were destroyed, and a portion of the Jewish population met violent deaths. The Jews resisted both militarily and diplomatically, but peace between the different factions of the city's population would be a long time coming.

Flavius Josephus, at one time commander of rebel troops fighting the Romans in the Galilee region, was brought to Rome along with his immediate retinue by the emperor Titus. He became a trusted follower of the emperor, and while in Rome composed his two major works. The first, written in Aramaic around the year 80 CE, was a detailed chronicle of the "Jewish War," of which only a Greek translation survives. Ten years later came a history of the Jews from their beginnings to the outbreak of the revolt against the Romans, written in Greek for a Roman readership.

The Breakdown of Jewish Society

Josephus offers a comprehensive account of the growing divisions within Judean society. Already around the time of the Maccabean uprising, three groups (he calls them "sects") whose origins can be dated back to the middle of the second century BCE had assumed their basic outlines: the Pharisees, the Sadducees, and the Essenes. Josephus speaks of them as three divergent philosophical schools that are nonetheless perfectly united on fundamental questions such as Sabbath observation, dietary laws, and the centrality of the Temple. What, then, were their differences?

The Pharisees (from the Hebrew *Perushim*, meaning those who separate or isolate themselves) wanted to recruit as many students as they could for instruction in the Torah, which they adapted to their times with new interpretations of God's "oral teaching." (These were later codified in the Mishnah and Talmud). By building a "fence around the Torah," they attempted to protect its core. Their interpretations, however, were influenced by the Hellenistic environment in which they took shape. The best example of this is the Pharisaic doctrine of a resurrection. The Hebrew Bible occasionally mentions a resurrection of the dead, but it is only under Hellenistic influence that the doctrine of a new life after death acquires central importance. This way (and only this way) can it be explained why there is not always a just punishment for the sinner and a well-deserved reward for the virtuous in this world. In the world beyond, as it was envisioned, injustices would be righted.

The Pharisees were opposed by circles linked to the priesthood, known as Sadducees (a name derived from that of the priestly family of the house of Zadok), who tried to lead lives as faithful as possible to the dictates of the Torah. For them only the Torah's written word had binding authority. This meant that they had no use for the doctrine of individual resurrection. Archaeological burial finds do indicate, however, that in the first century CE there might have been at least vague notions of some kind of existence after death among circles close to the priesthood. How can we otherwise explain a coin found inside the skull of the High Priest Caiaphas at an excavated gravesite? This is clearly a burial gift that accords with the Greek custom of paying an obol to Charon for transporting a dead person across the river Styx.

Among the apocalyptically-minded opponents of the Hasmoneans there were also some who intended to lead an eschatological war of the "Sons of Light" against the "Sons of Darkness." This group, of which we have an abundance of evidence from scrolls discovered at Qumran by the Dead Sea, is often identified with the Essenes chronicled by Josephus. This though the Essenes were arguably more like a heterogeneous movement consisting of several groups. The Qumran Essenes withdrew into the desert near the northwestern shore of the Dead Sea, where they lived in a monastic-like setting, did not allow any private property, and maintained a radical distance both from the Temple cult of the high priests and the rule of the Hasmoneans. The group viewed itself as God's emissary in a coming eschatological war that would result in the Temple being purified once again and the enemies of God destroyed.

It was ultimately the Pharisees who were able to prevail against the two other factions. Even though what they were preaching in their own name was separation, one reason they were ultimately successful was their willingness to incorporate new ideas from the world around them, among them doctrinal innovations such as resurrection. They came into close contact with political power in Judea until, under the reign of Queen Salome Alexandra (76–67), they actually began to conduct the affairs of state under their leading representative Shimon ben Shetach (Simeon ben Shetah). The fraternal struggles that ensued between Salome's two sons, Aristobulus II and Hyrcanus, ushered in the end of Hasmonean independence. Their rivalry made it easy for the Romans under Pompey to assume actual control inside the country. From now on Judea would be no more than a Roman vassal state. For the Pharisees, this loss of sovereignty was no insurmountable catastrophe. They appealed to those Biblical passages that recognized only God as Israel's king. In the same way, they said, the judge Samuel had initially refused to appoint a king over Israel and had only acquiesced after a long period during which the people insisted that they wanted to be like other nations. If God alone was now the legitimate king of the Jews, and if the Romans granted them domestic religious autonomy, the Pharisees might have an easier time implementing Jewish teachings than they would under the disgraced Hasmonean kings.

Maintaining a balance between self-preservation as a minority and adjustment to the surrounding majority would remain a distinguishing feature of Judaism's subsequent development. The Hasmoneans had come to power in order to remove a foreign cult but ended up as radical Hellenizers; the Pharisees defined themselves by separation from their surroundings, but they internalized some of the surrounding world's central concepts. In much the same way Judaism would later maintain itself as an independent minority that was never quite shut off from its surroundings, be the context Babylonian or Spanish, German or Polish, North African or American.

Revolt and Decline

There is a certain irony in the fact that the Romans, the very people who, when they were just timidly emerging as a power, had helped the first Hasmoneans onto the throne through a military alliance against the powerful Seleucids, were now, at the height of Roman power, administering a death blow to the Hasmoneans. The last remnants of sovereignty in the Hasmonean state, which had de facto already been abrogated in 63 BCE by Pompey's conquest of Judea, finally disappeared a quarter century later. The Romans dissolved the Hasmonean dynasty in name by appointing the Idumean Antipater their highest administrative official in Judea. The Idumeans, having only recently converted to Judaism, were viewed as parvenus by the old elites. The marriage of Antipater's son Herod to Mariamne, the granddaughter of two Hasmonean kings, was calculated to bolster the legitimacy of the new ruler.

From now on King Herod would rule by the grace of Rome, and he was merciless as he set about killing the last of the Hasmoneans, first and foremost the entire family of his wife Mariamne. She was executed, along with her mother Alexandra and her grandfather Hyrcanus II, and Herod had her brother, the last Hasmonean High Priest Aristobulus, drowned in a pond in Jericho. Josephus' characterization of Herod, accordingly, is scathing: "A man he was of great barbarity towards all men equally, and a slave to his passion; but above the consideration of what was right; yet was he favored by fortune as much as any man ever was" (*Antiquities*, Book 17, 8:1). Admittedly, Herod also left a legacy in stone that displays another side of the ruler. He was the greatest builder Judea had ever known. He had the Temple renovated and new cities established; topping the list were the magnificent port city of Caesarea and a rebuilt Samaria, renamed Sebaste after the Greek name of Augustus, where Herod promoted the imperial cult. It hardly comes as a surprise that the tax burden for these undertakings, along with the king's despotism, left his people with few positive memories of King Herod.

After the death of Herod in 4 BCE, Archelaus, one of his sons, was able to rule over Judea for a few years, but in 6 CE he was deposed by the Romans, who from now on exercised direct rule. They were admittedly dependent on cooperation with a local elite, which they found among the large landowners who first attained power and wealth under Herod. The old elites, especially the ancestral high priestly family, were driven from their positions or even out of the country. The "new ones," by contrast, had not previously played any role in governmental affairs; they were hence an artificially created political elite, and so held in little regard inside their own society. The new religious leadership was regarded by major sections of the people as illegitimate. Economic relations also changed after the death of Herod. The gap between rich and poor widened. After the great renovation of the Temple had been concluded, unemployment rose, while at the same time the rural population suffered the effects of a series of bad harvests. In addition, there was an appreciable growth in population owing to a relatively high birth rate. Opposition groups emerged that found support in the countryside and occasionally took justice into their own hands. There was overall a gradual but perceptible collapse of authority that from time to time erupted into chaos. The blame for this deterioration was placed on the Roman administration, which refused to convene the popular assemblies still customary under the Hasmoneans.

Against this background, it took only a minor crisis to trigger an open revolt. In the year 66 CE, in the largely Greek city of Caesarea, a group of Greeks sacrificed poultry directly in front of the synagogue on the Sabbath. As a countermove and protest against a lack of protection by Roman troops, some young priests decided to suspend the usual sacrifices made on behalf of the Roman rulers in the Jerusalem Temple. This sparked a rebellion. In retrospect, this uprising against the Roman world power was found to fail. Why the insurgents were nonetheless convinced they had a chance of winning is something that cannot be explained by rational arguments alone. One factor that played a role was their profound belief that their God was more powerful than the gods of the Romans and would, in the end, lead them to victory. Convinced of their God's omnipotence, the insurgents threw caution to the winds and tried fooling their adversary into thinking that they were stronger than they really were. In the long run, of course, such a tactic would be useless against Roman military might.

It would be a simplification, nonetheless, to see only the protest of the Judeans against the Romans. As was already the case at the time of the Maccabees, and would later be the case during the Bar Kokhba revolt, the struggle against alien rule was accompanied by severe intra-Jewish conflicts. At least three rival groups and their leaders—Eleazar ben Simon, John of Giscala (Yohanan ben Levi), and Simon bar Giora—quarreled over precedence in the independent Jewish state that lasted from 67 to 70 CE. The Sicarii (from a Greek name meaning "dagger men") a group notorious for turning up in a crowd of people and committing murder with knives concealed under their cloaks, were motivated not necessarily by ideological zeal, but also by pay.

The insurgents' considerable, if temporary, successes rested in part on turmoil within the Roman world. After the death of Nero in 68, the army commander Vespasian needed to withdraw from the region, and he became emperor himself a year

The Arch of Titus in Rome was erected in 70 CE and shows the triumphal procession of the victors who defeated Jerusalem. Among the booty, the plundered objects that stand out are the menorah (the seven-armed candelabra) along with several other items from the Temple (a golden table as well as trumpets). These cultic objects were stored in the Temple of Peace in Rome.

later after a ferocious succession struggle. His son Titus, after a siege that was demoralizing and exacted numerous casualties, finally vanquished the city of Jerusalem and its inhabitants. In August (on the 10th of Av) in the year 70, his troops destroyed the Temple, which was both the religious symbol of the Jews and the center of their military resistance. This calamitous defeat at the hands of the Romans pushed the ferocious intra-Jewish struggles that were taking place at the same time into the background of collective memory and historical writing. The revolt in Jerusalem was followed in the year 73 by a final sequel: the mass suicide of the Zealots who had entrenched themselves at the hill-fortress of Masada.

The failed revolt marked the deepest incision ever in the history of the Jews. Their central sanctuary was destroyed. The half shekel that had been paid as a tax for the maintenance of the Temple in Jerusalem was now replaced by the *fiscus juda-icus* for the Temple of Jupiter Capitolinus in Rome. Entire Jewish villages were destroyed by the war, and the population of Judea was reduced by as much as a third, according to some estimates. Jews were allowed to keep practicing their religion, but for many centuries restoration of state sovereignty was no longer a realistic option, even if more uprisings against foreign domination by the Romans were to follow, revolts that would also be met with bloody repression.

In the period following the destruction of the Temple, according to tradition, the oral teachings of the rabbis were set down in writing. This was the origin of the Mishnah and the Talmud. In an episode from the Haggadah, five rabbis gather at Bnei Brak and discuss the Exodus from Egypt: Rabbi Eliezer, Rabbi Joshua, Rabbi Eliezar ben Azariah, Rabbi Akiba, and Rabbi Tarfon. In this German Haggadah from the year 1460 they are depicted in contemporary clothing with garments made of heavy fabrics, silk, and brocade.

5. From Jerusalem to Yavneh
THE DIASPORA LEGITIMATES ITSELF

According to a Talmudic legend, Yohanan ben Zakkai, one of the most important Jewish law teachers of the first century CE, let himself be carried out of a Jerusalem under siege in a coffin. In the Roman camp outside the city he encountered the emperor Vespasian, who granted Yohanan's request to found a house of learning in the little town of Yavneh, located south of Jaffa near the Mediterranean coast. Not suspecting that this request would guarantee the continued existence of Judaism, the emperor granted him this wish. Historical scholarship has long proceeded from the assumption that we are dealing here with a founding legend about the Yavneh academy that was concocted later. The historical Yohanan was more likely to have been brought to Yavneh as a Roman prisoner en route to a penal colony. Yet it is legends like these that became the source of a new Jewish consciousness that would endure for centuries to come. The old governmental center with its political and cultic focal point had been destroyed, and what took its place was a spiritual center. Initially in Yavneh, but soon at many other sites, the interpretations of the Torah that the Pharisees regarded as an oral teaching parallel to the written Torah were also committed to writing.

From Oral Tradition to Written Commentary

Yohanan's legendary act of feigning death may allude to yet another survival tactic used by the Jews after another defeat.

Josephus and Philo have described cases in which the Jews were threatened with punishment and reacted by threatening suicide. The response of whoever was in power at the time was to revoke or postpone their punative actions. Josephus himself, after his troops had been defeated, was sealed in a cave where he confronted the possibility of suicide. And Yohanan played dead in order to save his people. In fact, it might be said that following the destruction of the First Temple by the Babylonians, the desecration of the Second Temple by the Greeks, and then the destruction of the Jewish polity by the Romans, the Jews had turned themselves into "survival artists." Each catastrophe required a different response. In the first case the response had been to fall back on a powerfully effective spiritual tradition, in the second the Jews reacted with a mixture of rebellion and accommodation, and in the third great catastrophe they responded, in part, by feigning death. Yohanan conceded that the Jews were finished as a political power, so he demanded "only" a spiritual living on. Once again, the formation of a holy writing was the key to survival. The Mishnah, written in Hebrew and edited by Judah ha-Nasi (the Patriarch), originated in the territory now called Palestine (after the Philistines) by the Romans. Over the next three centuries it was followed by the Gemara, composed in Aramaic in two different versions: the one in Galilee, and the other, more important, version in Babylonia. The Gemara is also called the Talmud, and together with the Mishnah it constitutes the most important written document of the Jews after the Bible. One should not imagine the Talmud as a law code that offers exact instructions requiring personal compliance. More typical of the structure of the text are debates between law teachers, the ahistorical character of which is immediately apparent because occasionally we hear rabbis from different centuries arguing with each other. Subsequent authorities determined whose opinion was binding, yet the minority opinion is also handed down, as a rule, in the Talmud.

This textual structure led to the formation of a technique of Jewish learning based on dialogue and dissent, a pedagogical style that has spread to several continents over many centuries.

What now took the place of the Jewish state was the Jewish Book, which became the "portable fatherland" of the Jews, as Heinrich Heine would later put it. No matter where one lived, the Bible and the Talmud provided both the foundations for daily life and a guide to deeper philosophical questions. Even if Yohanan ben Zakkai had not really founded the academy in Yavneh, the legend later told about him certainly did quite strikingly reflect the way in which the Jews had internalized the notion that Judaism could survive without a state of its own. The secret of this Diaspora people's millennium-long existence may lie in its unswerving faith in this idea.

The teachers ("rabbi" means "my teacher," and occasionally the honorary title "Rabban" was also used) now acquired a prominence comparable to that which the priests had enjoyed before them. The title of "rabbi," which is not attested prior to the period of the Second Temple, thereafter becomes a central element of Jewish society, so central that the era about to commence is often called rabbinic. How did one become a rabbi? Initially, and above all, this happened through study; but it was not long before the process also required entering into an explicit teacher-student relationship and a formal ordination at the end of the course of studies. If priests oversaw the Temple service, rabbis were associated with study and legal interpretation. Rabbinic Judaism emerged from the Pharisaic tradition, the Pharisees being the only sect (as Josephus called them) to survive the demise of the Temple, yet it represented a new phase in the development of the Jewish religion.

Compared with what we know of their religious doctrines, political disputes, and military conflicts, much less information has come down to us about the private life of Jews in the period following the destruction of their sanctuary. By and large, the picture that emerges is one that does not fundamentally differ from that of the surrounding culture. In the many villages and less numerous cities in mostly Jewish Galilee, Jews are attested in almost all occupational groups; they are involved in agriculture, handicrafts, and trade. Money changers assumed an increasingly important role as trade became more complex. Urban markets, which were held in *agorae* on the Greek model, attracted tradesmen from distant places. The sources testify to robust relations between the Jewish and non-Jewish population, and not only in the area of trade. Jews could live next door to non-Jews, and there was mutual assistance in private matters. Yet rabbinic discussions indicate a perceived need to draw boundaries on social contact.

The language of the Jews in the first centuries CE was barely distinguishable from that of the surrounding peoples. Like their neighbors, they communicated in Aramaic inside Judea and the Galilee, and in the Diaspora they spoke whatever language was customary. Greek often shows up in official communications, and numerous Greek loanwords slipped into the discussions of the rabbis. To be sure, the Mishnah was composed in Hebrew, but the language of the Bible declined in importance as a spoken language. Hebrew became the language of study and prayer that it would remain for centuries to come.

Though women's lives were for the most part restricted to house and family, we also have numerous examples of women who pursued careers. These included those engaged in traditionally female professions such as midwives, but there were also women in the characteristically male trades, such as selling foodstuffs and helping with the harvest. In any event, the man was obligated to provide his wife with the basics. These included food, a place to sleep, new clothes once a year, permission to wear jewelry and drink wine, a certain amount of pocket money, as well as permission to frequent the bathhouse, visit friends and family members, and participate in family festivals as well as burials. While polygamy had not been abolished among the Jews, it was certainly seldom practiced. As was the case with their non-Jewish neighbors, sons were more desired than daughters, but in contrast to their neighbors, there are no sources indicating that the Jews practiced female infanticide, a fact that amazed some Roman observers. The ability to write became a source of high status in the period, so much so that a father's duties came to include teaching his children both a profession *and* Hebrew. Whoever wanted to continue his education would do so in the *beth ha-midrash*, the house of study. This did not have to occupy a special building; teaching could take place in private houses, on the market square, or even in vineyards, as we have been told in the case of Yavneh. One was instructed in jurisprudence, but also in wisdom teachings. Synagogues—where a congregation would gather to pray, rather than to offer sacrifices as in the Temple, and which were not tied to a specific location—took their place in Jewish observance as an addition to the Temple. The idea that one could get spiritually close to the invisible God anywhere opened the way for the spread of Judaism as a universal religion.

The land of Israel did not, for the time being, lose its central role within the Jewish community, now rapidly spreading across major parts of the Roman Empire. In Palestine there existed—alongside such Hellenistic cities as Caesarea, transformed by Vespasian into a Roman colony, and Flavia Neapolis (today Nablus), near Shechem, with its magnificent Temple of Zeus on Mount Gerizim—a network of Jewish cities such as Yavneh and Lod. The Sanhedrin, the highest Jewish court of justice, was reestablished, initially in Yavneh, later in the Galilee. From here, in this period, were issued such key decisions affecting the unity of the Jewish people as the assignment of dates for the new moon in the Jewish calendar. In absence of a geographic center, religious unity was guaranteed only if all Jews celebrated their holidays at the same time. To these rulings were added other decisions of Jewish religious law, or *Halakha*. A special authority from the House of Hillel (the most important law teacher) was Rabban Gamaliel, who at the end of the first century was able to assert a claim to leadership of the Yavneh academy that was recognized both inside Israel and beyond.

The task at hand was to replace all the functions that the Temple and political center in Jerusalem had fulfilled with other practices. These practices now included daily prayer and newly structured holiday rituals. The changes may be illustrated by the example of the Passover festival. In Temple times sacrificing the paschal lamb had been a central component of the festival. Thereafter this was replaced by a communal meal on the eve of the festival within a specific ritual setting, the recitation of the Passover Haggadah. The commandment to eat unleavened bread for a week remained in force.

Under Hadrian (117–138) it initially looked as if Jerusalem might be rebuilt, but the emperor's policy took an about-face. He decided instead to build a Hellenistic city on the site, with a temple to Jupiter Capitolinus. The imminent transformation of the Jews' dormant capital into the center of a heathen cult triggered the uprising under Bar Kokhba that ended in the year 135 with brutal punishment of the Jews and a definitive end to their hopes for national restoration. As in previous uprisings, not all Jews joined the revolt; once again there was intra-Jewish dissension.

At first Bar Kokhba and his followers achieved some astonishing triumphs. The Romans suffered such harsh losses that Hadrian, in a letter to the Senate, dispensed with the usual clichés about how he and his troops were doing well. Yet there was no way that an ultimate triumph of Roman supremacy could be avoided. For the Jews this defeat would have even more serious implications than the destruction of the Temple sixty-five years earlier. With the fall of Bar Kokhba's last fortification in Betar, southwest of Jerusalem, not only were the Jews' last hopes for rebuilding a state of their own destroyed; the defeat also consigned to a distant future any concomitant messianic hopes that the Jews might harbor. When Rabbi Akiba, later tortured to death as a martyr, described Bar Kokhba as the "King Messiah," the answer given by Rabbi Yohanan ben Torta and recorded in the

This coin shows an image of the Temple in addition to the festive palm branch (lulav) for Succoth (the "Feast of Tabernacles"), and it indicates that the rebels had access to a mint in Jerusalem after the Bar Kokhba uprising against the Romans. Whether this means that they had really brought Jerusalem under their control, on the other hand, is not clearly proven.

Jerusalem Talmud (Ta'anit, 4:8, fol. 68b), was: "Grass will grow on your cheeks and still the son of David will not have come."

And so on the ruins of the old Jerusalem Hadrian built a new city, Aelia Capitolina. Jews were not allowed to set foot there, except on the 9th of Av, in order to mourn on the day commemorating the destruction of both Temples. Key practices prescribed by Jewish law, such as circumcision and observance of the Sabbath, were forbidden on penalty of death by Hadrian's decrees, as were houses of study. The most important law teachers convened in Lod and decided that, under the pressure of events, they had to bow to all of Rome's dictates in order to guarantee the Jews' survival, though they made an exception for public idolatry, murder, and incest. Under Hadrian's successor Antoninus Pius (138–161), almost all anti-Jewish laws were rescinded. Only the prohibition on circumcising people who wanted to adopt Judaism remained in force. Jews were once again allowed to practice their religion freely. When Emperor Caracalla made all subjects of the Roman Empire into citizens in the year 212, Jews, too, were promoted from subjects who were merely tolerated to Roman citizens with full rights.

The Rise of Christianity

The destruction of the Temple may have had been a decisive factor in the ultimate success of the initially Jewish sect that radically separated the concept of salvation from the goal of restoring political sovereignty and would later become its own religion under the name of Christianity. In addition to the Biblical, Apocryphal, and pseudepigraphical texts already mentioned, those writings that found their way into the canon of the New Testament also serve as important written documents about that period of Jewish history. We are here less interested in the question of what these texts tell us about the historical Jesus than in what they say about the cultural background of Jesus' earliest adherents.

In the religiously pluralistic Jewish society of the time, there was no shortage of charismatic healers who claimed magical and exorcistic powers, or of prophets, often apocalyptically inclined, who preached repentance. John the Baptist certainly belonged to the latter category. Jesus of Galilee himself roamed the countryside as a preacher whose message was especially addressed to the poorer strata and marginal groups in society. Since he appeared not only as a faith healer, but also as someone who questioned the authority of the Torah, he increasingly came into conflict with the Pharisees as well as with the Temple aristocracy, which finally turned him over to the Roman authorities.

In sermons that provoked the establishment, Jesus heralded an imminent End of Days when the existing Temple would be replaced by a better, a perfect Temple. There were certain similarities between his teachings and the teachings at Qumran, but such resemblances are more easily explained by the general popularity of apocalyptic beliefs than by Jesus' possible membership in that group. Even after Jesus' crucifixion, ordered by the Roman governor Pontius Pilate, his adherents constituted only one of many sects within the Jewish population. It was only as an escalating number of non-Jews both adopted Christian teachings and set aside the Torah's commandments that the break with Judaism occurred. While the destruction of Jerusalem and the Temple amounted to an unprecedented national catastrophe for the Jews, Christians regarded it as confirmation of their belief that the death of Jesus had ushered in a new chapter in history, in which the Temple and its entire cult of sacrifice had become superfluous.

Though Christianity as it later developed would have a decisive role in shaping the history of the Jews, the person of Jesus himself does not occupy a significant place in the consciousness of Jews of later generations. Occasionally, to be sure, there is a medieval Jewish text that tries to seek revenge for Christian persecution of the Jews by disfiguring the story of the Christian religion's founder, but for most Jews Jesus remained at best one of many teachers of law, and at worst a heretic and false messiah. Only in the nineteenth century did Jewish researchers turn seriously to Jesus the Jew and his history.

For Christian history writers of later eras, it is frequently the figure of Jesus and his milieu that is the focus. They read Jewish sources from this period with one-sided interest in the development of Christianity, and every now and then purported mentions of Jesus are even smuggled into older texts and presented as authentic. In the Christian interpretation, Christianity was now replacing the out-dated Jewish religion.

The center of Jewish learning and jurisdiction for Palestine's institutions shifted in this period toward Galilee in the north of the country. In Usha there was a new Sanhedrin, and new houses of study arose in Bet Shearim, Tiberias, and other cities. The chairmen of the Sanhedrin, the patriarchs (*Nasi* in Hebrew), viewed themselves as scions of Hillel, a claim that implied descent from the Davidic house. The Church Father Origen once compared the power of the patriarchs to that of kings. Domestically, they were regarded as chief justices and legislators who also had the right to ordain new teachers; externally, they were the highest Jewish officials, representing Jewry in Palestine and the Diaspora to outside authorities.

It was not until the fourth century that Christianity became the dominant power. Emperor Constantine first permitted it as a religion in 313, then a short time later made it into the state religion. An offspring of Judaism had ascended to political power over its parental faith. The consequences for the Jews were mixed. On the one hand, the Christian emperors as well as the Church Fathers gave special consideration to their mother religion, an attention they did not bestow on the heathen religions whose adherents would sooner or later convert to Christianity. On the other hand, a boundary line had to be sharply drawn precisely because of the new faith's proximity to Judaism, especially since Christians understood Jews not only as God's people but also as a nation of deicides.

Thus it was that ambivalence shaped the relationship between Christians and Jews from the very outset. In 325 the synod at Nicaea passed a variety of measures that aimed at a stricter separation between the two religions. Formally, this was undertaken by calculating holidays differently: In the future, Easter would no longer coincide with the Jewish festival of Passover. Old synagogues were allowed to remain, but no new ones could be built. Under Theodosius II Jews were turned into second-class citizens once and for all. In the Codex Theodosianus, compiled between 429 and 438, they were excluded from the army and all public offices. Under no circumstances would they be allowed to hold any offices in which they might exercise power over Christian subjects. This precept remained in place well into the modern era. Another long-lived aspect of the Theodosian legislative code was its frequently repeated association of Jews with heretics and heathens. The concept *religio*, previously used for both Christians and Jews, would now be applied only to the Christian religion, whereas Judaism would be deprecated as *superstitio*. The Codex Theodosianus did, however, ensure that Jews could practice their religion, and it protected their property, including their synagogues. This though several years before (in 415), the last patriarch, Gamaliel VI, had already lost the privileges of his office. The institution of the patriarchate ended with his death.

Church fathers like Hieronymus (340–420) and Augustine (354–430) laid the theological foundations for the Christian policy on Jews. Jews should remain alive in order to testify to the authenticity of the Old Testament and so that they might be converted at the End of Days. Yet at the same time they had to be humiliated in order for the truth of Christianity to be demonstrated on earth. This two-sided theological doctrine remained a cornerstone of Christian policy toward the Jews for more than a millennium: it was not acceptable to kill them, but necessary to discriminate conspicuously against them.

Most Jews took up residence outside the Christian world. After the Mishnah was concluded at the beginning of the third century, the center of Jewish life moved steadily eastward. Thus, it was Babylonian academies, especially the ones in Nehardea, Sura, and Pumbedita, that became the preeminent institutions of Jewish learning. To this day, the Babylonian Talmud is regarded as more important than the Palestinian or Jerusalem Talmud. The most important Jewish communities were also to be found outside Christian-ruled territory, in Parthian-and Sassanid-ruled Babylonia, where there had been continuous Jewish settlement for nearly a millennium. The Babylonian Jews, whose language was Aramaic, were certainly very aware of their deep rootedness in Mesopotamia, from which Abraham had once struck out for Canaan, and to which the elite of the destroyed kingdom of Judah had later been transported. Local traditions attempted to fabricate a line of unbroken continuity

Since the end of the nineteenth century, Jews increasingly perceived Jesus as part of the Jewish society of his time. In the painting *The Twelve Year-Old Jesus in the Temple* by Max Liebermann, Jesus is pictured in the midst of Jews praying in a nineteenth-century synagogue. In its original version the portrait had shown Jesus with a hooked nose, shoeless, and wildly gesticulating. Liebermann changed his depiction after an exhibit of the painting in Munich had led to public protests and even a discussion in the Bavarian state parliament.

reaching back to the earliest Jewish exile. A corresponding institution to the patriarchate in Israel was the office of the exilarch in the Diaspora, which continued to exist even after the patriarchate was dissolved. The exilarch (*resh galuta*), who was allowed to maintain his own court, also traced his line back to King David.

Under the rule of the Sassanids, who practiced the Zoroastrian religion, the Jews seemed, as a rule, to have lived without suffering any significant persecutions and to have been treated

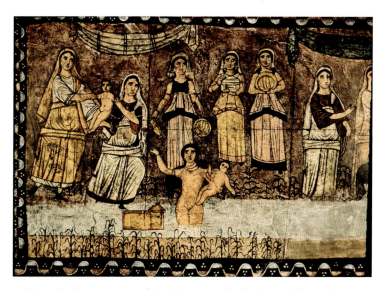

The resplendent synagogue of Dura Europos on the Euphrates offers insight into the life of the Jewish Diaspora in the middle of the third century. In contrast to later synagogue ornamentations, it is evident here that there were no inhibitions on depicting humans, as seen in the depiction of the baby Moses being found.

better than the Christian minority. A fourth-century Christian cleric by the name of Aphrahat complained that the Jews derided the Christians because of their lower status and lamented the fact that God was not coming to their aid. Our sources are much too sparse to draw any general conclusions about this, but it is certainly plausible that Jews were better off than Christians. Unlike Christians, Jews did not pose any danger: they were too few in number and had no state of their own. There is also no clear picture regarding contacts and mutual influences between Jewish and Zoroastrian culture. A reading of the Babylonian Talmud shows clearly that there must have been close neighborly relations. On occasion it is mentioned that Jews and non-Jews lived in the same house, that their clerics exchanged gifts on each others' holidays, and that there were definitely numerous similarities in their ideas about magic.

אלמא יחתאג אלי אנה אמרי וכוזפיהא מאא
ומסח כה אלכבז   ושרח חכמאיה
לפרקא ופלילה אלפסחהו אני יצלח הדא
אלפטור וירפע וישתרים מן כאקי אלבקול מתל
כרפס ובדבר ופצל מקד אר מא ויצלח עבאג
מן תנדה וגוז וסמסם יעגן בכל וסמי חליק
וירפע לופטאו נאור סלק וארז ומאלח וביץ
וירפע גמיע ערדך אלי ליילה לכאמקה עשר
מן ניסן פאול מא יטעמ אחד לבית יוב
אן יקרס עליכאס שראב בוראפרי הגפן
                    תם   קדוש פסח

בָּ‎אר‎וּ‎ךְ‎ יְ‎יָ‎ אֱ‎לֹ‎הֵ‎ינ‎וּ‎ מֶ‎לֶ‎ךְ‎ הָ‎עוֹ‎לָ‎ם‎ אֲ‎שֶׁ‎ר‎ בָּ‎חַ‎ר‎
בָּ‎נ‎וּ‎ מִ‎כָּ‎ל‎ עָ‎ם‎ וְ‎רֹ‎מְ‎מָ‎נ‎וּ‎ מִ‎כָּ‎ל‎ לָ‎שׁ‎וֹ‎ן‎ וְ‎קִ‎דְּ‎שָׁ‎נ‎וּ‎
בְּ‎מִ‎צְ‎וֹ‎תָ‎יו‎ וַ‎תִּ‎תֶּ‎ן‎ לָ‎נ‎וּ‎ יְ‎יָ‎ אֱ‎לֹ‎הֵ‎ינ‎וּ‎ מוֹ‎עֲ‎דִ‎ים‎ לְ‎שִׂ‎מְ‎חָ‎ה‎
חַ‎גִּ‎ים‎ וּ‎זְ‎מַ‎נִּ‎ים‎ לְ‎שָׂ‎שׂ‎וֹ‎ן‎ וְ‎יוֹ‎ם‎ חַ‎ג‎ הַ‎מַּ‎צּ‎וֹ‎ת‎ הַ‎זֶּ‎ה‎
זְ‎מַ‎ן‎ חֵ‎רוּ‎תֵ‎נ‎וּ‎ בְּ‎שִׂ‎מְ‎חָ‎ה‎ מִ‎קְ‎רָ‎א‎ קֹ‎דֶ‎שׁ‎ זֵ‎כֶ‎ר‎
לִ‎יצִ‎יאַ‎ת‎ מִ‎צְ‎רָ‎יִ‎ם‎ כִּ‎י‎ בָ‎נ‎וּ‎ בָ‎חַ‎רְ‎תָּ‎ אוֹ‎תָ‎נ‎וּ‎ יְ‎יָ‎
קִ‎דַּ‎שְׁ‎תָּ‎ מִ‎כָּ‎ל‎ הָ‎עַ‎מִּ‎ים‎ מוֹ‎עֲ‎דֵ‎י‎ קָ‎דְ‎שֶׁ‎ךָ‎ בְּ‎שִׂ‎מְ‎חָ‎ה‎
וּ‎בְ‎שָׂ‎שׂ‎וֹ‎ן‎ הִ‎נְ‎חַ‎לְ‎תָּ‎נ‎וּ‎ בָּ‎אַ‎תָּ‎ה‎ מְ‎קַ‎דֵּ‎שׁ‎ יִ‎שְׂ‎רָ‎אֵ‎ל‎

The oldest surviving Haggadah comes from the Islamic world and is a section in the prayer book of its most important religious philosopher, Saadia Gaon, who lived in the tenth century. The Hebrew Kiddush blessing is preceded by an explanation of the Seder in Arabic, though this is also written using Hebrew letters.

6. From Medina to Baghdad
UNDER ISLAMIC RULE

It was the journey of a non-Jew that would introduce the biggest change in Jewish society since the destruction of the Second Temple. When Muhammad departed from Mecca for Yathrib (later known as Medina), he took the first steps in the triumphal march of Islam that, within a single generation, would bring the entire region between the eastern Mediterranean, the Red Sea, and the Persian Gulf—and therewith the vast majority of Jews—under the rule of Islam. Between the seventh and thirteenth centuries, nearly 90 percent of all Jews lived in Islamic territories, which at that time were far more advanced than Christian Europe, both culturally and economically. The Jews who had been dispersed among different kingdoms were now united under Islamic rule, and they adopted Arabic, the language of the civilized world. The almost universal prestige enjoyed by the Talmud and rabbinic authorities from Mesopotamia to the eastern Mediterranean was also associated with political parameters conducive to Judaism's "standardization."

Among the families of Medina that hosted Muhammad, there were branches of Jewish tribes living on the Arabian peninsula. It is impossible to reconstruct how long they had resided in the oasis towns of Hejaz and in Yemen, but it is certain that they made up a considerable portion of those Arab cities' populations at the time of Muhammad's birth in 570. They spoke Arabic, had Arabic names, and were part of the local culture. Some features of their Jewish tradition had seeped into the surrounding culture, as had some traditions of the Christians living in the region. So it is not surprising that Muhammad, like many of his contemporaries, was acquainted not only with the Biblical stories, but also with later Jewish and Christian interpretations of the Bible.

Muhammad saw the Jews as natural allies in the struggle against heathen society. He recognized the Biblical prophets as prophets for Islam as well, and he hoped that the Jews would accept his new religion as their truth as well. The refusal of most Jews to adopt Islam led to a military conflict that resulted in the expulsion of two Jewish tribes and the annihilation of a third. In the Koran one finds traces of both respect for the Jews of the Bible and of Muhammad's conflict with the Jews of Arabia.

Theological and Legal Foundations

The position of the Jews under Islam, rather like their place under Christianity, is characterized by a permanent tension between a principled toleration and simultaneous humiliation. The theological relationship between Christians and Jews was, however, a closer one, since the religion's founder came out of Judaism himself. This closeness gave rise to friction that did not exist in the relationship between Muslims and Jews. The scripture that was holy for the Jews was also sacred to Christians, although the latter accused their "elder brethren" of not interpreting it correctly. In the Christian view, God's "New Covenant" had replaced the "Old Covenant," and the Jews had played out their historical role. In addition, the Jews were branded as deicides for allegedly having brought Jesus to the cross.

There were clearly fewer theological sources of conflict between Judaism and Islam. While Islam conceived of itself as the purer form of monotheism (the Christian doctrine of the Trinity and its sacred pictorial representations were far more suspect!), and while both Jews and Christians were accused of having corrupted Holy Scripture, the Koran had not replaced the Old Testament, Muslims did not regard themselves as the "new" Jews, and the fatal accusation of deicide was absent. Christians and Muslims shared disappointment at their inability to persuade the Jews to adopt their respective religions. But whereas the continued existence of Judaism posed a very specific theological problem for Christians, for Muslims Judaism was no more than an annoyance standing in the way of their effort to spread the Muslim faith to all the peoples of the world. In addition, Muslims recognized that Judaism, like Islam, was a religion of laws, that there were definite similarities between *halakha* and *sharia*. There were similarities as well in matters of everyday life; similar dietary laws, for example, including special rules for slaughtering animals. Given these congruencies, it should come as no surprise that many Jews greeted the Muslim conquerors in formerly Christian areas of the Roman Empire as liberators.

What was the legal situation of Jewish—and Christian—minorities under Muslim rule? To begin with, we need to emphasize that by no means were either Jews or Christians without rights or outside the law. The foundation of their legal status was the so-called Pact of Umar, which tradition ascribes to the second Caliph Umar, who ruled between 634 and 644.The actual content of the Pact is only known from versions dated some centuries later. In this document, which takes the form of a letter from the Christian community to its Muslim ruler, the Christian subjects affirm that they will accept a number of restrictions in order to live in peace under Muslim rule. The *dhimmi*, which initially included adherents of the "religions of the book" such as Jews and Christians, but then later came to include other religious communities as well, were accordingly allowed to practice their religion within the Islamic territories. But they were not allowed to build any new houses of God or even to restore old ones that had been destroyed; existing places of worship were not allowed to be of greater height than mosques. The *dhimmi* were not permitted to ride horses, carry weapons, proselytize, or publicly flaunt their religion. The influence of Romano-Christian legislation with respect to Jewish subjects is clearly evident. But one may also recognize an influence running in the opposite direction. *Dhimmi* were to be distinguished from those around them by way of speech and clothing. The ordinance introduced by Pope Innocent III prescribing a badge on the garments of Jews was thus inspired by Islamic models. In addition, subsequent laws prescribed that non-Muslims were not allowed to hold any state offices.

Of central importance was a tax already mentioned in the Koran, the *jizya*, which all *dhimmi* had to pay to guarantee their safety. Not only did it pose a financial burden, but it was also meant as a manifest way of demeaning non-Muslims. Testimonies to a variety of other degrading practices, such as a blow to the scruff of the neck, have come down to us. Nevertheless, Jews in territories ruled by Islam could invoke their payment of the *jizya* in order to underscore their claim to protection. A fundamental difference between the legal position of the Jews under Islamic rule and the way they were treated in Christian areas is that in the latter Jews were usually the only non-Christian minority, so that a unique "Jewish legislation" was enacted. Under Islamic rule, by contrast, Jews were subject to the broad category of legislation that applied to all adherents of religions of the book.

As *dhimmi*, the Jews were certainly not citizens with equal rights, and yet for most of them their legal position under Islam represented an improvement over their previous situation. For Christians and Zoroastrians, by contrast, two groups who had previously been masters of mighty empires, the situation had drastically worsened. They now found themselves to be "second-class citizens." Perhaps that is why there were many more Christians than Jews who converted to Islam. An additional difference had to do with political power. The Christians

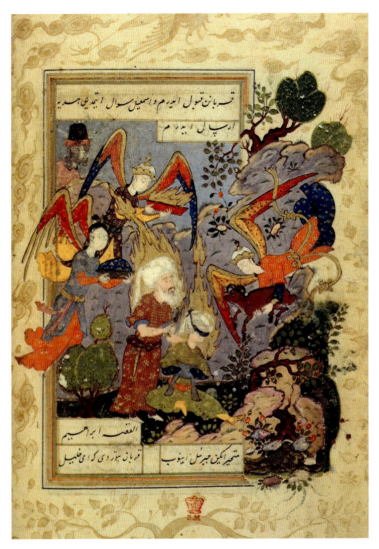

In a Turkish manuscript, "The History of the Martyrs from the Family of Mu-hammed" by Fuzuli from the end of the sixteenth century, Abraham is shown bringing his son Ishmael—and not, as in Jewish tradition, Isaac—to the sacrificial altar.

were aware that they had a powerful imperium behind them, the Byzantine Empire, whereas the significantly smaller minority of Jews had no such state. This meant that the Muslim rulers did not need to fear any conflicts of loyalty on the part of their Jewish subjects, whom they therefore frequently allowed into higher positions of power than was the case with members of the Christian population.

Exactly how the relevant laws on minorities were implemented de facto was a matter for the local authority. We know from a number of sources that some restrictions were little more than theoretical constructs during the first few centuries of Muslim rule in the Near East. For example, although horse riding was forbidden to Jews, the exilarch rode on a horse through Baghdad in a showy public ceremony during his inauguration. The documents that have come down to us from the tenth, eleventh, and twelfth centuries lead one to surmise that Jews dressed exactly the same way as their Muslim neighbors. New synagogues were built almost everywhere Jews lived, and there were even some churches whose rebuilding would surely have been forbidden if the letter of the law had prevailed. Somehow, the Muslims were able to arrive at legal interpretations that permitted these laxities. Nevertheless, it was by no means self-evident that synagogues would be built and renovated. When the Jews of Fustat (Old Cairo) were accused of having built a new synagogue in the year 1038, they had to bring forth Muslim witnesses who testified that this was really an old building that had been in the city before the Muslim conquest. The prohibition against non-Muslims holding state office was also frequently circumvented. It would hardly have been possible to administer an expanding Muslim empire without employing high-ranking Christians and Zoroastrians in Iran. And from Muslim Spain we hear of important Jewish statesmen, up to and including an army commander. Even so, there were also complaints against such appointments, which suggest that the

In the Ben Ezra synagogue in Old Cairo (Fustat), built in 882, the most valuable collection of medieval Jewish documents was found at the end of the nineteenth century.

formal legal prohibitions had by no means fallen into oblivion. Indeed, they would be rigorously followed in centuries to come.

Economic Life

We are informed at great length about the economic life of the Jews in the Mediterranean region by way of a unique discovery made at the end of the nineteenth century in the *genizah* of a synagogue at Fustat (Old Cairo). A *genizah* is a depository for papers that contain the name of God and therefore may not be thrown away. These include not only holy writings, but also private and business letters that usually begin with the set phrase "in the name of God" or similar formulas. The collective picture we get from the Cairene discovery, which today is stored in scattered archives from St. Petersburg to New York and from Cambridge to Jerusalem, is the panorama of an entire society. Private letters from the eminent scholar Maimonides were found here alongside business letters from Jewish and Muslim traders and records of rabbinic rulings.

Under Islamic rule, Jews were represented in almost all professions, in manual trades as well as in agriculture, in commerce as well as among physicians and government officials. There was no analogue to the Christian guilds that excluded Jews. At markets they did not occupy separate places, but as a rule sold the same goods at the same place as Muslim merchants. Trade did not have the negative connotations that it had in Christianity, and the sources confirm that there were numerous Jewish merchants dealing in long-distance and retail trade, and that there were working relationships between Jews and Muslims in the same firm. In these cases rabbis permitted Jews to work on Friday, while Muslims could work on Saturday, with the profits going to whichever partners were working on the day in question. Jewish traders who frequently moved from one locality to another were by no means an exception. In short, the role of the Jew as "stranger" that was typical for the Christian Middle

Ages did not apply in the Islamic region. Dealing in money was just one of many commercial activities that Jews also practiced in the Islamic realm, but in contrast to Europe, this was mostly done within the Jewish community. Unquestionably, as with every religious minority in medieval society, Jews occupied a lower social position in Islam, just as they did in Christendom. Yet time and again, individuals succeeded in breaking out of this niche and occupying socially important positions.

Most Jews lived in the urban centers of the Islamic world. Like every religious and ethnic group, they were concentrated in specific streets or neighborhoods, but there was no such thing as "purely" Jewish quarters. Since Jews followed special dietary laws that were quite similar to those of the Muslims, the latter were able to eat in Jewish (but not in Christian) homes. It was easier for *dhimmi* to participate in the cultural achievements of the Islamic world than for "unbelievers" to take part in Christian culture. Only a few Jews in Europe learned Latin, which was strongly associated with theological discourse. Arabic, by contrast, was not only the colloquial language of many Jews, but also the literary language of many Jewish scholars. It was only natural that Saadia Gaon, Judah Halevi, and Maimonides would publish their philosophical treatises in Arabic. Saadia Gaon even used Arabic terms for Jewish religious concepts. He talked about God as "Allah," about the Hebrew Bible as the "Koran," and about the *hazzan*, the prayer leader or cantor, as an *imam*.

The respect that was accorded Judaism in parts of the Islamic world was keenly noted by Jewish travelers from Europe. For example, Benjamin of Tudela, who traveled from Christian Spain to the Middle East in the twelfth century, marveled at how Muslims revered the Jewish prophet Ezekiel and undertook pilgrimages to pray at his grave. A short time later, the traveler Petachia of Regensburg was astonished to observe that even the graves of famous rabbis from the Mishnah were visited by Muslims. Persecution and expulsion of the Jewish minority were not unknown in the Islamic world, but they were exceptions to the rule. Only three major waves of persecution are known to us. Under Caliph al-Hakim (996–1022), who was viewed by both some contemporaries and later observers as mentally ill, and who is said to have issued a great many irrational orders, numerous synagogues and churches are supposed to have been destroyed. Many Jews fled his kingdom, and others converted to Islam. His son, however, allowed them to return to Judaism and rescinded his father's discriminatory measures. A pogrom against the Jewish community took place in the Muslim Berber state of Granada in connection with the murder of Joseph ibn Nagrela, the son of one of the most famous Jewish courtiers, Samuel ha-Nagid ibn Nagrela, in 1066. Here, too, the riots proved to be relatively short-lived, though they showed how vulnerable were even those *dhimmi* who had risen to positions of great honor in Muslim society. Longer and more serious were the persecutions undertaken by the Almohads, North African Berber tribes who brought wide portions of northern Africa under their control and presented both Jews and Christians with the alternative between death and adopting Islam. The persecutions of Jews in Yemen around 1172, which resulted in the conversion of a large part of the community, are known to us only through the missive sent by Maimonides, himself a refugee from Cordoba, to his coreligionists in Yemen. On the whole, these persecutions represented an exception within an overall relationship that, while not always harmonious, was nonetheless comparatively conflict-free.

Spiritual Life

For centuries the most important center of spiritual life for Jewish communities under Islamic rule was in Mesopotamia, between the Tigris and the Euphrates, an area that had already played a central role for the Israelites in Biblical times. In the middle of the eighth century, Baghdad replaced Damascus as the seat of the caliphate, after the Umayyads had to admit defeat at the hands of the Abbasids. A triumvirate determined what the Jewish power structures would be in this center of Jewish scholarship. In addition to the already mentioned exilarch (*resh galuta*), who occupied the Jewish community's highest political office, considerable influence was also exercised by the two *geonim* (singular: *gaon*), the principals of the most important Talmud academies in Sura and Pumbedita. From Baghdad important legal decisions went out to every corner of the Jewish world, mostly in the form of *responsa*. These were letters in which law teachers examined concrete questions of religious law. The *responsa* (in Hebrew *she'elot u-teshuvot*, meaning "questions and answers") form has been maintained to this day.

In contrast to the exilarchs, whose office was dynastic (their ancestors would be traced back to King David), the *geonim* were chosen for their erudition. There were always conflicts and disputes over authority between the different occupants of this office, best exemplified by the most famous *gaon*, Saadia ben Joseph (892–942). He was the author of philosophical works in Arabic as well as of mystical writings composed in Hebrew, and he translated parts of the Bible into Arabic.

Within the power structures of Babylonian Jewry, he did not shy away from conflict. Saadia Gaon directed his sharpest attack against a Jewish group that originated in the eighth century and had wide appeal during his lifetime. These Karaites refused to accept the Talmud as an "oral teaching" inspired by God and recognized only the Bible itself as holy scripture. Naturally, even the Karaites could not take the Bible literally, and they developed their own interpretations and adaptations, especially when it came to calendrical calculations, Sabbath laws (for example, they would not allow any candles to burn after the start of the Sabbath), and dietary laws. The rabbinic and Karaite schools of thought increasingly moved apart. Karaite Jews recognized neither the gaonate nor the exilarchate and had their own authorities. Saadia Gaon in particular took up the cause against this sect and, thanks to the influence he exerted, rabbinic Judaism prevailed. The Karaites did, however, become widespread between the tenth and twelfth centuries, initially in Palestine and Egypt, and later in the Byzantine empire and in Russia as well. Today there are still tiny Karaite communities in Russia, Poland, Turkey, the United States, and especially Israel.

Saadia's polemics against the Karaites have only come down to us in fragmentary form. By contrast, we possess large parts of his philosophical writings, especially his main work, *The Book of Beliefs and Opinions*, in which he becomes the first medieval thinker to attempt harmonizing rationalist Greek philosophy with the teachings of Judaism, presenting the Torah as revealed reason. Saadia thereby laid the groundwork for many other Jewish philosophers, and especially for Maimonides, who lived in Saadia's homeland of Egypt three centuries later.

Along with intense discussions about the correct interpretation of the Torah, there were equally heated debates about the coming of the messiah. Of the numerous messianic movements that took place during those centuries, only a few are known to us. As a rule, what happened was that a charismatic figure was declared the messiah, and was expected to redeem the world at some specific time—and then, when the foretold date came and went without any noticeable change, people returned to the realities of everyday life. The messiah's followers might have sold their worldly possessions so that they could set off for the Holy Land, and often they were subjected to the ridicule of their non-Jewish neighbors. The best-known case was that of David (actually Menachem) Alroy (or Al-Ruhi), who in twelfth-century Kurdistan initiated a messianic movement the offshoots of which could be traced all the way to Azerbaijan, Iran, and Iraq. On a certain night he was to lead the Jews of Baghdad on wings to Jerusalem. At the appointed time numerous people, hoping for imminent salvation, took to the roofs of their homes. When they were still awaiting their messianic flight the next morning, they became objects of ridicule in the neighborhood.

But messianic movements, which continued to exist in Judaism until well into the modern era, do illustrate one significant
point. Many Jews, in spite of their centuries-long rootedness in
their surroundings, continued to feel as if they were in exile and
waited longingly to return to the Holy Land. Attachment to the
land of Israel was also expressed in numerous prayers that were
recited three times daily. Many Jews undertook a pilgrimage to
Israel at least once in their lives, and some set out to die there.
This deep inner bond was also evident in financial support for
the community in the homeland. Emissaries traveled throughout Jewish communities worldwide and collected money for the
Jews residing in Israel.

In Palestine itself a small yet vital Jewish community continued to exist. A special component of that community was
the Masoretes (from *masora* meaning "tradition"), who were
active in the Galilee and attained considerable stature in the
tenth century. It is hardly an exaggeration to say that they were
responsible for a second canonization of the Hebrew Bible. To
be sure, the books to be included in the Holy Scriptures had
been selected long ago, but it was the Masoretes who decided
which of these books' competing versions would be considered
valid, and they defined the authoritative way to read them,
both by vocalizing the Bible's Hebrew letters (since the alphabet contains only consonants) and by fixing the proper accent
marks for public Torah readings. The diacritic marks placed
by the Masoretes underneath and above the Hebrew letters,
as well as the punctuation marks they set for sentences, can be
found to this day in prayer books and printed Bibles (though
not in the Torah scroll used for recitation in the synagogue).
The Palestinian center could not, admittedly, compete with
the more powerful communities of the Jewish periphery, in
Babylonia and (later) Spain. Yet, until the eleventh century, it
did constitute an important secondary arena of Jewish history
that would only decline in importance with the turmoil of the
Crusades.

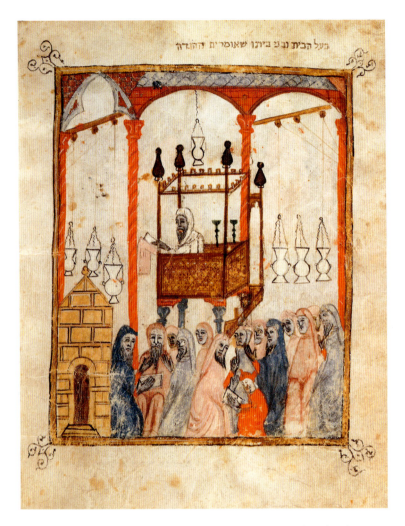

על הבית נבע ביתו שאומרים ההודה

This Haggadah, produced in mid-fourteenth-century Barcelona, has thirty-four full-page scenes that resemble the splendidly illustrated Golden Haggadah, so that it is has been called the "Sister Haggadah." This scene shows a recitation by a cantor in a synagogue whose entryway portal is portrayed in miniature on the bottom left. At the top there is this sentence: "The man of the house and his family read the Haggadah." Since, as a rule, such readings take place at home and not in the synagogue, it could be a little-known custom that is being illustrated here.

7. From Sura to Cordoba
SEPHARAD—JEWISH CULTURE ON
THE IBERIAN PENINSULA

IN THE TENTH CENTURY, so it is told, a Muslim mariner, perhaps the famous Ibn Rumahis, seized a ship that had set sail from the southern Italian port of Bari; on board were four rabbis from the Babylonian academies of Sura and Pumbedita. On behalf of the academies, the rabbis were collecting money for the dowries of indigent brides. The scholars were ransomed for a large sum of money by the major Jewish communities of northern Africa (Kairouan and Alexandria), as well as by the community in Cordoba, and they ultimately rose to great prominence in their new communities. Among the hostages was Rabbi Moses ben Enoch, who upon his arrival in Cordoba made his way to the Talmud school there and began studying under Rabbi Nathan. Upon hearing his new student's learned observations, Rabbi Nathan is reported to have immediately resigned his post and proposed Rabbi Moses as the city's new chief rabbi and judge. Under its new spiritual leader, Cordoba became a site of Jewish scholarship, independent of the Babylonian centers.

This legend, which was recorded by the Toledan philosopher Abraham ibn Daud in his twelfth-century *Book of Tradition* (*Sefer ha-kabbala*), symbolizes the transfer of the center of Jewish life from Mesopotamia in the East to the Iberian peninsula in the West and Jewish Iberia's spiritual independence from Babylonia. By this time, in fact, Cordoba and Toledo had acceded to the legacy of Sura and Pumbedita.

One must ask, in the first place, what the term "Spanish Jewry" meant in this period. Strictly speaking, there was no such entity as "Spain" in the Middle Ages. In addition to the region's ever-shifting Muslim dominions, there were also several Christian kingdoms on the Iberian peninsula: alongside Castile and Aragon, for example, there was Leon in the north, Portugal in the West, and Navarre in the east. Only after the 1469 marriage of Ferdinand and Isabella, both heirs to their respective thrones, did a Spanish nation-state come into existence, a state that then went on to incorporate the last remaining Islamic territories around Granada. But even in the absence of any unified political rule, the Iberian peninsula had obtained a uniform name, *Sepharad*, in Jewish terminology. In Jewish consciousness, the map of Europe is also a Biblical map, as described (for example) by the prophet Obadiah (1:20): "And the captivity of this host of the children of Israel, that are among the Canaanites, even unto Zarephath, and the captivity of Jerusalem, that is in Sepharad, shall possess the cities of the South." The Zarephath that the exiles from Israel were supposed to have reached was located on the Phoenician coast, and Obadiah's Sepharad was in Asia Minor. Later, when Jewish settlement extended as far as Europe, the actual geography of the Jewish people may have changed, but in their collective imagination they remained rooted in the Biblical world. Thus Zarephath became France, and Sepharad the Iberian peninsula. To this day, in Modern Hebrew, these Biblical terms denote the two European states of France and Spain.

A "Golden Age"?

A major part of the epoch that later observers would call the Iberian "Golden Age" took place under Muslim rule in "al-Andalus." The victory of the Muslims at Xeres de la Frontera in 711 began their rapid conquest of the Visigoth empire, in which the Jews had been harshly excluded through numerous laws enacted by Christian councils. In contrast to this unhappy previous chapter in Ibero-Jewish history, the rule of the Umayyads really did initiate a Golden Age, the beginning of which is usually dated to coincide with the foundation of the caliphate in Cordoba by Abd al-Rahman III in 929. While most of the cultural creativity of Spanish Jewry took place under Muslim rule, the usual subdivision into a tolerant Muslim and an intolerant Christian society is an oversimplification. Under Christian as well as under Muslim rule, it was possible to regard Jews in ways that could be either friendly or hostile. Both the New Testament and the Koran contained a great many passages that allowed Jews to be honored as elder brothers and sisters, but material that could be invoked to justify Jews' disenfranchisement and marginalization was equally plentiful.

The history of the Jews during what was almost a millennium in Iberia testifies all too well to this mixed record. When the Muslims conquered the Visigoth empire, the Jews living there experienced this as liberation from Christian subjugation. Over the next several centuries they enjoyed the permission to practice their religion relatively freely, coupled with widespread opportunities for participating in every aspect of social life. But with the triumph of more radical Muslim rulers from northern Africa, first the Almoravids and then the Almohads, the tables turned. If, in previous centuries, Jews had fled Christian for Muslim regions, now they were leaving the Muslim south for the Christian north. The *Reconquista* that was advancing through the peninsula did not automatically mean the end of Jewish life. The partition of the peninsula into these two zones of political rule, moreover, blurs our picture of cultural identities that were far more complex. Even in the Christian realm, poets and philosophers cultivated the Arabic language and continued to participate in the mixed culture that had originated here.

What, then, were the achievements of the so-called Golden Age? Between the tenth and twelfth centuries, the Jewish communities on the Iberian peninsula were to produce major poets, philosophers, Biblical exegetes, scientists, and statesmen. It is characteristic about their achievements that several of these qualities were often united in a single person. Thus, for example, Hasdai ibn Shaprut, born in Jaen at the beginning of the tenth century, was not only a close political adviser of Caliph Abd al-Rahman III, a high official supervising customs inspections, and head of the Jewish community, but also the translator of an important medical manual from Greek into Arabic and a promoter of Hebrew language and literature. He officiated as a diplomat in negotiations between the caliphate and Christian rulers and established at his court in Cordoba a center for Hebrew literature and linguistics. By conducting linguistic research into Hebrew and refining the Biblical text, he continued along the path started by Saadia Gaon and the Masoretes.

The debate between the two most important scholars at Hasdai's court, Menachem ben Saruk and Dunash ibn Labrat, is characteristic of a rivalry between proponents of Arabic and Hebrew that also took place within the Jewish community of the tenth century: Menachem, who had arrived at Cordoba from Tortosa in the north, came to prominence not only as a prolific poet, but also owing to his *Machberet* (meaning "Notebook"), the first Hebraic dictionary composed in Hebrew. According to him, one could not transfer the metric verse system used in Arabic to an

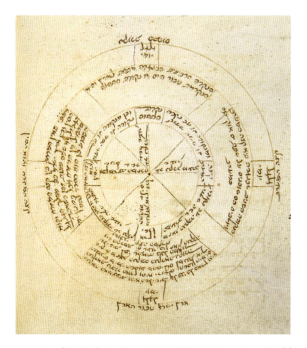

In a manuscript of the Sefer ha-Kuzari by Judah Halevi, produced in fifteenth-century Spain or Italy, one sees this sketch of the celestial spheres.

autonomous Hebrew language. But this was precisely what Dunash, his rival who had arrived at Hasdai's court in Cordoba from Fez in Morocco, aimed to do. For Dunash not only Arabic poetry, but also Arab grammar, served as models for Hebrew. This debate showed how both languages' claims to divine origins—whether revealed in the Bible or the Koran—had been translated into intra-Jewish discourses.

Perhaps the most versatile Jewish politician and scholar was Samuel ibn Nagrela, originally from Cordoba but active in Granada and better known by his Hebrew title, Shmuel ha-Nagid ("Samuel the Prince"). At the court of Granada, he ascended to the rank of vizier and army general; while in the Jewish community he was distinguished by his considerable Talmudic erudition. His writings in verse are regarded as some of the greatest treasures of medieval Hebrew poetry. In these poems he immortalized his experiences with warfare as well as his devotion to God and the Jewish religion. To this day, some of his literary creations in the form of *piyyutim*, religious-liturgical poems, have been incorporated into Jewish services around the world. Yet his family history clearly illustrates the tragedy and insecurity of Judaism's lot as well. His son became a victim of court intrigue in an episode that marks the beginning of the end of the "Golden Age." The fragmentation of the caliphate into numerous smaller principalities, the *taifas*, led to political instability, strengthened the Christian north of the country (Toledo was conquered by the Christians in 1085), and ultimately led to the invasion of Berber tribes from northern Africa, the Almoravids (who crossed the Straits of Gibraltar in 1086) and later the Almohads.

Poets and Philosophers

The most important Jewish thinkers of the twelfth century were Judah Halevi, who lived part of his life in Christian Toledo, and Maimonides (Moses ben Maimon), born in Muslim Cordoba. Judah Halevi's poems are among the most moving creations of Hebrew literature, giving expression to his longing for the land of Israel. In what are probably his most famous lines (here in the anthology translated by T. Carmi), he asks:

> O Zion, will you not ask how your captives are—
> the exiles who seek your welfare,
> who are the remnant of your flocks?
> From west and east, north and south, from every side,
> accept the greetings of those near and far. . . .

Among the few illustrated manuscripts of Maimonides' *Guide of the Perplexed* is this illuminated work, commissioned by the physician Menachem Bezalel in Barcelona in 1348 and probably made by a Christian artist. The illustration for the introduction to Part 2 shows a scholar holding an astrolabe in his hand and engaged in a dispute with his students.

For Judah Halevi, religious insight took precedence over the rational cognition of the philosophers. It was his firm belief that the Jews and the land of Israel were of the utmost importance in human history. The people of Israel was like a noble vine that could only yield perfect grapes on the proper soil (Israel) and with the proper cultivation (observing the religious precepts). His most important philosophical work appeared in Arabic under the title *Book of Refutation and Proof on Behalf of the Despised Religion* (better known as *Kuzari*). Within the framework of a historical narrative about the conversion of the Khazar king Bulan during the late eighth century, Judah Halevi attempted to demonstrate the superiority of the Jewish religion over other religions, as well as over philosophy. Not least of all, this was meant to infuse the Jews of the Diaspora with a new self-confidence. The Kuzari elite, at least, really had adopted the Jewish religion, which has led some historians to attribute the origins of Eastern European Jews to this kingdom, located on the lower reaches of the Volga and along the Caspian Sea.

Like Judah Halevi, the family of Maimonides—also known as Rambam (from the initial letters of his Hebrew name, Rabbi Moses ben Maimon)—fled from its home in Cordoba in 1158/59. On the Iberian peninsula a less tolerant Berber dynasty, the Almohads, had by now come to power. When Maimonides was thirteen years old, the Almohads had closed all the churches and synagogues in Cordoba. Outwardly, from now on, all subjects were regarded as Muslims, including Maimonides' family. Why they chose to spend the next several years in Fez, of all places, a Moroccan city under the dominion of the same Almohads who ruled Spain, is unclear. One possibility is that surveillance of Jewish converts to Islam was less strict there. That interpretation seems to be indicated by a letter from Maimonides' father in 1159, in which Maimon offers words of

This astrolabe, meant for calculating the positions of stars, has a Judeo-Arabic inscription using Hebrew letters and is from Spain or northern Africa around 1300. It demonstrates the interest Jewish scholars had in astronomy. Jews made major contributions to the development of the ancient astrolabe in the Arab world, and at the court of Aragon they were employed in manufacturing astrolabes.

encouragement to Jews who were compelled to turn away from Judaism. This served as a model for Maimonides' later letter about conversion. In Fez, Maimonides himself began to study Jewish subjects and medicine and, at the age of twenty-three began writing his commentary on the Mishnah. In 1165, finally, his family journeyed on to Fustat, so-called Old Cairo, where Maimonides became court physician to the sultan and leader of the Jewish community.

In addition to his medical tracts, Maimonides wrote a number of Talmudic works in Hebrew, culminating in a systematic legal compendium, the *Mishneh Torah*, as well as philosophical works in Arabic, of which the *Guide to the Perplexed*, completed in 1190, is of special importance. This remarkable book is addressed to a small intellectual elite, for whom Maimonides demonstrates that the Biblical text should be understood on two levels: in a literal sense that is disclosed to everyone, as well as in an allegorical sense that can only be discerned by the philosophically-trained reader.

With this implicit proposition that only the study of philosophy elucidates the deeper meaning of the Biblical text, Maimonides made many enemies among his contemporaries, and would make even more in future generations. But in the Jewish Enlightenment movement of the eighteenth century, which strove to reconcile Jewish tradition with modern thinking, the *Guide of the Perplexed* would be rediscovered and become a central text.

Many Jews in medieval Spain devoted themselves to scientific writings, whether in astronomy, geography, or medicine. Jews also played an important role as intermediaries and translators between cultures on the Iberian peninsula. Often it was Jews who translated Arabic works—including numerous texts originally written in ancient Greek—into Latin (sometimes indirectly via Hebrew), thus making these texts available to European scholars. Jewish translators worked at the court of Frederick II, as well as at the court of King Charles I of Naples.

Maimonides was esteemed not only as a legal teacher and philosopher, but also as a physician whose works in Latin achieved wide circulation throughout Europe. But Maimonides' teachings did not go unchallenged. Even in his lifetime many scholars rejected his compendia of religious law, and especially his idea that studying his systematic work, the *Mishneh Torah*, would spare a student any need to consult the plethora of individual sources. His rationalist philosophic writings stirred up even more resistance. The campaign against his philosophy lasted beyond his death. In 1233 Maimonides' opponents convinced the Inquisitors in Montpellier that his writings contained heresies liable to have a pernicious influence not only on the Jewish but also on the Christian community. This cleared the way for a systematic examination of Jewish literature, culminating in the burning of the Talmud, as well as of Maimonides' books.

וְלֹא נָתַן לָנוּ
אֶת הַשַּׁבָּת דַּיֵּנוּ
אִלּוּ נָתַן לָנוּ
אֶת הַשַּׁבָּת
וְלֹא קֵרְבָנוּ לִפְנֵי
הַר סִינַי דַּיֵּנוּ
אִלּוּ קֵרְבָנוּ לִפְנֵי
הַר סִינַי
וְלֹא נָתַן לָנוּ
אֶת הַתּוֹרָה דַּיֵּנוּ
אִלּוּ נָתַן לָנוּ
אֶת הַתּוֹרָה

The Birds' Head Haggadah from the early fourteenth century is the earliest separately preserved illustrated Ashkenazic Haggadah. Probably owing to the Biblical prohibition against depicting human beings, the figures are distorted by the placement of bird-like heads on their bodies. They are wearing the "Judenhut"—the typically yellow tall conical hat enjoined upon German Jews.

8. From Lucca to Mainz
ASHKENAZ—THE ROOTS OF CENTRAL EUROPEAN JEWRY

"**Rabbi Moses**, son of Kalonymus, son of Rabbi Judah, was the first [from the Kalonymus family] who left Lombardy, he and his sons Rabbi Kalonymus and Rabbi Yekuthiel.... For King Charles brought them with him out of the land of Lombardy and settled them in Mainz, and there they were fruitful and multiplied greatly, until God's wrath struck all the holy communities in the year 1096."

So wrote the famous Rabbi Eleazar of Worms in his family chronicle around 1220. The migration of the Kalonymides from Lucca to Mainz in the ninth century is one of the best-known founding legends of German Jewry. A millennium later a presumed descendent of the same family, a nephew of the poet Karl Wolfskehl of the Stefan George circle, would invoke this story in his own family chronicle: "I was able to ... trace back ... the family of the Kalonymides ... to the year 870. At that time there resided in Lucca Moses ben Kalonymus the Elder, with whom the tradition of the Kabbalah on European soil had begun.... Kalonymus ben Meshullam ... [,] like his ancestor a great scholar, was personal physician to Emperor Otto II. He

saved the emperor's life in the battle against the Saracens at Co-
trone near Taranto on July 13, 982. As a reward, the emperor
brought him to Germany and settled him in Mainz, where his
gravestone is still preserved." Their fabled beginnings—bound
up with the fate of the emperor, and even with the well-being
of the empire—may have been invented, but it is certain that
the Kalonymides personified the origins of Central European
Jewry in Ashkenaz, origins that are to be found in the south,
arguably in Italy.

Ecclesia and Synagoga

Just as the Hebrew term *Sepharad* represented the Iberian peninsula, the Jews also had a term of Biblical origin for medieval
Germany. *Ashkenaz* shows up in Genesis (10:3) as a descendent
of Noah's son Japheth, whom Jewish tradition regards as the
progenitor of the northern peoples. It was in the Rhine region
that the most important communities of medieval Ashkenaz
arose, especially the three communities forming the German
acronym SCHUM. SCHUM is comprised of the three initial letters of the cities Speyer (the Hebrew *shin*), Worms (in
the Hebrew alphabet the letter *vav*, equivalent to the German
consonant *w*, can also be used as the vowel we know as *u*), and
Mainz (Hebrew *mem*). When Jews later migrated out of German cities and territories, mostly in order to head east, they
took the designation "Ashkenazim" along with them.

Among the Jews of the Middle Ages various founding legends circulated that dated the presence of their ancestors in
Ashkenaz back to pre-Christian times—an apologetic aimed
at countering Christian accusations that Jews were responsible
for Jesus' death. If their ancestors were already living along the
Rhine and Danube at that time, so the argument went, how
could they have had anything to do with the crucifixion? These
accounts surely belong to the realm of legend, but an actual

document, dated 321, contains the oldest mention of Ashkenaz Jewish settlements (in Cologne). A continuous Jewish presence in the region since that time, however, is not attested. Only at the end of the Carolingian era can we begin to talk about continuous residence in what later became German territory. Thus, it is said that Charlemagne sent the Jew Isaac, along with two Frankish nobles, as an emissary to the caliph Harun al-Rashid. It caused a sensation when Bodo, court chaplain to Emperor Louis the Pious, converted to Judaism: Instead of completing a pilgrimage to Rome, he moved to the Iberian peninsula and married a Jewish woman. Around 825 Louis the Pious issued three grants of privilege guaranteeing to Jewish merchants protection for their lives, exemption from taxes, the free exercise of their religion, and the establishment of rabbinic courts for intra-Jewish legal matters. Moreover, their heathen slaves were not to be baptized against the will of the Jews. This benevolent treatment of Jews under the Carolingians triggered clerical resistance, which was expressed in five letters written by Agobard, Archbishop of Lyon, between 821 and 829. The themes of many anti-Jewish polemics later made by the Church can already be found here.

To this day, numerous medieval streets named "Judengasse" testify to the likely settlement of Jewish communities, as do (in many cases) certain place names, such as Judenburg or Villejuif. Yet we should not forget that only a small minority of Jews lived in Ashkenazic throughout the Middle Ages; the majority were under Islamic rule, and most of the Jews within Christendom resided in the Byzantine realm. Prior to the eleventh century there were no Jewish communities comparable to these anywhere in Ashkenaz.

By no means all the Jews in medieval Europe were merchants; at the outset they included many craftsmen and silk weavers, glass blowers and dyers. Wine producing was a Jewish trade, as were livestock breeding and horse breeding. The legal positions of Jewish tradesmen were initially defined by individual grants of privilege, which might later be extended to the Jewish community as a whole. In time the legal position of the Jews deteriorated, as did their occupational structures. Enfeoffment, or the mortgaging of land, began to require that a Christian oath be sworn, and in consequence there were soon no longer any Jewish peasants. Craft trades came to be governed by guilds that admitted only Christians. Only in a few of the larger Jewish communities were Jews able to continue working as craftsmen, and so occasionally they formed their own guilds. Commerce was the main field that remained open to Jews; the prohibition on charging interest enacted by the Third Lateran Council of 1179, which barred Christians from lending money at interest to other Christians, led to an increase in the ranks of Jewish money traders. Driven in this manner into specific occupational groups, Jews became not only religious but also economic outsiders. In many districts they were exclusively perceived as moneylenders—an occupation that earned them many enemies.

In larger cities, Jews often settled close to the synagogue. In 1084, when Bishop Ruediger conceded to the Jews living in Speyer the right to build a wall around their quarter, this was part of a grant of privilege to the community. The bishop was convinced he could "make a city out of the village of Speyer" if he invited Jews. As the historian Salo Baron later noted, initially the ghetto gates could only be shut from the inside and not from the outside. Yet this raises the question: Why did the Jews want a wall of their own in addition to the city walls? The answer would be demonstrated, in a manner only too gruesome, just a few years after the privilege of Speyer had been granted.

For Ashkenazi Jews, the First Crusade in 1096 meant devastation, destruction, and often a choice between forced baptism and death. When the crusaders, made up of peasants and adventurers, marched eastward in order to liberate Jerusalem from the Muslims, many were overcome by religious fanaticism long before they reached their goal. Why wait until one got to the Holy Land in order to slaughter the "unbelievers"? There were infidels right here in Europe! A few church dignitaries, like Archbishop Ruthard of Mainz, himself threatened by the crusaders, offered the Jews protection and refuge, but that did little good. Chronicles of the time offer horrifying accounts of Jews gruesomely murdered by crusaders. In Regensburg they were summarily driven into the Danube with a cross held over them, as a way of converting them to Christianity. Later, to be sure, the emperor allowed the survivors to return to their original faith, since forced conversion was not regarded as legitimate. In the cities along the Rhine, many Jews chose death over baptism and put an end to their own lives. Entire Jewish communities were wiped off the face of the earth. The booty stolen from Jews was frequently divvied up among the crusaders and various authorities, both worldly and clerical. When the crusaders arrived in Jerusalem in 1099, they also destroyed the Jewish community there and set fire to the synagogue where Jews had taken refuge.

The experience of the Jewish martyrs killed during the crusades gave rise to several ways of commemorating the dead that became institutionalized and retain their validity in Judaism to this day. Following the model of the Christian *liber memorialis*, Jews created so-called books of remembrance (*Memorbücher*, in the singular *Memorbuch*) in which the martyrs' names and dates were recorded. It was at this time, too, that mourners began to recite the old Aramaic Kaddish prayer in memory of close relatives, to commemorate the annual anniversary of their death as a *yortsayt* with special rituals, and four times a year to say a special prayer (*yizkor*) in memory of the deceased. In this era, too, it became a custom to visit the graves of relatives, from whom one expected help for the living.

The First Crusade and those to follow demonstrated that the Jews were a relatively small and weak minority whose worldly possessions could easily be purloined, in spite of imperial protection. This would be borne out not only during subsequent crusades, but throughout the Middle Ages. In light of the increasing threats, the legal status of the Jews took on special significance. In the most recent scholarly research, opinion is divided on how the legal situation of the Jews compared to that of the Christian population. While some historians emphasize the lower status of the Jews, which led to their gradual disenfranchisement and ultimately to their expulsion from numerous territories, others remind us that the Jewish population was entitled to some rights that the bulk of the Christian population, the peasant serfs, lacked. In the feudal social system the latter were often subject to the despotic authority of their lords, could not change their place of residence, and were often plagued by famine. Jews, by contrast, were either directly subject to the Holy Roman Emperor or, in states outside the Empire, were (most of the time) subject to whatever royal power was in place. Hence, in theory, they received protection from the highest sovereign authority: "We are not servants of servants, but servants of kings." This "vertical alliance," however, was often purchased at the high price of "horizontal conflicts" with power hierarchies lower down on the feudal scale. The Jews' high-placed protection often proved to be protection that was too remote to be effective. Especially when the king or emperor was abroad, or when there was an interregnum, there could be violent riots against Jews.

Most historians agree that the legal position of the Jews gradually worsened. Toward the end of the Middle Ages, Emperor Henry IV, in light of the threat from the crusades, repeatedly exercised the role of protector of the Jews. He allowed forcibly baptized Jews to return to Judaism, ordered a legal investigation into their stolen property, and in the imperial peace of 1103 he placed the Jews, along with other minorities, under special protection. In 1236, in an expansion of this privilege to all Jews in the Holy Roman Empire, Frederick II began to refer to Jews for the first time as *servi camerae nostri* ("serfs of our chamber"), thereby applying to the Jews the concept, coined by Pope Innocent III in 1205, of (chamber)-serfdom (*Kammerknechtschaft*). To be sure, the word *servi* ("serfs" or "servants") had a negative connotation (as for example when Innocent III talked about how the Jews should always be viewed as slaves, their punishment for the killing of Christ). But since they stood outside the feudal social structure, no literal enslavement or serfdom was thereby implied. Among the privileges renewed by Frederick II were the Jews' right to freedom of trade, to practice their religion, and to take oaths according to their own law. During the late Middle Ages the *Judensteuer* (Jewish tax) made up the largest share of revenues for the imperial chamber. The tax became indispensable, and was in fact such a rich source of capital that some rulers used it ruthlessly. One example of such ruthlessness is provided by the Austrian Duke Albrecht V, who rid himself of "his" Jews in 1420/21, when they were no longer economically profitable to him. He had the poor Jews expelled and the two hundred richest burned on a large funeral pyre. He expropriated their property and cancelled outstanding debts owed to Jews.

Starting as early as the twelfth century, various legal provisions limited the social and honorific status of Jews within medieval society. In the Mainz imperial peace of 1103 they were declared *homines minus potentes*, which placed them on the same level as clerics, merchants, and women. Gradually this grew into an absolute prohibition against carrying weapons. The Papal bull *Sicut Judeis*, renewed time and again since the first half of the twelfth century, emphasized the fundamental right of Jews to life and to practicing their religion and at the same time the need for discrimination against and humiliation of the community adhering to the Jewish religion. Both factors were in play, but the pendulum of Church policy always moved in the direction of the second, towards marginalizing the Jews. In the Fourth

At the end of the fifteenth century, the "Master of the Ursula Legend" depicted this pair, found on many churches, of a triumphant Ecclesia and a broken Synagoga. The figure of the synagogue was painted in Oriental costume with a turban, in order to emphasize her foreign character. A blindfold symbolized her blindness toward the message of the Christian Bible.

Lateran council in 1215, Pope Innocent III toughened the ordinances that forbade Jews from holding any public office, prohibited them from being seen on the street at Easter time, and required them—like the Muslims designated as Saracens—to be recognizable based on their clothing. The latter provision led to all sorts of markings on Jewish garments, the first of which were probably enforced in England, and only later (beginning in the fifteenth century) in the Holy Roman Empire.

The deterioration of relations between church and synagogue that began in the thirteenth century can be attributed, not least of all, to two new clerical orders, the Dominicans and

the Franciscans. They took a radical stance against all non-Christians and undermined the fundamental toleration of Jews that had been the Church's doctrine since the time of Augustine. In order to gain leverage over the Jews, they branded the Talmud, first and foremost, as a heretical writing. One could see (so their argument ran) that the Jews no longer oriented their everyday lives around the Bible's Old Testament, but instead around the Talmud; they had become (at least in Christian understanding) apostates to their own religion. Therefore the Church needed to intervene as a guardian of "genuine Judaism," so to speak. Later, Gregory IX was one of several popes who had copies of the Talmud confiscated. In 1242 the French king Louis IX, after a "religious disputation" staged as a trial against Judaism, consigned twenty-four wagonloads of Talmudic literature to a funeral pyre, and Pope Innocent IV followed his example. Today, only a single complete medieval manuscript of this, the most widely studied Jewish writing, survives. It is kept in the Bavarian State Library in Munich.

The official accusations leveled against Jews were reinforced by anti-Jewish folk myths. Since the twelfth century stories had been circulating about ritual murder and the desecration of the Host. They emanated from England (initially from Norwich in 1144) and France (Blois in 1171), and then rapidly spread across Germany (with a ritual murder accusation in Würzburg in 1147 and tales of desecration of the host in the town of Beelitz in Brandenburg prior to 1247). According to these legends, Jews had a predilection either for killing little Christian children before Easter and using their blood for ritual purposes or for purloining the Hosts from churches and stabbing them with a knife in order yet again to desecrate the body of Christ. Although popes, emperors, and kings insisted that defamations of this kind should not be given any credence, belief in them persisted among the lower clergy and the masses. And no wonder, as the sites where the bodies of children or desecrated Hosts were discovered soon became places of pilgrimage, medieval tourist attractions that brought lots of visitors and money into the local economy. What is worse, Jews were often arrested after these kinds of accusations and only released in exchange for money, or else simply killed and their property confiscated. Even as late as the twentieth century, such legends surfaced in a number of places, giving us vivid evidence of the phenomenon.

In the fourteenth century, to accusations like these was added the charge that Jews had poisoned the wells and so initiated the plague. The first such instance occurred in 1321 in France. Jews, purportedly at the instigation of Moorish kings, were alleged to have incited lepers to poison the wells. Here we see how conspiracy theories functioned in the Middle Ages: The majority begins to imagine that various marginal groups are banding together to do them harm, and this suspicion supplies the pretext for bloody, sometimes extensive persecutions.

The ritual murder legend of Trent shows up in Hartmann Schedel's "Weltchronik" ("World Chronicle") from 1493. According to that legend, around Easter in 1475 the body of a twelve-and-a-half year-old boy named Simon was found, and Jews were held responsible for his murder. Although the bishop and the pope, after an exhaustive investigation, concluded that the Jews were innocent, the rumor persisted, both in this depiction and elsewhere, for centuries.

The Jews were victims of such persecutions in 1298 at the instigation of a ringleader by the name of Rintfleisch, and again in the 1330s under the command of a man known as "King Armleder," an impoverished knight banished from his homeland. Both waves of violence spread across broad sections of southern Germany. The persecutors rampaged most fiercely during the plague years, 1348–1350.

Pictorial representations of Judaism were calculated to leave no doubt about which religion had triumphed and which one ought to submit. A standard practice was to place two statues side by side in a church, the one depicting a victorious *Ecclesia* with a crown and scepter, the other a vanquished *Synagoga* with eyes blindfolded (symbolizing the Jews' blindness to religious truth) and holding a broken staff (representing the loss of worldly power). Other depictions demonized Jews as inhuman creatures who suckled on a pig (the *Judensau* or "Jews' sow") and had horns on their heads like the devil. Medieval dehumanization of the Jews went so far as to describe them as giving off their own *foetor judaicus* (Jewish stench) and to suggest that Jewish men menstruated.

The theological and pseudo-theological accusations that fueled anti-Jewish sentiment were bolstered by economic motives, which ultimately led to the Jews being ostracized and often expelled from wherever they resided. For rulers, the Jews had their uses so long as they possessed money. They paid for the protection they received with special taxes and were, moreover, obligated to grant kings and princes loans when necessary. Things became difficult when the Jews were no longer able to pay their taxes or were not contributing much to monetary commerce. It was for this reason that the Jews were expelled from England in 1290. They were followed in the fourteenth century by the French Jews, and in the late Middle Ages by the Jewish communities of numerous German territories and of almost all German cities in the West. The traditionally disparaging attitude of the Church toward commerce had begun to change, but it changed in such a way as to favor the emergence of a Christian merchant class. Jews were excluded from the mercantile guilds on the grounds that they were not able to swear a Christian oath. At the same time the growing complexity of trade meant that charging interest could no longer be prevented, with the result that the Church discovered backdoor ways of getting around its prohibition on usury. There was less and less need for the Jews, and they were increasingly viewed as unwelcome competitors, especially in urban areas. In proportion to the Christian population's improving economic situation (again, especially in cities), things got worse for Jews. In the Holy Roman Empire they were forced to leave the cities, with the exception of Frankfurt, Worms, and Prague. Christian competition was the major factor accelerating this expulsion. Nuremberg was at the tail end of the trend by 1499, and Regensburg by 1519.

Where did the Jews go after they were driven out? The British Isles they had to leave completely; in France there remained enclaves to which the Jews could flee, such as the papal region around Avignon and the county of Provence. It was similar in the German states. The occasional prince of one of the smaller states might see a chance to augment his coffers by taking in Jews. But beginning as early as the Middle Ages, the prevailing direction of Jewish migration was unmistakably eastward, in the direction of Poland.

As a minority, Jews had little ability to protect themselves physically. But they did react to the increasing hatred directed against them. Just as Christians looked down on Jews, Jews looked down on Christians. In fact conflicts along these lines between Judaism and Christianity went further than those between Judaism and Islam. Most Jews could sympathize with some aspects of Islam; it was after all a substantially aniconic religion with an unequivocally monotheistic stance. In the eyes of many Jews, by contrast, the Christian definition of Jesus as the son of God, the characterization of Mary as the mother of God, the ubiquitous crucifix, and the adoration of the saints all indicated that human beings were being elevated to the rank of God. Yet it was precisely those Jews living under Christian rule who were most cautious about defining their neighbors as idolaters. With idolaters any kind of relationship, including trade, was to be avoided, and restrictions of that sort would make survival as a

This prayer book made in Mainz in 1427/28 contains the lamentations recited on the ninth of Av to commemorate the destruction of the two Temples in Jerusalem. This pictorial depiction refers to the persecutions under Antiochus Epiphanes in the second century BCE, yet it also alludes to current expulsions from German cities. The lamentations in this prayer book also include recitations for the Jews murdered in Würzburg, Rothenburg, and Nuremberg.

tiny minority barely possible. This circumspect attitude did not, however, prevent some Jews from expressing their disdain when they passed by a church or a crucifix. Especially around the time of Purim, which commemorated the wondrous (and very violent) liberation of the Jews from their persecutors in the Persian empire, there were verbal attacks on Christians, often with the aim of avenging harms inflicted and thereby gaining a measure of sense of relief. The boisterous Purim festival, which in quite a few respects resembles the Christian Carnival, frequently coincides with the penitential period of Lent that precedes Easter.

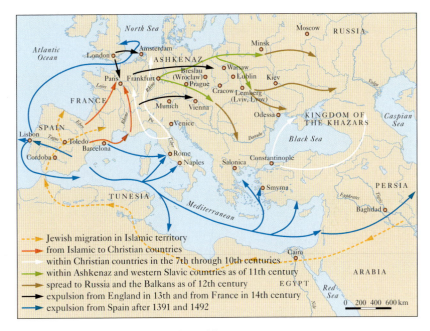

Migrations and expulsions in the Middle Ages.

It would surely have made a negative impression on Christians to see Jews celebrating joyously and getting drunk, especially in that season. In addition, during the Middle Ages the villain Haman was often associated with Jesus, so it was not unknown for Jews to take out their frustrations with their tormentors on the object of the crucifix. An additional way of defending themselves against the triumphant daughter religion was to compose polemical books, among which some of the most popular were those entitled *Toledot Yeshu*, which depicted the life of Jesus in a negative light. We would be getting a false picture of Jews and Christians, distorted by modern notions of tolerance, if we imagined them as friendly, respectful neighbors. But the reverse conception, that there was nothing but mutual hate and contempt, also feeds on false stereotypes. To be sure, Jews often did live near their synagogues during the Middle Ages, but not in an enclosed ghetto. And the Jewish quarters were often also in close proximity to the city's cathedrals and markets. Contacts with the Christian world were not rare at the level of everyday life, and in some places they went beyond purely commercial relations. Jews were often knowledgeable about Christian customs and practices, as were some Christians about Jewish ones. And even if one community did reject the other's religion, there was subliminal cross-influence. Jewish customs for starting school resembled Christian practices, some of the crusaders' liturgical motifs found their way with slight modifications into the chronicles of Jewish martyrs, and the cult of holy sites was similar in both religions. The thirteenth century *Sefer Hasidim*, the most important book of the German-Jewish pietists, the Hasidei Ashkenaz, may have been full of anti-Christian polemics, but at the same time it gave evidence of numerous contacts between Jews and Christians.

Jewish Communal and Congregational Life

Jewish communities had a tightly structured administration, at the head of which stood the *parnas* (leader, *literally* "provider") as well as the *tuve ha-ir* (town notables). The *shamash* (community caretaker) was the sole paid official. The community enjoyed substantial legal autonomy when it came to dealing with disputes among its members, which ran the gamut from assigning fines and prison terms to imposing the ban (*herem*), the act of excommunication from the community. Since there were no supreme regional authorities, the various courts and rabbis were autonomous and had freedom of action. There was not yet any real professional rabbinate, and most rabbis also pursued other professions.

The most renowned Ashkenazic religious authority of the tenth and early eleventh century was Rabbenu Gershom from Mainz, also known as Me'or ha-Golah (the "Light of the Exile," ca. 950–1028). Among his numerous *responsa* (rabbinic legal opinions), the most famous was the one that prohibited polygamy. In this regard, we should remember that the Bible not only permits polygamy, but that in fact polygamy was the norm. We need only think back to the patriarchs and to kings like David and Solomon. For Jews under Muslim rule, too, polygamy was completely taken for granted—and this well into modern times. Rabbenu Gershom's decision, which was initially just made for the community in Mainz, confirmed a longstanding trend away from taking multiple wives, and his ratification of monogamy has been recognized by all Ashkenazic Jews from the tenth century on. Rabbenu Gershom also decided, among other things, that men could not divorce without the consent of their wives, that they should not be allowed to travel away from home longer than eighteen months, that they had to provide for their wives during their absences, and that they must remain at home at least six months after returning from a journey. We have hardly any documents pertaining to the women of medieval Ashkenaz. There are, however, indications that some were quite learned and had studied both Torah and Talmud.

Rabbenu Gershom had numerous famous students, a few of whom directed the yeshiva (Talmud school) in Worms. Among the students who came here to study there was the best-known Ashkenazic scholar of the Middle Ages, Rabbi Shlomo ben Yitzhak, known as Rashi (1040–1105). He came from Troyes in northern France and wrote what is still to this day the most widely read Biblical commentary, and not coincidentally the first book printed in Hebrew (1475). His commentary on the Talmud was distinguished for its conciseness and its clear explanations of complex passages. His grandsons and their students wrote their own commentaries on the Talmud, exegeses that became known under the name *Tosafot* (Additions).

A page from the Darmstadt Haggadah, produced at the end of the thirteenth century, shows men and women studying. Although this activity was reserved for men, as a rule, some sources indicate that there really were exceptions.

Accordingly, Rashi's scholarly progeny themselves are called the Tosafists.

At the same time, Jewish mysticism was experiencing a florescence in the territories between the Danube and the Rhine. Several centers of the Hasidei Ashkenaz emerged, notably in Regensburg (Judah ben Samuel, ca. 1150–1217) and Worms (Eleazar ben Judah, ca. 1165–1230). These "Pietists from Ashkenaz" highlighted asceticism and martyrdom in religious practice. In contrast to Jewish scholars in France, who had a more studious focus, the German-Jewish mystics strove to go beyond learning and—in a way that was entirely analogous to Christian mendicant orders—take on greater burdens than the law required.

The precarious situation of Ashkenazic Jewry in the late Middle Ages is illustrated by the most famous German rabbi

A school scene from the Coburg Pentateuch of 1395: The teacher brandishing a rod has his student recite the famous maxim that the legal scholar Hillel used to summarize the Torah: "Do not do to your neighbor what is hateful to you." The backdrop setting is that of a medieval city.

of the thirteenth century, Rabbi Meir of Rothenburg (ca. 1215–1293). Rabbi Meir, who left behind over a thousand *responsa* as well as poetry and Talmud commentaries, is described in some sources as a kind of chief rabbi for the entire Holy Roman Empire. He pushed through majority voting in Jewish communities, thereby doing away with the practice of giving special privileges to elders and scholars. When the economic situation for Jews in Germany worsened and large numbers of Jews sought to leave the empire, King Rudolf I prohibited their departure. Rabbi Meir was caught trying to leave for the Holy Land and imprisoned in 1286. He was detained and until his death doggedly refused his coreligionists' attempts to ransom him for large sums of money.

Humanism and Reformation

In the age of humanism, there was a revival of interest in the Hebrew language and, by extension, in Jewish culture as well. The study of Kabbalah (Jewish mysticism) became widespread among Christians, who gave it Christian interpretations. Some Christian scholars, like Pico della Mirandola, learned Hebrew in order to understand Kabbalistic teachings. The original text of the Hebrew Bible also met with greater interest. This was not, however, always associated with a more positive attitude toward Jews. Thus, for example, the great humanist Erasmus of Rotterdam was known for his hostile attitude toward Jews. By contrast, the philosopher Johannes Reuchlin (1455–1522), although he regarded the conversion of the Jews as desirable, nonetheless repeatedly defended them against denunciations. When a baptized Jew, Johannes Pfefferkorn, joined his fellow Dominicans from Cologne in demanding that Jews have their books taken away, Reuchlin protested so vehemently that he had to stand trial for defending the Talmud and other Jewish literature.

Martin Luther, too, expressed a positive view of Jews in his early writings, which included a 1523 tractate entitled *Das Jhesus Christus ein geborner Jude sey* (That Jesus Christ was Born a Jew). When the Jews did not respond as he expected, however, and did not become followers of his new teaching, Luther radically changed his tone. His anti-Jewish writings climaxed with the 1543 tractate *Von den Juden und iren Lügen* (On the Jews and

Their Lies), in which he called for synagogues and houses of the Jews to be burned, their rabbis to be prohibited from teaching, and their freedom of movement to be restricted. To be sure, one needs to see Luther's intolerance in the context of the similarly rude tone he took against the Pope and the Turks. But his outbursts did not miss their mark. Princes of the Protestant persuasion and aligned with Luther immediately enacted severe anti-Jewish ordinances. Jews were even forbidden passage through Saxony.

In Josel (or Joselmann) of Rosheim (1480–1554), the "commander and governor of the Jewish community in the Empire," German Jews found a spokesman (*shtadlan*) who committed himself to their well being in a variety of situations. In numerous audiences with Emperor Charles V, the Alsatian native Josel obtained letters of safe conduct for Jews. He was also able either to prevent imminent expulsions of Jews (from Alsace, for example) or at least to secure passage through regions from which they had been expelled. At the Augsburg Imperial Diet in 1530, he emerged victorious from a disputation with the convert Antonius Margerita, who had written an anti-Jewish diatribe. Margerita was thereupon expelled from Augsburg. He also publicly opposed the anti-Jewish writings of Luther and refuted his accusations. No other German Jew in the centuries before or after Josel of Rosheim achieved this level of recognition as a political advocate for Jewish causes throughout the Holy Roman Empire.

When the Jews were expelled from the Iberian peninsula at the end of the fifteenth century, they also took along a share of their cultural artifacts. These included the oldest Spanish Haggadah, which was made in Barcelona in 1350 and found a new home, presumably in Italy, after the Jews' expulsion from Iberia. In 1896 it was sold to the National Museum in Sarajevo, where it was saved several times at great peril, for example, by the museum's librarian during the German occupation in World War II and then again during the Balkan war in 1991. The picture shows a Jewish family at a table laid out for a meal.

9. From Lisbon to Venice
EXPULSIONS AND THEIR AFTERMATH

ISAAC ABRAVANEL came from one of the most renowned Sephardic families, which traced its ancestral line back to no less a figure than King David himself. Isaac's ancestors lived in Seville, in Valencia, and in Portugal. He himself was born in 1437 in Lisbon, and as a young man distinguished himself both for rabbinic learning and philosophical aptitude. He must have proved himself in practical matters as well, for at an early age he was appointed by King Alfonso V to administer the king's finances. As was often the case in such circumstances, the good favor and patronage he enjoyed came to an end with the death of the king, whose successor, John (João) II, suspected him of conspiracy. In 1483 Abravanel left Portugal, where he was sentenced to death in absentia, and made his way back to his family's home, to Castile, where he was again entrusted with a position of responsibility in the service of the royal household. He even helped finance the conquest of the last Muslim enclave in Granada by the Catholic royal couple Isabella and Ferdinand. None of this would be of any help to him only a few years later when the royal couple, having completed the "Reconquest" in 1492, decided to create a united Christian Spain and forced

Jews to choose between baptism and exile. Isaac Abravanel worked feverishly, even offering large sums of money, to stop the expulsion. But the decision of the Spanish crown was irrevocable. Abravanel made his way to Naples, where he again entered royal service. A short time later the city was captured by the French, who did not tolerate any Jews in their realm, and Isaac again had to set off. He headed first to Messina, then to Corfu, in 1496 to Monopoli on the Adriatic coast, and finally in 1503 to Venice. Here he demonstrated his abilities once more in negotiations between the Republic of Venice and the Kingdom of Portugal. His descendents lived in Italy, England, Holland, and the Ottoman Empire, a distribution that is emblematic of the settlement pattern of those expelled from the Iberian peninsula.

Prelude to Expulsion

The *Reconquista*, the ongoing reconquest of Spanish lands by Christian forces, does not suffice as an explanation for the expulsion of the Jews from the most important center of Jewish life in the Middle Ages. As we have seen, some Jews even fled from the Islamic part of the peninsula into the Christian districts. In Christian Spain, too, Jews continued to experience several centuries of a fruitful existence. Jewish craftsmen had their own guilds; there were Jewish smiths and weavers, farmers and merchants. The ordinances requiring Jews to wear special badges were ignored more often here than in the rest of Europe, scholarship found an important center both in Christian and Muslim Spain, and the art of building synagogues and illustrating books flourished there. Many Jews held high office at Christian courts, as was the case of Samuel ha-Levi Abulafia, who was finance minister under King Pedro IV (1350– 1369). His former mansion, which can still be seen in Toledo today, allegedly also became El Greco's residence.

But in spite of these marks of tolerance the fourteenth century did indeed see a reversal of fortunes for Jews on the Iberian peninsula. Religious fanaticism increased perceptibly, and Jews as well as Muslims were seen as standing in the way of the Reconquista's timely fulfillment. The situation escalated at the end of the century, following inflammatory speeches by fanatical itinerant preachers. The great Jewish quarter of Seville was set on fire in 1391, an event that ushered in a decade of ongoing destruction of Jewish life on the whole Iberian peninsula. The Queen Mother Catherine fell under the influence of hate preaching by the Dominican monk Vicente Ferrer, who found a comrade in the baptized Jew Paul of Burgos. Acting as regent for the underage John II in Castile, she issued an edict in 1412 that deprived Castilian Jews of all their rights, drove them out of all public offices, and decreed the strict social segregation of Jews and Christians. Ferrer now roamed the country preaching sermons to convert the Jews in synagogues, which he and the fanatics accompanying him occasionally had immediately transformed into churches. Within just a few years about 20,000 Jews had adopted the Christian religion, most of them out of fear for their lives. This mass movement of baptism gave rise in the first half of the fifteenth century to the group known as "New Christians," also called *conversos* (converts) by the Spaniards.

In the second half of the fifteenth century, there were stepped-up efforts to ascertain whether these New Christians might secretly be practicing Jewish customs. Finally, in 1478, the Spanish Inquisition was established in order to deal definitively with the question. Informers denounced their formerly Jewish neighbors, accusing them of cleaning their houses on Friday, wearing newly washed clothes on Saturday, or not eating pork. Such actions sufficed for an indictment of "Judaizing." The Inquisition did not have any legal leverage against Jews who remained true to their faith; they could only condemn Christians charged with heresy.

The archives of the Inquisition are full of case records allowing us to reconstruct the everyday life of the period from a new perspective, even as these documents help us understand the perfidy involved in some indictments and court decisions. Of special value to the Church was the deterrent effect that came from publicly carrying out sentences, often in the context of a carnival-like spectacle, the high point of which was an execution by burning at the stake. In some cases the Inquisition even had bodies exhumed so that they could be posthumously convicted of transgressions and then publicly burned. The first of these spectacles (auto-da-fés) took place in 1481, and within a year three hundred New Christians died at the stake in Seville alone. Before the practice was abolished in the nineteenth century, an estimated nine thousand auto-da-fés took place in Spain, Portugal, and their colonies.

In the eyes of the Inquisition, the Jewish communities that continued to exist represented the greatest threat to New Christians in danger of backsliding. The Grand Inquisitor Torquemada therefore urged the royal house to expel the Jews from Spain completely. On March 31, 1492, barely three months after the conquest of Granada, the royal couple signed the "General Edict on the Expulsion of the Jews from Aragon and Castile" in the Court of the Lions of the Alhambra in Granada. The Jews were given four months' time to either adopt the Catholic religion or leave the country.

Between one hundred and two hundred thousand Jews are believed to have fled Spain, a large share of them initially to neighboring Portugal or to tiny Navarre, the only countries they could reach by land. Navarre was unable to withstand the pressure from its larger neighbor to the south and issued an edict similar to Spain's in 1498. In Portugal, where the Jews were initially permitted to remain for a brief time, King Manuel signed an edict of expulsion as early as December 1496, according to which the remaining Jews had till October 1497 to leave the

וְתִשְׁלִי וִירוּשָׁרֵיְדֵנוּ אֵל אֵל

Wall decoration at the El Transito synagogue in Toledo, built by Samuel ha-Levi Abulafia. Abulafia became involved in court intrigue, was denounced and arrested, robbed of his possessions, and finally died under torture. The Jews were collectively held responsible for his alleged transgressions, and an attack on the Jewish quarter of Toledo in 1355 is said to have resulted in more than 1,200 deaths. The synagogue and its entire property fell to the king. After the expulsion of the Jews in 1492, the synagogue was turned into a church. In 1877 it was declared a national monument. Since 1970 it has served as a national museum of Spanish-Jewish art.

country or be baptized. Unlike the Spanish sovereigns, however, Manuel wanted to keep those Jews whom he considered vital to the economy in the country, and so in 1497 he had almost all of Portugal's Jews converted by force. These numerous New Christians continued to live in their old neighborhoods, practicing the same professions, and they often married among each other. In the course of several generations most became Christians in more than name, connected to Judaism only by a distant memory. A minority, however, surreptitiously clung to Jewish traditions and were contemptuously referred to by the native population as *Marranos* (pigs). After 1506 they were allowed to emigrate, and over the following two centuries many of them officially returned to Judaism. In 1539 the Inquisition's courts in Portugal began to follow the Spanish example of carefully monitoring whether the New Christians really had discarded all the Judaizing tendencies of which they were suspected.

After 1497, Jewish life on the Iberian peninsula was extinguished, and it would remain so for centuries. This meant that there was no longer a Jewish presence anywhere in all of Western Europe. And yet the Spanish Inquisition continued for centuries its mission to keep the Christian religion "pure." It enacted the first racial laws, which made so-called *limpieza de sangre* (purity of blood) a requirement for certain offices and titles. In practice this meant that New Christians, regardless of how loyal they were to their new faith, were excluded from certain professions and public positions.

In the New World

Some refugees tried their luck in the new colonies on the other side of the Atlantic. There is no proof to confirm the speculation that Columbus himself came from a New Christian family that had once been forcibly baptized. But there is also no doubt that New Christians did support his voyages of discovery as financiers and translators, and that he regarded the land he had discovered as a reflection of Biblical geography. In subsequent generations, conjectures that the ten lost tribes of Israel were to be found among the American Indians repeatedly made the rounds. Christians as well as Jews lent credence to these theories.

The history of the Jews in the New World during the sixteenth and seventeenth century is marked by many of the same problems as faced European Jews, as well as by opportunities for a new life under new circumstances. It should come as no surprise that the state of affairs that followed the expulsions from Spain in 1492 and Portugal in 1497 persisted in these countries' New World colonies. The Inquisition was extremely active in Latin America, but there was also a liberal policy in the Netherlands that led to a concentration of Jewish traders in the Dutch colonies. In what was (for the time being) the Netherlandish part of northern Brazil, the Jewish community made up about half of the white population, estimated at 3,000, until the Portuguese conquered Recife in 1654. Jewish settlements in the Dutch colonies of Curaçao and Surinam lasted longer. The first synagogue in the Western Hemisphere was founded in 1665–67 in a place called Jooden Savanne in Surinam. At the end of the eighteenth century, over 1,000 Jews lived among the 13,000 inhabitants of Paramaribo, the capital of Surinam. At the same time, the Jewish community in Curaçao consisted of 1,500 members. These were very impressive numbers when compared with the Jewish communities of Europe: In the early modern period there were only a few German cities that had more Jewish residents than Paramaribo or Curaçao! The Jews in the Dutch Caribbean also became important, not least of all as mediators between the Dutch and the Spanish.

Sephardim in Northern and Central Europe

Most refugees, admittedly, did not head westward as they left Iberia, but rather toward the east and north. Here, since the sixteenth century, the spirit of humanism and enlightenment had been spreading, as represented by scholars like the Dutch Calvinist philosopher Hugo Grotius. Without evincing a markedly positive attitude toward Judaism, Grotius did advocate tolerance on pragmatic grounds. In 1615 he was asked by the States of Holland and West Friesland for an expert opinion on the Jews. At the beginning of his report he listed, still entirely in the medieval tradition, all the faults and errors of the Jews. These he attributed to anti-Jewish policies on the part of Christians. He went on to advocate the right of the Jews to live in Holland. But as they could neither be converted by force, nor be left bereft of religion, they must retain the right to practice their religion freely. Admittedly, even Grotius continued to advocate certain restrictions. Thus, he argued that the number of Jews should be limited, they should be forced to listen to Christian sermons, and they should not be allowed to hold any public office, although their choice of profession should otherwise be largely open. It would take another half century before John Locke, in his letter *Concerning Toleration* (1689), insisted more forthrightly that neither Jew nor Muslim nor heathen should be excluded from the political community owing to his religion. Jews should be granted the right to build synagogues, because, as Locke rhetorically asked, "Is their doctrine more false, their worship more abominable, or is the civil peace more endangered by their meeting in public than in their private houses?"

In northern Europe, too, new centers of Jewish life emerged because of the absorption of *conversos*. England had been the first European country to expel the Jews (in 1290). When Shakespeare immortalized the Jew Shylock in *The Merchant of Venice*, there was still no official Jewish settlement in England. Only about a hundred Marranos lived in London, among them the court physician to Queen Elizabeth I, Roderigo Lopez, who was executed in 1594 after he was accused of plotting to kill the queen. As political and economic conditions worsened in 1609, this community also disappeared.

Only toward the middle of the seventeenth century did a Marrano community resettle on the British Isles. Under the Lord Protector Oliver Cromwell, England finally came around to readmitting a Jewish population. Political reasons like a shared aversion to the Spanish crown certainly played a role. The most prominent motives, however, were economic and

The centers of the Sephardic Diaspora after the expulsion of 1492.

religious. Both are articulated in a book by the Amsterdam rabbi
and printer Manasseh ben Israel, *Esperanca de Israel* (1650), the
Latin translation of which he dedicated to the English Parliament. He asserted that the Jews must be settled in all four cor-
ners of the world before the final coming of the messiah—and
yet in England there was no Jewish settlement. Cromwell's supporters, who had overthrown the monarchy, were only too glad
to lend credence to this kind of messianic rapture. Although
the Whitehall Conference convened by Cromwell in December
1655 was unable to decide on a formal readmission of the Jews, it
did make it easier for those Marranos already living in England

to acknowledge their Judaism openly. They thereupon founded their own synagogue and a cemetery. After the Restoration, the monarchy tolerated this Sephardic community, which gradually increased and was supplemented by an Ashkenazic one.

The former Spanish Netherlands had granted asylum to a number of Marranos who were able—unofficially at first, then openly—to return to the religion of their ancestors. At the beginning of the seventeenth century, every Dutch city established for itself the legal status of its Jewish residents, with the result that their position varied considerably from place to place. In some cities Jews could actually become citizens, while in others they were not even allowed to reside. In Amsterdam they were allowed to take up residence, but they were not accepted into any guild. During the decade of the 1630s Amsterdam replaced Venice as the most important center of the Western Diaspora. In contrast to most of the great centers of Sephardic emigration, however, the Jewish community of the city was new and did not encounter established traditions. Conversely, Judaism was also new to most of Amsterdam's Jews. To be sure, certain basic features of the religion had been passed down by way of family tradition, but the recipients of these diluted legacies were often people whose ancestors had already long since been baptized Catholic, who had never practiced the Jewish religion, and who (of course) did not understand any Hebrew. They often maintained contact with their relatives on the Iberian peninsula who had remained Catholic, spoke Portuguese among themselves most of the time, and translated the most important Jewish books with any religious content into Spanish, which came close to assuming the status of a sacred literary language. The culture of the motherland remained close to their hearts, and they had many a Spanish play performed on an Amsterdam stage. Some wrote their own poetry and prose in Spanish. They dressed like their Christian neighbors, which has led art historians to wonder whether Rembrandt's purported portrait

This anonymous copperplate engraving from the late seventeenth century shows the imposing Sephardic synagogue of Amsterdam built by Elias Bouman in 1671–75. In the seventeenth century it was by far the largest synagogue in Europe and served as a model for the construction of new synagogues in America.

of Manasseh ben Israel might not in fact depict a Christian scholar. In Amsterdam there was no ghettoization as in Frankfurt or Venice, Prague or Rome. (Rembrandt, after all, actually lived in the Jewish quarter and used Jews from his immediate neighborhood as models for many of his Biblical figures.)

The members of the "Spanish and Portuguese Jewish nation" were initially split into several different congregations. This was, among other things, a reflection of differences between religious free thinkers and the more orthodox among the Jews. They closed ranks, however, vis-à-vis the Ashkenazic Jews, who also formed their own congregation in 1649. The feelings of cultural superiority among the Sephardim went so far that Sephardic men who married Ashkenazic women were excluded from their congregation. Although (or perhaps one should say precisely *because*) the Sephardic community of Amsterdam had to create its own traditions, it soon came to be regarded as exemplary for its organizational structures, education, and physical appearance. It was, in a sense, the first modern Jewish community. As of 1675, it was also perceived as such by the outside world because of what was then the most palatial synagogue in Europe. In contrast to most of the older synagogues, this *Esnoga* was not hidden in a back courtyard or behind inconspicuous outer walls (as in the Venice ghetto); instead, with its deliberate architectural echoes of the Jerusalem Temple (a model of which was making the rounds) and with its jacaranda wood imported from Brazil, it was the conspicuous sign of a newly emerging self-confidence.

The Jews of Amsterdam occupied a leading role in religious scholarship, Hebrew publishing, and economic activity during the seventeenth and eighteenth century. Their institutions included one of the best-organized and most modern Jewish school systems of its day. Ashkenazic observers were impressed by the orderly and systematic nature of a curriculum in which classes were taught in six distinct study units, morning and afternoon, on Hebrew language and grammar, the Bible, and rabbinic literature. The lingering influence of the Jesuit school system of Spain and Portugal, where many of the older community members had grown up, was unmistakable in this structure. Even though the Ashkenazic community, composed of German and Polish Jews, soon outnumbered the Portuguese, the most prominent members of the Ashkenazic community still came from among the Sephardic group.

The family of Manasseh ben Israel belonged to this group, as did that of the philosopher Baruch Spinoza. Uriel da Costa, who had held a high administrative office in Portugal and returned to Judaism in Hamburg in 1616, also headed for Amsterdam in order to practice the Jewish religion openly. His conflict with the Jewish community there highlighted in a radical and tragic manner the gap between that community's insistence on strict Jewish norms and a generation of Marranos who had grown up outside Jewish tradition. Da Costa had come of age in a Christian environment without formal Jewish education or any opportunity to study Jewish sources. For him, Talmud and rabbinic interpretations had no meaning; his Judaism was derived directly from the Bible. When he openly admitted this, the Jewish community excommunicated him in a humiliating ceremony. He had to prostrate himself at the entrance to the synagogue and let those entering the building tread over his body. While the ban was being recited, all the candles in the synagogue were extinguished, exactly as if the life of a person were being snuffed out. Contact with other Jews, whether private or for business reasons, was prohibited to those on whom such a ban was laid. Da Costa repented and returned to the bosom of the community, but he was unable to square this with his conscience and soon thereafter took his own life. Shortly before his suicide he wrote an autobiographical study in which he reaffirmed that he had only wanted to keep the commandments of Moses, and restated his conviction that the Jewish community had moved away from Biblical Judaism through the innovations they had introduced into the original faith.

His younger contemporary Spinoza, who was also excommunicated by the community, succeeded in becoming the first modern Jew to disengage from the Jewish religion without becoming a Christian. He wanted to uphold his independence as a thinker and preferred working as a diamond polisher to accepting an appointment to teach philosophy at the University of Heidelberg. Spinoza feared being unable to act and think unfettered in a professorial chair. His *Tractatus Theologico-Politicus* was the fruit of those doubts that his change of conviction, combined with the associated constraints it imposed, had nourished in him.

In Spain and Portugal, the refugees who later returned to Judaism, and often their ancestors as well, had officially lived as Christians, attended churches, and received instruction in the tenets of Catholic religion. In contrast to the Jews of the Middle Ages, and unlike their contemporaries coming from a different background, they were fully conversant with the religion, customs, and language of their surroundings; on the other hand, they often became acquainted with the Jewish religion and Hebrew language only after emigrating and had their first contact with a community openly practicing Judaism only after several generations. This may help explain many a dissident teaching by a Da Costa or a Spinoza, as well as the special character of the Sephardic communities.

There were a number of less well-known descendents of the New Christians, who shared those doubts, distanced themselves from every organized religious community, and became free thinkers, though without the more famous dissenters' aptitude for clothing their ideas in philosophical garb. Although far from being religiously observant, they often felt solidarity with other descendents of Spanish or Portuguese Jews, with the *Nación*, and the prosperous among them expressed "national feeling" or "ethnic solidarity" by various forms of social assistance. They stayed connected via family ties both to the Marranos who had remained behind on the Iberian peninsula and to the members of the new Jewish communities. The rich merchants among them often had honorary titles bestowed on them by the same governments of Spain and Portugal that would not tolerate any kind of Jewish settlement on their own territory. They formed a well-connected trading network in northern Europe, the Iberian peninsula, and the Caribbean, a network that they further extended through marriage. Abraham Diego Texeira took the Swedish queen Christina into his household in Hamburg after her abdication. After emigrating to his new homeland of Bordeaux, Isaac Israel Suasso, who had grown up as Antonio Lopez Suasso, was made the Baron of Avernas-le-Gras in the southern Low Countries (Brabant) by King Charles II. The legendary riches of a few families so dominated perceptions of this community that it is often forgotten that most Sephardic Jews were hardly among the economically privileged classes in their new homeland.

While Amsterdam was certainly the most important Jewish community in the North Sea region, during the seventeenth century Hamburg had also become a center for Sephardic and, shortly thereafter, also for Ashkenazic Jews. The first Spanish-Portuguese Jews settled in this Hanseatic city at the end of the sixteenth century. In the beginning they did not openly practice their faith. By the middle of the seventeenth century, their numbers had grown to 600, yet the city still did not allow them to worship in public, only privately. They were not allowed to build a synagogue. When they were also confronted with commercial restrictions in 1697, most of them left Hamburg. A few settled in the neighboring Danish town of Altona; the majority left for Amsterdam.

In Italy

A small segment of the Iberian Jewish population settled in southwestern France, where they privately practiced Judaism while officially being viewed as Christians until the eighteenth century. But the most important stream of refugees poured across the Mediterranean. Italy, where there had been Jewish communities since pre-Christian times, became one of the refugees' havens. Rome had the only large Jewish community in Europe with an unbroken line of continuity going back to Antiquity. In the Middle Ages Italian Jews had been responsible for major cultural achievements, especially in southern Italy.

Yet even here there were expulsions linked to developments on the Iberian peninsula. Sicily was a possession of Aragon, and in 1492 it also expelled its Jewish inhabitants, up to 40,000 according to some estimates. The same fate befell the Kingdom of Naples, which fell into Spanish hands in 1541. Northern Italy with its numerous small city-states now became the focal point of Jewish life: in Padua and Mantua, Venice and Ferrara, in Tuscany and the Papal State. Most Italian Jews of the Middle Ages were neither Ashkenazic nor Sephardic; they had their own rites and their own traditions. Starting in the fourteenth century, however, more and more German Jews arrived in northern Italy, and by the sixteenth century, after a few generations, the Sephardim who had fled Iberia were dominant.

The immigrants' diversity was reflected in the variety of Italian synagogues. In Venice there were at least eight, defined by the background of their members, and in Rome's ghetto five synagogues were housed within a single building: an Italian one, and next to it Ashkenazic, Sicilian, Castilian, and Catalonian synagogues. The sixteenth and seventeenth centuries brought contradictory developments. In 1516, on the one hand, in the former iron foundry district (*getto*) of Venice, the city's rulers created the ghetto, a segregated district that would later lend its name to similar Jewish enclaves throughout the world. Although the Jewish population grew enormously over time, Jews were confined to this small residential quarter, where they were only allowed to build higher. The Papal policy of Paul IV, who as Cardinal was already known for his public burning of the Talmud, soon ordered the construction of such ghettos well beyond Venice, and particularly in Rome. Shortly after his election as Pope, he issued the Papal bull *Cum nimis absurdum*, which asserted that it was absurd to show love and patience for those who had been punished by God. Jews everywhere should be forced to live in segregated quarters that they should not be permitted to leave at night or during Christian holidays, they should wear yellow hats so as to be recognizable as Jews, be forbidden from pursuing any honorable profession (they should only be allowed to peddle and trade in old clothes), and they should not retain any Christian servants.

In spite of this legally prescribed social segregation, it was precisely in Italy that a hermetically sealed lockdown of the Jewish community did not succeed. We have reports of numerous encounters between Jewish and Christian scholars. Jews took part in Italy's cultural Renaissance, contributing to its achievements. Numerous Jews worked as dance teachers, singers, and musicians. Salomone de Rossi's early seventeenth-century synagogal compositions are fully consonant with the music of his time. He was, after all, the conductor of the Duke of Mantua's orchestra. In historiography, Jewish chroniclers took an interest in secular post-Biblical history for the first time. Admittedly, this new and critical type of scholarship was restricted to a very small circle, and some rabbis strictly prohibited the reading of these texts. A more widespread phenomenon was the large number of Jewish physicians who received training at the University of Padua, in spite of all the restrictions and humiliations to which they were subjected. The Papal bull *Cum nimis absurdum* formally prohibited Jewish physicians from treating non-Jewish patients, but the reality was often different.

The contacts that existed between the Jewish and the Christian population are expressed in two important, though not necessarily (in every respect) typical, biographies. In his autobiography, Leone Modena, one of the most dazzling scholars of Venice, tells not only of his dabbling in alchemy and his passion for gambling, but also reports with pride that numerous Christians flocked to the Grand Synagogue to hear his sermons. Sara Coppia Sullam is one of the few Jewish women of the early seventeenth century who has left documents for the historian.

Jews and Christians socialized in equal measure in her salon in Venice, and numerous of her writings, poems, and pictures have come down to us.

The most important Sephardic community to develop in Italy since the end of the sixteenth century was the one in the newly established free port built by the Medicis in Livorno (Leghorn). Here a tolerant wind prevailed. Jews were freed from the odium of having to wear special badges, and they were permitted to own homes. Livorno was the only major Italian community that did not have a ghetto. The number of its Jewish residents, who spoke Spanish and Portuguese (as colloquial languages) among themselves, grew rapidly. By the end of the seventeenth century, about 2,400 lived in the port city, making it the largest Jewish community in Italy after Rome.

The changes described here have brought us from medieval to early modern Jewish society. The centers of Jewish life have relocated eastward, from the Iberian peninsula to northern Europe, Italy, Poland, and the Ottoman Empire. The expulsions of 1492 and 1497 have introduced a new degree of mobility into Jewish society, and through their immersion in Christian culture, many who have returned to Judaism are now creating a hybrid culture that integrates elements of the Christian world into their rediscovered Jewish universe.

In addition, new Jewish law codes are making possible an opening to the surrounding world, as the Jews create new ways of maintaining their beliefs. The explosion of knowledge as a result of the printing press further contributes to cultural exchange among the different Jewish cultures. Printed works from Venice are read in Brody, books from Constantinople in Hamburg. New colloquial languages that combine Hebrew components and characters with local vernaculars are emerging among the refugees from the Iberian peninsula and the German territories. In view of all these developments, the authority of the rabbis and of traditional community structures is on the decline.

The greatest challenge to traditional authorities at the onset of the modern era, however, will come from messianic-mystical movements. These had, to be sure, never completely disappeared from Judaism, but they are expanding now, carried along on waves of unbridled enthusiasm.

The Messiah rides into Jerusalem on an ass, as foretold in Zechariah (9:9). Messianic hopes repeatedly cropped up in Jewish history, and in the sixteenth and seventeenth century they were at their height. When this Haggadah appeared in Mantua in 1560, memories of the pseudo-Messianic figure David Reuveni were still fresh in the minds of Italian Jews.

10. From Khaybar to Rome
MESSIANIC AND MYSTICAL MOVEMENTS

Jewish Messianism in the Sixteenth Century

Among the many remarkable figures drawn to cosmopolitan Venice, David Reuveni was undoubtedly one of the most peculiar. Coming from Alexandria in the autumn of 1523, his dwarfish physique clothed in Oriental garments caused a stir in the city where the ghetto had been set up seven years earlier. Even his background was shrouded in myth. He claimed Khaybar as his home, that oasis on the Arabian peninsula from which Muhammed had once expelled Jewish tribes, and which had not been mentioned since as a place of Jewish residence. Reuveni's assertion that his brother Joseph ruled over a powerful Jewish kingdom made up of the remnants of the lost Biblical tribes of Reuben, Gad, and Manasseh also must have struck later historians as a fable out of the Thousand and One Nights. Nevertheless, when Reuveni claimed that his Jewish kingdom in the East would drive out the Turks, his proclamation fell on sympathetic ears, not only among his co-religionists, but in the Christian world as well.

Pope Clemens VII let Reuveni ride into Rome on a white horse and gave him an audience. He supplied him with a letter of recommendation to the Portuguese king, and in November 1525 Reuveni, sumptuously equipped, was granted entry into a kingdom where officially there were no longer any Jews. It is not surprising that the arrival of an emissary from a Jewish kingdom would elicit messianic feelings among Portugal's forcibly baptized Jews. An official at the royal court, Diego Pires, was so impressed by this Oriental prince that he returned to Judaism under the name Solomon Molcho, underwent circumcision, and left Portugal for the Ottoman Empire, where he studied Kabbalah in Salonica and let himself be celebrated as the messiah. When it became apparent that nothing would come of Reuveni's promises, and that his appearance was fomenting messianic unrest among the Portuguese Marranos, Reuveni also fled Portugal. A few years later the two met again in Italy and traveled to the Imperial Diet in Regensburg, where they insisted, in spite of warnings from the leading Jews of Germany (including Josel of Rosheim), on meeting Emperor Charles V. This time their initiative ended tragically, and they were sent to jail in Mantua. As a Catholic who had reconverted to Judaism, Molcho was condemned in December 1532 by a court of the Inquisition and burned at the stake. Reuveni presumably died in Spanish custody.

The question remains as to who this Reuveni really was and what might have driven him to concoct such a story. Was it a personal craving for recognition or a weak grip on reality? Whatever the case, certain messianic ideas that took hold in the period no doubt played a role. According to their proponents, only the war described in the Bible between the world empires of Gog and Magog could bring about the age of salvation, a war of the worlds that, it was hoped, would be brought about through the involvement of the Holy See. More evidence for this interpretation comes from the name of Reuveni's supposed brother, Joseph. According to one Jewish tradition, the messiah from the house of David who would bring about world peace would have to be preceded by a warlike messiah from the house of Joseph.

We can only speculate about Reuveni's origins. His own claim to have come from Khaybar hardly sounds plausible. Jews did live in some faraway territories—in India, China, Ethiopia, and Yemen. Only gradually, in this age of exploration, did their presence in these remote places come to be noticed on the old continent. In India, especially in the south around the city of Cochin, there were several Jewish communities, a few of which traced their origins back to Biblical times. In China things apparently went so well for the small Jewish community, centered in Kaifeng, that over the course of several centuries it assimilated completely into the majority population. Ethiopian Jews trace their origins back to the period of the Bible, some maintaining that they came from the ten lost tribes of the Biblical northern kingdom of Israel. And there are sources, including an epistle written by Maimonides, that attribute great antiquity to the Jewish communities of Yemen. Reuveni may have come from one of these communities, which to European eyes were exotic enough to have produced such a figure.

In the Ottoman Empire

The Ottoman Empire, the object of Reuveni's military interest and the place where Solomon Molcho let himself be celebrated as the messiah, was then experiencing what seemed like an unstoppable political and economic ascent. In 1453 the old Christian metropolis of Constantinople had fallen into the hands of the sultan. Istanbul became the capital of an empire whose borders would soon stretch from Algeria in the west to

Babylonia in the east. When émigrés from the Iberian peninsula sought refuge in the Empire of the Sublime Porte, they
found major Jewish communities already established there,
some with Byzantine origins (the "Romaniot" communities),
and others whose origins were partly Near Eastern and partly
Ashkenazic. It fit in with Ottoman policy to settle new population groups in the capital so that the city would develop into
a cosmopolitan center of even greater importance. Some accounts would have it that a formal invitation went out to the
Jews expelled from Spain; this is likely myth, but there can be
no doubt that the door was open for the immigrants to settle in
Istanbul and other centers of the Ottoman Empire. In big cities
they would often organize themselves into landsman associations of a kind, centered on synagogues and institutions that
served refugees from specific regions: Catalonia, Andalusia, or
Portugal. In Istanbul alone during the sixteenth century, there
were supposed to have been forty-four synagogues. In 1608 the
count for the city was twenty-four Romaniot congregations
with over 1,000 families, eight Spanish congregations, four
Italian, two Ashkenazic, one Hungarian, one Karaite, and two
that could not be further identified. By the end of the seventeenth century the picture had been radically transformed.
Now over two thirds of the Jewish population in the city was
Sephardic, and only a goodly quarter came from the Romaniot
community. At around 20,000 Jewish residents, Istanbul and
Salonica were by far the world's largest Jewish communities,
more than double the size of any of the communities in Amsterdam, Prague, Frankfurt, and Livorno, not to mention the
Polish communities.

The restrictive regulations that Islamic law applied to the non-
Islamic *dhimmi* were often overlooked, especially in Ottoman
metropolises like Istanbul, Salonica, and Izmir (Smyrna). The
sultan's highest priority was that the Jews pay their taxes and

Donna Gracia Mendes Nassi was also known as "La Signora" among the Jews who came from Spain and Portugal. She administered an international financial business, influenced politics in Venice and the Ottoman Empire, and contributed to making Tiberias a Jewish settlement again. This medallion with her portrait was made by the Italian artist Pastorino de Pasterini in 1553.

prove useful in building up the economy of this aspiring world power. Jews were active in almost all occupations. Often held together by family ties or common heritage and language, a network of Sephardic families took shape in the port cities of the Mediterranean and the North Sea. In Salonica, where they formed the largest population group in the city, as well as in other centers of the Ottoman Empire, they assumed a leading role in textile manufacture and trade. But they worked as artisans and fishermen as well. In some cases they formed their own guilds, while in other instances they joined existing ones.

An exceptional position among the Sephardic immigrants
was occupied by Donna Gracia Mendes (Beatrice de Luna
Miquez), who was born into a family of New Christians in 1510.
When her husband, an important banker in Lisbon, died in
1535, Donna Gracia inherited his fortune. When the Inquisition gained momentum in Portugal in 1536, she emigrated first
to Antwerp, and shortly thereafter to Venice and Ferrara,
where the family began to live openly as Jews. Only after her
arrival in Istanbul were diplomatic honors extended to her and
to her nephew Joseph Nassi. Joseph, known in Portugal as
João Miquez, in Venice as Giovanni Miches, and in Spain and
Flanders as Juan Miguez, was appointed by Sultan Selim II as
the Duke of Naxos, an island that the sultan had only recently
wrested from the Venetians. Gracia Mendes and her nephew
repeatedly demonstrated their solidarity with persecuted Jews
in other territories. Thus, in 1555, they tried to organize a boycott of the Italian port of Ancona, where Pope Paul IV was
taking brutal action against New Christians. Nassi was the
first Jew to plan and implement a resettlement of Jews in the
Holy Land, specifically in the region around Tiberias on Lake
Kinneret (the Sea of Galilee). (Messianic hopes were conse-
quently invested in him, shortly before his death.) His plans
for the Holy Land, however, were doomed to failure, since this
economically rather unattractive land attracted few Jewish immigrants. A family as highly esteemed and prosperous as that
of Joseph Nassi and Gracia Mendes was certainly an exception,
and it was only possible under the conditions of relative tolerance that prevailed in the Ottoman Empire.

The newly emergent Sephardic Diaspora differed in many
respects from the communities that had preceded it in the
Middle Ages. While Sephardic Jews in the Iberian states had
sought religious and national integration, in the Ottoman
Empire they inhabited a multicultural state in which different

nations retained their language and culture. They had brought Spanish along with them into exile and, well into the modern era, communicated with each other in the language known as Judeo-Spanish or Ladino. The expulsion from Spain had brought heretofore latent messianic expectations back to the surface. The reception accorded Reuveni and Molcho may be a manifestation not only of revived messianic expectations, but also of new aspirations to intervene actively in the course of history—compensation for one of their most serious humiliations. At the same time, in the Jews' country of origin, a systematic reinterpretation of Jewish mysticism emerged that smoothed the way for a much more consequential messianic movement.

As early as the Middle Ages, important rabbis had migrated to Palestine from Europe. One need only think of Yehiel of Paris, who left his country after a religious disputation that ended with the burning of every single copy of the Talmud, or Moses ben Nachman (Nachmanides or Ramban), who had likewise fled Europe after a disputation in Barcelona and then, after a brief stay in Jerusalem (like Rabbi Yehiel), settled in Akko. But the conquest of Palestine by the Ottomans in 1517 set in motion an immigration movement of far greater volume. The Jewish communities in the Holy Land that were now just starting to grow again were only able to stay afloat economically through donations from their co-religionists in the Diaspora. Emissaries (*shlichim*) from Palestine traveled the world visiting Jewish communities that regarded it as an act of charity to provide financial support for Jews living in Israel under economically trying conditions.

Kabbalah and Messianism in the Seventeenth Century

A significant new center of Jewish scholarship emerged in the sixteenth century in the city of Zefat (Safed) in the Galilee.

Here the scholar Jacob Berab, swayed by a conviction that the messianic age was imminent, tried to reintroduce rabbinic ordination (*semikhah*), which had not been practiced since the fifth century. It was in Safed, too, that the most important codifier of Jewish teaching, Joseph Caro, worked. His *Shulkhan Arukh* (The Set Table) is regarded to this day as the foundation for every Jewish religious codex to which Jews anywhere in the world look when they need orientation about religious practice. This compendium was later supplemented by an Ashkenazic version written by the Cracow rabbi Moses Isserles, a book Isserles aptly entitled *Mappah* (The Tablecloth).

Safed was, above all, home to the most important Kabbalists of the sixteenth century, Moses Cordovero and especially Isaac Luria. The latter was born in 1534 in Jerusalem, the son of a father who had emigrated from Germany and a Sephardic mother. He is regarded as the founder of a new mystical system of thought, Lurianic Kabbalah. His teachings, which revolved around messianism, shaped the new prayer books that were gaining wide circulation as they came out of the first Hebrew printing houses in Italy. As imparted to his student Chaim Vital, Luria's teachings supplied the intellectual scaffolding for the most important messianic movement in the history of modern Judaism.

The man on whom that movement's hopes were pinned, undoubtedly the most colorful Jewish figure from the second half of the seventeenth century, came from Smyrna (Izmir). Shabbetai Zevi was born in 1626, supposedly on the 9th of Av, the day on which, according to Jewish tradition, both the First and Second Temples had been destroyed. His unusual behavior (his biographer Gershom Scholem regards him as manic-depressive) and his messianic gestures led to his banishment from Smyrna, and then later from Istanbul and Salonica. He first declared himself the messiah in his hometown in the year

1648, a year that, according to some numerical speculations, represented the end of days, and in which there also were terrible anti-Jewish massacres in the Ukraine. In that momentous year, Shabbetai signaled his messiahship by publicly declaiming the holy and unpronounceable name of God.

His messianic movement, however, did not begin in earnest until after a journey that he took to Cairo and Palestine, where he encountered Nathan of Gaza, who announced that he was Shabbetai's "prophet" and then proclaimed Shabbetai as messiah in 1665. In a letter written by Nathan, which was disseminated from Livorno and Amsterdam to Constantinople and Lvov, the plan for salvation was explicitly foretold step by step:

> A year and a few months from today, he [Shabbetai] will take the dominion from the Turkish king without war, for by [the power of] the hymns and praises which he shall utter, all nations shall submit to his rule. He will take the Turkish king alone to the countries which he will conquer, and all the kings shall be tributary unto him, but only the Turkish king will be his servant. . . . "In the seventh year the son of David will come." The seventh year, that is the Sabbath, signifying King Shabbetai. At that time the aforementioned rabbi [Shabbetai] will return from the river Sambatyon, together with his predestined mate, the daughter of Moses . . . mounted on a celestial lion; his bridle will be a seven-headed serpent and "fire out of his mouth devoured." At this sight all the nations and all the kings shall bow before him to the ground. On that day the ingathering of the dispersed shall take place, and he shall behold the sanctuary all ready built descending from above. There will be seven thousand Jews in Palestine at that time, and on that day will be the resurrection of the dead that have died in Palestine. . . . The resurrection outside the Holy Land will take place forty years later. (Scholem, *Sabbatai Sevi*, 273–274)

The false Messiah Shabbetai Zevi is depicted as a crowned king in a prayer book of the Sabbateans from Amsterdam (*Tikkun keria le-kol laila ve-yom*). He is surrounded by angels and guarded by lions. In the lower frame he is shown with the princes of the twelve reunited tribes. According to the printer's mark, this book was published in the "year of the Messiah 5426 [–1666], Year 1."

Initially, the movement spread among mystically oriented Jews in Palestine. When it was placed under a ban by the religious authorities in Jerusalem, Shabbetai Zevi returned to his native city of Smyrna and, joined by his followers, occupied the Sephardic synagogue there. He had the old rabbi dismissed, appointed a new one, and brought much of the synagogue under his control. In the meantime, thanks to his charismatic personality, his well-versed heralds, and an atmosphere rife with expectation, he acquired adherents throughout the entire Jewish world. But Jewish communities, from Poland to the Rhineland and from northern Africa to the North Sea, were deeply split into factions of followers and factions of opponents of this "messiah." Among Shabbetai's followers, the feeling that redemption was at hand frequently outpaced all rational objections. Many sold all their worldly possessions and readied themselves to answer an imminent summons to the Holy Land, from which they expected redemption to proceed. All manner of recent events, from the readmission of the Jews into England to the terrible massacres of the Cossack uprising in the Ukraine in 1648, were viewed as signs and birth pangs of a Messianic Age.

For Shabbetai Zevi himself, however, history took an unfavorable turn. Convinced of his mission, he made his way to the sultan in Istanbul. In February 1665, worried by the movement's unstoppable momentum and by unrest in the empire, the sultan had Shabbetai arrested and gave him a choice between being killed or converting to Islam. When Shabbetai Zevi opted for conversion, most of his followers realized they had been deceived. His most loyal devotees, however, would not desert the cause, even after Shabbetai Zevi died under rather luxurious prison conditions in 1676. They interpreted his conversion as a necessary step in the process of salvation and continued secretly to maintain their faith in Shabbetai Zevi as the messiah.

The whole episode of the messianic movement shows how eagerly Jews were awaiting their redemption, how intensively they continued to feel tied to the land of Israel, and how strong were the ties that bound the Sephardic and Ashkenazic communities in spite of all their differences. And there was one more thing that all this messianic enthusiasm made clear: the enormous importance of the Kabbalah, of Jewish mysticism, for broad segments of the population. Indeed, Shabbetai Zevi's success would hardly have been conceivable were it not for the widespread influence of the Lurianic Kabbalah. His followers even attempted, by invoking a complex cosmological construct, to justify his break with Judaism and his various transgressions of Jewish religious law in theological terms: As a result of a cosmic accident during the process of creation (this theology of "redemption through sin" claimed), a portion of divine energy had fallen into the abyss of the universe. So long as this part of God remained in that dark abyss, so too would there always be a bit of good contained within evil. Salvation would only be achieved when the last remaining traces of divine energy were retrieved from the abyss and returned to their source. But for this to happen, the forces of good had to descend into the evil. The messiah had therefore betaken himself into the realm of evil in order to gather up the divine sparks and bring about redemption.

This cosmic theory could also explain the Jews' situation of exile. Just as God himself was in exile after the cosmic accident, so too did humankind find itself banished from Paradise and the Jewish people from its ancestral homeland. The expulsion from Iberia was interpreted as the final act of that total dispersion, which now needed to be followed by an ingathering of all the Jews in their land.

The shakeup following this messianic movement had long-term repercussions for Jewish life. Other mystical movements, of which Hasidism would prove to be the most successful, were to follow. But any actual messianic expectation, of the kind still associated with David Reuveni or Shabbetai Zevi, had to be postponed to an indeterminate future in the wake of these false messiahs' disastrous ends. The wounds that opened throughout the entire Jewish world as it split into "believers" and "nonbelievers" in the pseudo-messiah would not heal quickly, and they would flare up again centuries later, when the boundaries of the division would run along entirely different lines.

זה השער לי' צדיקים יבואו בו

ספר

זבח פסח

המאחר הזה הוא פירוש כתבנית
הפסח פרשיות ודרושים וטעמים
ככבדי חדש' לא סעדות כראשונים
מתוקים מדבש וכופת נופים ' חכרו
שר וגדול בישראל ד'ן ינחק אברבנאל
זנל כן השר דון יהודה
אברבנאל זצ'ל

סתחלמו המלאכ'ב' היום נ' י' אלול
כאנת ויעבמד ב'ן סביתים
וכיך החיים נסתנפה כפצרה

נדפס בכפר ביסטרוד'יץ
תחת השר ז'ידעם שקי
ובתכתר מלכות ריתן כרחן דנ'ד
ירום הודו ותכאא' מלכותן אבר:

על ידי כלונימוס רז יה'ר'ר
מרדכי יפ'חז'ל

The first Haggadah printed in eastern Europe comes from Bistrowitz in 1592
and was the only book printed in Hebrew in that city. An explanation for
this unique publication was offered by the printer Kalonymus ben Mordecai
Jaffe on the title page reproduced here. He indicates, referring to a Biblical
verse (Numbers 17:13) , that he had fled Lublin because of a plague there and
settled for a short time in Bistrowitz.

11. From West to East
A NEW CENTER IN POLAND

THE POLISH-BORN ISRAELI WRITER S. Y. (Shmuel Yosef) Agnon opened his 1916 *Buch der polnischen Juden* (*Book of the Polish Jews*) with Polish Jewry's best-known founding myth: "Israel saw how the suffering was constantly renewed, how the impositions multiplied, how the persecutions grew, how the bondage became great, how the rule of evil brought to pass one disaster after another and piled on expulsion after expulsion, so that Israel could no longer stand up to its haters—and so it set out on the roadways and looked and inquired after the paths of the world as to which might be the right road it should take in order to find rest for itself. Then a note fell down from Heaven: Go to Poland! . . . And there are some who believe that even the name of the country issues from a holy source: the language of Israel. For so spoke Israel when it arrived there: *po-lin*, that is to say: Here pass the night! And they meant: Here is where we want to pass the night until God gathers together again the dispersed of Israel."

A Tolerant Reception

This popular legend had its origin in the generous reception that Poland gave to Jewish refugees from Western and Central

Europe during the late Middle Ages and the early modern period. To the same degree that more and more territories, from Germany's cities to Spain and Portugal, expelled their Jewish population, Polish kings made an effort to settle Jews in their country. Colonization by Christians from the West had declined, and the influx of Jews was viewed as beneficial, augmenting the population of the cities and encouraging trade in this sparsely settled country. After Duke Boleslaw V, in the Statute of Kalisz (1264), encouraged the settlement of Jews (by routinizing and regularizing the conditions of Jewish residence in Poland), and King Casimir granted comprehensive privileges to the Jews of Lesser and Greater Poland in two charters (in 1334 and 1364), the flood of immigrants never ran dry. This was equally true of the kingdom of Lithuania, where little clerical resistance was to be expected as the country had only recently been Christianized (in 1385). Conditions for Jews in Poland and Lithuania were, thus, more favorable than for those in what remained of Jewish communities in Western Europe. Jews were exempted from the jurisdiction of all but the crown courts and were allowed to have their own courts. Synagogues and cemeteries were protected from desecration, and intra-Jewish autonomy was preserved to the greatest extent possible. Disseminating slander about Jewish involvement in ritual murder was made a punishable offense. In 1534 King Sigismund I proclaimed, against the will of the Sejm (the Polish parliament), that the Jews in his kingdom did not have to wear special badges on their clothes. Thus, the most famous Polish-Jewish scholar of the sixteenth century, the Cracow rabbi Moses Isserles, could write: "In this country there is not such a ferocious hatred of Jews as in Germany. May it remain this way until the arrival of the Messiah!" And there was this report from a papal legate in 1565: "In these territories there are great numbers of Jews who are not as despised as is elsewhere the case. They do not live in a state of degradation, and they are not restricted to despised professions. They own land, they engage in trade, and they study medicine and astronomy. . . . They bear no distinguishing insignia, and they are even permitted to bear arms. In short, they possess all civic rights." (Cited by Heiko Haumann, *A History of East European Jews*, [Budapest and New York: Central European University Press, 2002] 15.)

Yet, from the very outset, this tolerant treatment of the Jews ran up against energetic resistance from the Catholic Church. As early as the Council of Breslau in 1267, there was a call for Jewish areas to be segregated from the Christian population, for Jews to wear horned hats, and for a ban on their using the bath houses and inns of Christians as well as on their holding public office. Starting in the middle of the fifteenth century with the rise of the Polish bourgeoisie, economic competition intensified, and the nobility, frequently in debt to Jews, grew increasingly antisemitic. As in the German and French Middle Ages, here too the "vertical alliance" between Jews and the highest political authority, the king, proved fragile and unreliable. And this made the position of the Jews at the bottom of this partnership precarious, since it was their ally at the top, the Polish king, who had to endure a major loss of power in relation to the estates represented in the Sejm during the fifteenth century. After some initial hesitation, Poland, too, began to drive Jews gradually out of trade and commerce, as well as to expel them from the larger cities. In 1483 they were thrown out of Warsaw, and in 1494, following anti-Jewish riots, they had to leave Cracow to settle in suburban Kazimierz. Only in 1867 were they allowed, with some exceptions, to resettle in Cracow proper.

During the sixteenth century it becomes increasingly difficult to talk about any uniform legislation on the Jews of Poland. In spite of renewed anti-Jewish resolutions passed by Christian synods (1542 in Petrikau), and in spite of many a legend about ritual murder or desecration of the host, the royal house did (in principle) succeed in securing the position of Jews. In contrast to the situation in the Holy Roman Empire, however, the Jews as a whole did not have the status of *servi camerae* in Poland; rather, they were subject to different legal orders in different cities and parts of the country. This development reflects the royal house's gradual loss of power. Already at the beginning of the sixteenth century, the power of the kings was being curtailed in favor of the nobles. King Sigismund I granted the nobility the right to treat the Jews in each one of their territories as they saw fit. The power of the cities also continued to grow. From this period onward, an increasing number of Jewish settlements were on private land, owned and administered by Polish nobles. Some, including Gdansk, Warsaw, and Lublin, did not accept any Jews. With the passing of the Jagiellon dynasty in 1572, there emerged an elected monarchy, appointed by the nobility in the Sejm. Within their own communities, however, the situation of the Jewish minority stabilized. The 1569 Union of Lublin in particular, which incorporated parts of Lithuania and Prussia into the Polish union of states, would prove to have a positive effect on intra-Jewish life. A state emerged that comprised numerous nations, religions, and language communities. Along with its neighbors Ukraine and Belorussia, the greater Polish-Lithuanian Commonwealth also attracted major immigrant communities of Germans and Italians. Aside from Catholic Poles, there were Protestants, Orthodox Christians, and a significant number of Muslim Tatars. Within this diverse assortment, the Jews made up about 3 to 5 percent of the total population in the middle of the seventeenth century, and up to twenty percent in the cities. These figures were much higher than in the rest of Europe, where Jews made up only a little over one percent of the population. The Jews living in Poland-Lithuania (up to 300,000, according to some estimates) were thus Europe's largest Jewish community.

Whereas the majority of the Christian population lived on the land as peasants, Jews, as we have seen, made up a significant portion of the urban population. In the mostly smaller cities where they lived, they worked in various fields of trade and crafts. Polish nobles in the eastern parts of the country frequently leased their property to Jews. Jews thus became managers of landed estates, and frequently also publicans, which meant that they sold not only schnapps, but also everything produced on the nobles' estates, to the peasants. As a rule, men and women divided up the work. Typically, the husband looked after the loan accounts and traveled around the country, while the wife took care of business on the market square, which often involved pawnbroking and minor monetary transactions. In public houses the wife would look after the preparation of meals, while the husband catered to the guests.

In many respects, the Jews in Poland existed as a kind of parallel society to the Christian community. While the Jewish population in the noble latifundia of the eastern regions was often the only mercantile element, the economic activity of Jews in the Polish towns further west did not differ significantly from that of the surrounding populations. Jews spoke their own language, Yiddish, which they had brought along with them from German-speaking Europe. Yiddish was based on medieval German dialects, supplemented by Hebrew and Slavic elements and written in Hebrew letters. Of course, the calendars of Christians and Jews in Poland were different, as was the case elsewhere. Jews observed their own holidays, and their weekly day of rest fell on Saturday rather than Sunday. Autonomous Jewish communities were headed by community elders (*tovim*) elected annually by all taxpayers and by the mayor-like head (the *parnas*). They made their own decisions about both religious and worldly affairs, beginning with guidelines for what food was permissible and extending to the improvement of streets in the Jewish quarter. The communities claimed many of the rights that had been in existence since the Middle Ages, including the power to permit or prohibit Jewish strangers from settling in

This drawing from the nineteenth century shows the eighteenth-century wooden synagogue of Mohylów Podolski on the Dniester in front of the Roman-Catholic and Orthodox churches of the same municipality.

their community. The bedrock of Jewish autonomy was an in-dependent legal system. It was headed, as a rule, by a respected rabbi whose influence extended well beyond the religious sphere. Actual communal affairs were run by the *kahal*, the Jewish com-munal administration, which was usually dominated by afflu-ent merchants. Jewish religious and communal laws regulated everyday life to such an extent that it is often difficult to discern a separation between the religious and worldly spheres.

Autonomy was not only expressed at the local level. Until the eighteenth century, the *Va'ad Arba Aratzot* (*Aratzos* in the Ashkenazic pronunciation), a council first convened in 1581 as a network of the autonomous communities of Poland-Lithuania (the "Four Lands" of Greater Poland, Lesser Poland, Volhynia, and Podolia) that would rule on supra-local disputes between Jews and would present a united front in dealings with outside authorities. Both the secular community heads and the religious authorities met, usually twice a year, at the great trade fairs in Lublin and Yaroslav. In no other European Diaspora community was there comparable countrywide representation of Jewish interests.

In addition to the factors that obviously separated Jews from Christians in Poland, there were things that bound them together. The culture of their everyday lives drew on similar sources. Popular belief in demons and ghosts was merely clothed in different garments. Jews and Christians alike sought out faith healers, wore amulets, and believed in the active power of certain sayings and formulaic prayers. The clothing of Polish Jews was borrowed from that of the surrounding population, and synagogue architecture conformed to prevailing architectural styles. Wooden synagogues with impressive mural paintings became widespread, beginning especially in the eighteenth century. The "typically Jewish" food of the Jews was, apart from conformity to ritual dietary laws, closely related to Polish cuisine. The melodies they used in their folk songs derived from the indigenous musical traditions of Eastern Europe.

In many respects, therefore, Polish Jews were part of Poland. They felt tied to the landscape and to their king, established political structures like those around them, supplemented these for economic purposes, and when it came to a variety of everyday matters were more like their Christian neighbors than they were like Jews in distant lands. By no means should this affinity be idealized, however. Jews and Christians in Poland did not always love each other, and their religious differences remained a source of ongoing tensions. Jewish leaseholders often stood at the frontlines: between nobles and peasants, Poles and Ukrainians. This became especially apparent in times of persecution.

Destruction and Rebuilding

When the Ukrainian Cossack Bogdan Chmielnicki triggered a revolt against the rule of the Polish magnates in 1648, his actions would have dramatic consequences for the Jews of Eastern Europe. The revolt had several components: At the national level it was an uprising against the Polish empire, at the social level a struggle of peasants against the large landowners, and at the religious level resistance by the Orthodox church against the domination of the Roman-Catholic. The Jews were drawn into this fight and targeted not only as religious and ethnic outsiders, but also as economic scapegoats. Most Ukrainian peasants did not even know the actual property owners whose land they worked; they dealt with them only through Jewish middlemen, who became the objects of their hatred. Hundreds of Jewish communities were razed to the ground during the disturbances, and tens of thousands of Jews were either killed or sold into slavery. These were, until the twentieth century, the bloodiest Jewish massacres in history. Contemporary reports depicted the atrocities in detail and characterized them as the "third destruction" (after the destructions of the two Temples in Jerusalem).

These events turned the tide of Jewish migration westward. Jews now left Poland and returned to the various German territories or fled to Amsterdam or to the Ottoman Empire. Others settled in the western parts of Poland, and some soon returned to their native towns. It is in fact astonishing how quickly the Jewish community in Poland recovered from the horrors. By the end of the seventeenth century, the country was again home to numerous institutions of Jewish learning, and its Jewish population was increasing rapidly. By the middle of the eighteenth century, it reached 750,000 and comprised nearly half of the country's urban population.

Even the centers of learning of the Polish Jews were only temporarily shaken by the massacres of 1648. Until the modern era Poland would remain the hub of traditional Jewish learning, from which rabbis and teachers would repeatedly be summoned to the West, so that they might disseminate Polish-Jewish erudition. Starting at the age of three or four, every Jewish boy was expected to attend a kind of primary school, often located in the teacher's room or *cheder* (Hebrew and Yiddish for "room"), where he would receive at least an elementary education in Torah and Talmud, be introduced to the world of prayers and Jewish law, and learn to read Hebrew script. The quality of the instruction and classroom size depended on what parents could afford to pay the teacher. Girls could also receive rudimentary instruction, but this was usually done by family members or by private teachers and was conducted in Yiddish. The real centers of serious learning were the *yeshivot* (*yeshivos*, in Ashkenazic pronunciation), in which the Talmud and rabbinic commentaries and codes were studied intensively. Only a minority of students had the opportunity to attend a yeshiva; most began working while still in their youth. The highest goal of yeshiva students (beginners were called *ne'arim*, the more advanced students *bachurim*) was to become familiar later in their studies with the finer points of Jewish law. As a rule, they would have finished their course of study, received the title of a *haver*, and established a family by the age of eighteen. They could then become teachers or Torah scribes, preachers, or even rabbis. In the latter case, they would spend additional years attending a yeshiva (or one of two other institutions, the communal *beth midrash*, a house of learning, or the more elite *klois*, a cloistered student residence) and eventually receive the title of *morenu* (our teacher), which was the equivalent of a rabbinic ordination.

The invention of the letterpress contributed both to the spread and democratization of Talmud study. By the middle of the sixteenth century Poland had become home to the most important Hebrew printing houses, whose work centered on publishing the Talmud. A standard format now emerged for a page of Talmud, which included, next to the text of the *Mishnah* and *Gemara*, the most important commentaries from the last several centuries. Whereas students had previously been dependent on their teachers' interpretations and were only seldom able to get hold of the actual books, the letterpress now enabled direct access to the sources, thereby enabling more than a tiny elite to study without intermediaries. Books less elitist in their content were also printed and spread to a wider readership; these included the writings of less prominent authors and the speeches of popular preachers. As a result, the monopoly on learning of the traditional authorities was increasingly questioned.

There was now also a special "women's literature" (or literature often read by women) published in Yiddish. The best-known compendia of Biblical texts and legends were the early seventeenth-century *Tsene-rene* (derived from the Hebrew Biblical verse in the Song of Songs, 3:11: "Go forth, O ye daughters of Zion, and gaze . . . ."), along with the *Mayse-Bukh* (Book of Stories), which contained numerous rabbinic tales. In addition, there was an extensive literature of *tkhines*, collections of certain prayers that were regarded as important for women and that were used above all for household purposes, in the *mikvah* (the ritual bath visited each month for purification after a woman's period), and for graveyard visits. The *tkhines* allowed women to immerse themselves in a world of religious deeds parallel to the world of men. Whereas men were obligated to attend synagogue three times a day, women (owing to their domestic and business responsibilities, and the assumption that only men had an essential place in the public enactment of religion) did not have to participate in daily congregational prayers, although they were certainly not barred from doing so in a separate room. At home the ritual duties incumbent on women included the obligation of *challah* (cutting off a portion of dough for baking) and *hadlakat nerot* (lighting Sabbath and holiday candles).

Hasidism

By the middle of the seventeenth century, Kabbalah began to enjoy increasing popularity in Eastern Europe, both as a subject of theoretical study and in its practical applications, from the production of amulets meant to bestow blessings, through the introduction of new prayers, all the way to physical practices. Kabbalistic rituals were now influencing behavior in major life events, at birth, marriage, or death. Advice from a faith healer, a *ba'al shem*, was sought in cases of illness.

One of these faith healers was Israel ben Eliezer, who had come to be known by the name *Ba'al Shem Tov* (Master of the Good Name). From contemporary sources we do not know much more about him than the fact that he lived in the small Ukrainian town of Miedzyboz and inspired the poor people of Podolia to take an interest in his teachings. With Hasidism (*Hasidim* are "the pious") his followers created a mass movement that posed an enormous challenge to a Jewish tradition fixated on the study of Talmud. According to Hasidic teaching, it was not only through rigorous study that one could get closer to God. There were many ways to approach Him: through intimacy with nature and through physical activities such as singing and dancing, as well as rocking back and forth during prayer. Joy and merriment took on a whole new devotional significance. Internalizing spirituality during prayer, up to the point of achieving a trance-like state, became more important than uttering the words of the prayer itself.

After the death of the *Ba'al Shem Tov* in 1760, his right-hand man, Dov Baer of Mezhirech, turned a small following into a movement. Dov Baer's movement began to gain respect, among other reasons, because he, unlike the movement's founder, was a renowned teacher who now granted Talmud study a more important place in the life of the Hasidim. By the end of the eighteenth century, Hasidism had split into numerous smaller groups, each of which followed its own spiritual leader, the *rebbe* or *tzaddik*. Their teachings were, for the most part, handed down orally in the form of folk tales, but some students published the most important texts of their masters. In contrast to a rabbi elected by a congregation, from the nineteenth century onward the *tzaddik* was often legitimated dynastically by ancestry. As a rule, the father was followed by the oldest son or, if he had no sons, by a stepson. Almost supernatural powers were ascribed to the rebbe. Coming into bodily contact with the rebbe—and not only with the rebbe himself, but even with the food and drink he had tasted—was just as holy an act as humming his melodies or telling his stories. As a result, pilgrimages to Hasidic courts enjoyed enormous popularity. In a certain sense, the rebbe was the equivalent of a Catholic saint.

In traditional Jewish circles, the Hasidim initially engendered intense resistance. They openly engaged in curiously ecstatic movements during prayer, they preferred the Kabbalah-enriched Sephardic prayer book to the traditional Ashkenazic ritual that was standard for the region, and they studied the *Zohar* with the kind of fervor usually reserved for the Talmud. In addition, they rejected the knives used by most Jewish butchers as not kosher and introduced their own knives. And finally, they turned against the authority of the rabbis and looked to their own rebbes. A major reason, therefore, for the conflict between the Hasidim and their adversaries (*Mitnagdim*, or *Misnagdim* in Ashkenazic pronunciation, is the Hebrew word for "opponents") was the question of authority. Introducing new rituals made it impossible for both camps to pray together; making new butcher's knives prevented eating together; and with the emergence of charismatic new rebbes, what the traditional rabbi said no longer counted. So it is hardly surprising that the "old" authorities mustered all their heavy guns against the Hasidim, and, as some historians argue, only thus created

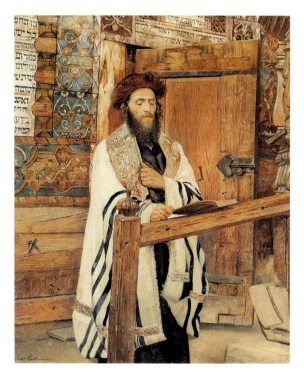

The Hungarian-born genre painter Isidor Kaufmann specialized in portraying Hasidic Jews. This painting from 1897/98 shows a Hasid in the wooden synagogue of Jablonow in Slovakia, whose four walls are adorned by colorful ornamentation.

a real movement. Moreover, they were irked by the neglect of Talmud study and by the apparent need of the Hasidim to give free rein to their often exuberant feelings, going so far as to often accuse the Hasidim of the excessive enjoyment of alcohol and tobacco.

Standing at the frontline of this conflict was the greatest rabbinic authority of his time, Rabbi Eliayu ben Shlomo Zalman, the "Vilna Gaon." Supported by the Jewish community of Vilna, he dedicated his entire life to Talmud study, which he carried out in the splendid isolation afforded him as a private scholar. In 1772 he excommunicated the Hasidic leaders and was, in turn, excommunicated by them. Vehement and divisive struggles over dominance in Jewish communities were not infrequent. Most often they reflected geographical differences. The Hasidim maintained the upper hand in generally less educated regions of the east (Podolia, Volhynia) and south (Galicia, Hungary), while the Mitnagdim prevailed in the citadels of Jewish learning, in Vilna and the other northern regions of Lithuania and Belorussia.

The movement surrounding the pseudo-messiah Shabbetai Zevi would have its own spectacular sequel in Poland. Even after his conversion and death, there were many parts of Europe where "believers" could not be dissuaded from viewing him as the messiah. Some of his Polish followers stayed in touch with the centers of the Sabbatean movement in the Habsburg and Ottoman Empires. Presumably, this was also true for the family of Jacob Frank, who had been disseminating Sabbatean teachings since the 1750s and had accused rabbinic Judaism of using the Talmud to distort Jewish doctrine. Citing the *Zohar* and other Kabbalistic writings, he introduced Christian elements such as the Trinity into his own teachings. Among the practices cultivated by his sect were deliberate transgressions of Jewish law, including sexual debauchery. Matters had reached the point that the Jewish authorities in Poland consulted Jacob Emden, a private scholar who had risen to the front rank of the anti-Sabbateans after a public dispute with the rabbi of the three communities of Hamburg, Altona, and Wandsbek, Jonathan Eybeschuetz, to whom Emden (quite correctly) ascribed Sabbatean practices. Emden recommended turning to the bishop of Kamenetzk-Podolsk for assistance. The bishop, however, sided with Frank and, at Frank's urging, convened a public disputation in 1757 between the rabbis of the region and the Frankists, a religious debate whose outcome, like those that took place in the

Middle Ages, was predetermined. The bishop declared Frank and his followers as the winners of the disputation, imposed a fine on the Jewish communities, and had all the copies of Talmud that could be found in Podolia publicly burned.

Fortified by this victory, Frank had himself proclaimed as the successor of Shabbetai Zevi, as well as of King David, and then betook himself to the bosom of the Catholic Church. The public conversion of Frank and 500 of his followers took place, with a number of Polish nobles participating, on September 17, 1759, in Lemberg (Lviv). The following day Frank had himself baptized one more time in Warsaw, with no less than King August III as godfather. But since Frank and his followers kept up their curious practices, they continued to be eyed suspiciously, now by the Church, and a year after his baptism Frank was finally arrested. He spent the last thirteen years of his life imprisoned in a fortress in Częstochowa. Many of the Catholic Frankists, who may have numbered 20,000, secretly adhered to certain Jewish practices, had their sons circumcised, and celebrated the Jewish Sabbath. Even inside Jewish communities, some families clandestinely preserved Sabbatean or Frankist traditions until the beginning of the nineteenth century. But by 1817, when the Russian Czar officially declared the Frankists Israelite Catholics, most of them were fully assimilated. Even so, many Frankists maintained a consciousness of their origins over several generations and stayed in touch with each other through family and business ties. Undoubtedly, both Sabbateans and Frankists contributed to the sense that the unified Jewish community was in the process of disintegration. Indirectly, they laid a cornerstone for the community's diversification, and ultimately for Judaism's modern divisions.

The Lower-Rhenish van Geldern family—ancestors of the poet Heinrich Heine—belonged to a Jewish upper class that could still have a hand-illustrated Haggadah like this one made as late as the eighteenth century. This domestic scene shows how adhering to Jewish tradition could be brought into accord with upward mobility. In the background a park-like landscape opens up, which highlights the manorial frame of the house.

12. From Dessau to Berlin
RURAL JEWS, COURT JEWS, AND ENLIGHTENMENT PHILOSOPHERS

CONVENTIONAL JEWISH HISTORIOGRAPHY knows no better motif for describing the start of the modern era than the journey undertaken by fourteen-year-old Moses ben Mendel from his hometown of Dessau to Berlin in 1743. This son of a Torah scribe was following his teacher, Rabbi David Fränkel, in order to continue his Talmud studies. Like all his co-religionists, Moses had to pay a humiliating special toll (the *Leibzoll*, a personal or "body tax") at every provincial border and submit to other discriminatory laws. He was allowed to remain in Berlin only because he had been hired as a private tutor by the prosperous factory owner Isaak Bernhard. Within a few years, Moses ben Mendel had become one of the most important philosophers of the Enlightenment. As Moses Mendelssohn, he enjoyed a close friendship with the playwright Gotthold Ephraim Lessing and won high acclaim from the philosopher Immanuel Kant.

As depicted by the first modern Jewish historian, Isaak Markus Jost, Mendelssohn's emergence signified a departure "from the heavy darkness that enshrouded all of Judaism

[into] ... the dawn of a beautiful day" that was breaking. If Mendelssohn was a new Moses to Jost, to the poet Heinrich Heine he was the modern Luther who would reform Judaism.

Between Beggar Jews and Court Jews

The light breaking through the darkness did not quite come without warning, despite what Jost and other historians would have had us believe. Changes in eighteenth-century German Jewry began earlier and more slowly. Upon his arrival in Berlin, Mendelssohn encountered a Jewish community very different from the one he had left behind in Dessau. In the various German territories of the eighteenth century, the Jewish community was characterized not so much by religious as by social conflicts. On the one hand, there were a few court Jews who had experienced a kind of social mobility hardly deemed possible heretofore, and who were often close confidants of their respective rulers. On the other hand, there were the *Betteljuden*, or vagrant "beggar Jews," who moved from place to place and were dependent on the good will of their co-religionists. In between was the bulk of Jewish society, which, after having been driven out of the cities and forbidden to compete in the trades, was mostly restricted to cattle dealing and to running small pawnbroking operations.

That men were not the only ones who were employed is shown by the memoirs of Glikl bas Juda Leib, as she called herself, or Glueckel of Hameln, as her editors later named her. Glikl was the daughter of two merchants from Hamburg. In 1660, at age fourteen, she was married to Chaim ben Joseph from Hameln. Although the couple had fourteen children, Glikl helped out by working in her husband's business. When her husband died in 1689, she initially carried on his business operations on her own. Later she was joined by her second husband, Hirsch Levy, from Metz in Lorraine. He, however, drove the business to financial ruin. Glikl's are the first comprehensive memoirs of a Jewish woman that we possess, and from them we learn not only a great deal about commercial life, but also about legends and family stories. Her memoirs also make it clear that some Jewish women in early modern times were able to acquire a Jewish and secular education, that they studied using a special women's literature (mostly compendia of Biblical texts, historical legends, and prayers), and that they participated in religious life.

The economic policies of the absolutist state would have a decisive influence on the fate of the Jews in the seventeenth and eighteenth centuries. According to the tenets of mercantilism, it was in a state's most vital interest to achieve a balance of trade surplus. This was to be accomplished by increasing state revenues and favoring the immigration of foreigners so long as they brought economic benefits to the country. More and more, religious motives took a back seat to economic interests. The realization that Jews could be productive members of the state took hold and led to the formation of a new economic elite among the Jews of Central Europe.

In the wake of the Thirty Years' War, the Emperor's authority declined, giving way to numerous smaller princely courts. These principalities needed to find entrepreneurs with experience minting coins and provisioning armies, as well as leaseholders for state monopolies who would look after economic growth and centralization in the territories of their princes. These new mercantilist recruits, moreover, would have to be a disinterested group without any possibility of gaining power on their own. The Jews were ideal. "Court Jews" were prepared, even in the most difficult of times, to procure all kinds of items, from animals for slaughter to jewelry. In the course of the Thirty Years' War they had already proven their worth as major army suppliers. Also important—and not least of all—were the necessary assets for obtaining title to merchandise. Without the credits of his *Hoffaktor* (court factor or agent) Behrend

Title page of the Yiddish memoirs of Glikl of Hameln in the transcription of her son Moses Hameln.

Lehmann, the Saxon Elector August the Strong would certainly not have managed to become King of Poland. And without the assistance of Leffmann Behrens, Ernst August of Hanover would never have become an Elector. One prince might hire numerous court Jews. Court Jews from thirty-five Frankfurt Jewish families were employed by August the Strong. Conversely, it was also often the case that one court agent might be engaged as an agent at several different courts. The Frankfurt banker Moses Löb Isaak Kann, for example, was employed in Mainz, Würzburg, Bamberg, and Vienna.

It was, of course, only a tiny minority of well-to-do Jews who made careers for themselves in this manner, but in the seventeenth and eighteenth century they could be found at numerous princely courts. Frequently they were the ones who, years after an old Jewish community had been expelled, would reestablish the core of a new one, fortified by members of their own family, attendants, and such functionaries as were necessary to a Jewish way of life (rabbis, teachers, and butchers). As a rule they also acted as representatives of their communities. They founded and financed such Jewish institutions as Talmud schools and Hebrew print shops. On the one hand, they enjoyed special privileges, such as being able to live outside the ghetto, not having to pay the "body tax" (*Leibzoll*), and being granted equality with Christian merchants at trade fairs. Sometimes they were even allowed to carry weapons. They had direct access to the prince, although they were completely and utterly at his mercy. There were even occasions when princes who valued the services of their court Jews nonetheless indulged in coarse jokes: August the Strong, for example, cut off the beard of his court Jew (with his own hands) in front of a dinner party.

The court Jew's biggest fear, however, was always the death of the prince whose favor he had enjoyed. At that moment there could be a radical reversal of fortune, and yesterday's favorite could become tomorrow's scapegoat. The most famous instance of such a turnaround was the case of Joseph Süss Oppenheimer (1698–1738). In 1732 he was appointed court agent by the Duke of Württemberg, Karl Alexander, and within a short period of time he rose to become the most important minister in his country's government. After the death of Karl Alexander, public anger at the duke turned on his court Jew, who was arrested on charges of embezzlement and sentenced to death. His sensational end was just as atypical of a court Jew's fate as his rapid rise had been, yet it illuminates the precarious situation of his co-religionists, even those in the highest positions.

Court Jews often worked for a princely house over several generations, which frequently meant that they also functioned as spokesmen for their co-religionists. Only in a few cases had their way of life and residence outside the ghetto put such great distance between them and the Jewish community that there were hardly any points of contact between community and spokesman. Usually court Jews had a close connection to the Jewish communities and contributed to their consolidation. Yet they were separated from ordinary community members by the extensive privileges they enjoyed. Frequently they were not under rabbinic jurisdiction, being subject instead to the prince's manorial court. They had direct access (*Immediatverkehr*) to the sovereign ruler at all times and did not have to pay the discriminatory body tax (*Leibzoll*), the special toll charged only to Jews and livestock at Germany's numerous border crossings. A relatively high number of their descendents converted to Christianity.

Often, as in the expulsion from Vienna in 1670, court Jews did not succeed (their best efforts notwithstanding) in averting dangers. On the whole, too, the role they played in the European economy has been exaggerated. They were one building block in the mercantile system, but the system would not have collapsed without them. Rich Christian merchant families like the Fuggers had vastly greater sums of capital at their disposal than did

The execution of Jud Süss on February 4, 1738, as a public spectacle: Thousands of onlookers watched his death on a twelve-meter high gallows at Stuttgart's place of execution. His mortal remains were kept on display in a cage for six years as a warning.

court Jews. The court Jews constituted an important new element in a Jewish community on the threshold of modernity, but they were certainly not the only agents of the impending transformation. In many cities, such as Königsberg, Magdeburg, and Breslau, the arrival of court Jews resulted in the reestablishment of Jewish communities, and many another community grew substantially as a result of their efforts. There were, however, also other motives for bringing Jews into a country, as we see illustrated by the case of the Sulzbach Count Palatine Christian August. Because of his interest in the Christian interpretation of the Kabbalah, the count had a Hebrew printing house established, which laid the cornerstone for a Jewish community.

The settlement of Jews in one part of the count's margravate led to the founding of other communities there. Thus, in the small market town of Floss, which was part of the territory of Sulzbach, a Jewish community emerged with a structure that was typical of Jewish villages we know from other regions. More often, it could be said, Jews and Christians lived next to each other, but not with each other. Even when there was no ghetto wall, there was often a visible line of demarcation. A river or a street might separate the Christian part of the village from the Jewish quarter. In Floss it was the *Judenberg* (the "Jewish hill"), first officially designated as such in 1736, on which the Jewish population lived, whereas the Christians resided in the town below the hill. The two groups maintained separate administrative structures. The Jewish settlement was subject to the exclusive jurisdiction of the Palatine-Sulzbach public authority in Sulzbach. Well into the nineteenth century it remained a politically autonomous commune with its own communal organs, leaders, and deputies, its own night watchman, and its own fire brigade.

Most points of contact arose out of commercial transactions. Many Jews of Floss were peddlers, their customers Christians. Since competitive pressures were also extreme among Jewish traders, in 1719 the government in Sulzbach divided the region into several trade districts, with just one trader allowed to work in each. Among Jewish traders these could be inherited, sold, leased, exchanged, or divided. Tradition has it that the Jews' Christian neighbors respected the town's other ritual space and

Zizenhausen terracotta figures enjoyed great popularity in petty bourgeois households during the nineteenth century. The church painter Anton Sohn started making them in his home town in 1799. The figures showed different scenes of country life, nostalgically transfigured. Jews usually took their place as traders in these statuettes, as in this depiction of the "goat trade."

sometimes even participated in celebrations, though frequently ascribing magical functions to them. Thus, for example, it might happen that Christian peasants would ascribe special powers to Jewish ritual objects, believing that they could affect the fertility of their livestock. Things were seen but little understood; well into the twentieth century, all manner of curious legends persisted around Jewish dietary laws and burial rites.

The majority of German Jews in the early modern period lived in the country, organized in so-called *Landjudenschaften*, corporate self-governing bodies for administering Jewish affairs that included all the heads of families in a particular territory. Their main function was to determine how the often oppressive taxes levied on Jews would be allocated, and they appointed the chief rabbi of their province as well as the community leader charged with representing the community to the outside world. There was no equivalent in Germany to the Eastern European shtetl. Only in southern Baden and Swabia were there larger Jewish communities with several hundred members. As a rule, Jewish communities consisted of just a few families and were widely dispersed. Frequently, far-flung cemeteries had to be used. Maps record *Judenwege* (Jewish lanes), some of which owe their origin to the Jewish religious law requiring that short, specially demarcated paths be used on the Sabbath. In most cases, however, the new pathways were built either to enable the Jews to circumvent discriminatory laws like the body tax and the death tax, or due to fear of anti-Jewish attacks by neighbors.

Southern German as well as Alsatian Jews displayed many distinctive features that were unknown among the Jews of Eastern Europe. They spoke a western Yiddish dialect (formerly called *jüdisch-deutsch* or *Judendeutsch*), which had much in common with the language of East European Jews but also showed major deviations, both in vocabulary and pronunciation. Some traditions, like the *Hollekreisch* (a ceremony for naming a child), Torah binders (painted ribbons of cloth for wrapping around the Torah scroll), and memorial books preserving the names of the community's deceased members and old customs, were limited to southern Germany. Even in their diet the Jews of southern Germany differed from their Eastern European co-religionists. They prepared kosher versions of German dishes, from sauerbraten and *Knödel* (dumplings) to *Stollen* and *Zwetschgendatschi* (Bavarian plum cake). Gefilte fish, bagels, and blintzes—all the popular East European dishes—were unknown to German Jews. For all Jews, however, it was important to prepare special

Sabbath dishes that could be put in the oven (often at the local bakery) on Friday afternoon and taken out on Saturday afternoon, since cooking was forbidden on the Sabbath. Overall, the best-known of these dishes was *cholent*, a stew made of beans, barley, meat, and potatoes. In southern Germany, by contrast, it was a sweet dish known as *Schalet* (later immortalized by Heinrich Heine, alluding to Schiller's Ode to Joy: "Schalet, ray of light immortal. . . ."). Southern German Jews did not call their Sabbath bread challah, but "Barches." Just as there were major differences among Polish Jewry regarding customs, pronunciation, liturgy, and diet, so there were also traits that distinguished the Jews of Baden from their Swabian counterparts and Alsatian from Franconian Jews. Hessian Jews, for example, adhered to the traditional liturgy from Frankfurt, while Franconian Jews followed the liturgy from Fürth.

Frankfurt, Prague, and Berlin

At the turn of the eighteenth century there were only a few cities that could claim to have sizeable Jewish communities. Among these were a handful whose Jewish communities had had a continuous presence since the Middle Ages. These few included Prague, Frankfurt-on-Main, and Worms. And then there were rapidly growing communities of more recent origin: in Hamburg, Berlin, Mannheim, Hanau, and Fürth. In 1462, when Frankfurt forced all its Jews to reside within the narrow confines of the city's *Judengasse*, this created what would be given the name "ghetto" half a century later in Venice: a municipal district inhabited exclusively by Jews, and which the non-Jewish authorities could lock from outside. Ghettos distinguished such cities as Frankfurt and Venice, but also Prague and Rome, from most Jewish communities in Central and Eastern Europe, where Jews lived in close proximity to one another to be sure, but were not wedged in behind locked gates. In spite of the cramped living conditions, the Jewish population in Frankfurt's Judengasse kept growing: It rose from what was initially 110 registered residents to 250 by the year 1520, then to 1200 six years later, and to 3,000 by 1610. Since the ghetto was not allowed to expand physically, one made do—as in Venice—by subdividing the houses and by raising them to include higher stories. In this period the community was in its heyday, both economically and culturally. Frankfurt's rabbis, like Joseph Juspa (Yuspa) Hahn and Jesaja (Isaiah) Horowitz, and its Talmud school rabbinic court enjoyed enormous prestige throughout Europe. There were conflicts simmering below the surface, however, that erupted in 1614, when a mob led by Vincenz Fettmilch stormed the ghetto, looted houses and shops, and expelled the Jews from the city. At the emperor's command, the agitators were arrested and executed in 1616. Thereupon the Jews were allowed to return. Not until Napoleonic troops invaded Frankfurt would the ghetto walls come down.

Frankfurt was overshadowed by only one other Jewish community, and that was Prague's. The Bohemian metropolis had already been a major center of Jewish life in the Middle Ages, but only in the sixteenth century did Prague's *Judenstadt*, as its ghetto was called, become a focal point of Jewish life in Europe. It reached its cultural zenith at the turn of the seventeenth century, under Emperor Rudolf II. Major financiers like Mordechai Meisel, who had large sections of the Judenstadt rebuilt, and Jacob Bassevi von Treuenburg, the first Jew to be elevated to the nobility by the Habsburgs, were not the only ones with connections to the court. Among those held in high esteem were the astronomer David Gans and Rabbi Judah Löw ben Bezalel (known as the High Rabbi Löw, or Maharal, from the Hebrew acronym for "Our Teacher the Rabbi Löw"), around whom would later grow the legend about the creation of the Golem, an artificial man. At the beginning of the eighteenth century, nearly every fourth resident of Prague belonged to the Jewish community.

It was the religious zeal of the empress Maria Theresa that put an end to this success story. On December 18, 1744, she signed a decree stating that all Jews had to leave Prague by the end of January, and all of Bohemia five months later. The ostensible reason was rumors that Jews had sympathized with the Prussian troops who had temporarily occupied Prague during the Austrian War of Succession. The reaction of Prague's Jews to the imminent danger of expulsion provides an example of active diplomacy, and it shows as well how Jews could indeed be politically effective even while lacking a political structure of their own. The community elders wrote a circular that was sent at wildfire speed to their co-religionists in Vienna, Frankfurt, Amsterdam, London, and Venice, as well as to court agents Wolf Wertheimer in Augsburg and Bendit Gumperz in Nijmegen. Most of the recipients immediately dispatched more copies of the letter, sending them on to Mantua and Munich, Hanover and Hamburg. Just two weeks after the expulsion edict had been signed, dozens of Jewish communities throughout Europe had been informed in detail about the peril facing thousands of their fellow Jews—and this in the middle of winter. Feelings of solidarity, and also of anxiety at the thought that their own (often already overcrowded) communities might have to offer the refugees asylum, drove them to take effective measures. Bendit Gumperz in Nijmegen requested assistance from the king of England; in Amsterdam a joint delegation of Sephardic and Ashkenzaic envoys met with representatives of the Estates General, which immediately had its ambassador lodge a complaint at the court in Vienna; Wolf Wertheimer asked his brother-in-law Moses Kahn, in service to the prince-archbishop of Mainz, to intervene with the latter, while Wertheimer's son Itzig led a delegation to the archbishop of Bamberg, the brother of the prince-archbishop of Mainz. The result was impressive. A month after Maria Theresa's edict was issued, a number of statements in favor of the Jews remaining in Bohemia, most of

A portrait from the picture series of the Prague burial society (*hevra kadisha*) around 1780 shows how the deceased was carried to the grave. The paintings in this series were originally hung in the conference hall where the society met for its annual banquet.

them economically motivated, arrived at the court in Vienna—from the English and Danish kings, from the Estates General of the Netherlands, from the prince-archbishop of Mainz, the Senate in Venice, the municipal authorities of the city of Hamburg, and even from Maria Theresa's mother.

Some of those sending these messages to Vienna were electors of the Holy Roman Empire who had the power to decide whether or not the imperial crown would go to Maria Theresa's husband, Francis of Lorraine. To gain their favor, she suspended the expulsion order and, in the end, revoked it entirely. Those Jews already expelled from Prague were allowed to return. The success of this joint action proved two things: first, that Jewish communities did not by any means take persecution lying down; and second, that at the middle of the eighteenth century political winds had begun to turn in their favor.

The emergence of a Jewish community in Berlin at the end of the seventeenth century must also be seen in this wider context.

The Jews had been driven out of Brandenburg in 1573, and it would take a century before they were allowed to resettle there. The community continued to grow under the rule of the Great Elector (Frederick William), until it reached forty families at the time of his death in 1688. Prussia's settlement policy was driven by mercantile interests and clearly defined. Only well-to-do immigrants involved in trade were invited. And the terms for Jewish immigrants were far more restrictive than those for Huguenots admitted at the same time. Only one child per family was allowed to remain, guilds were still closed to Jews, and religious services had to take place in private quarters. Nonetheless, the community's population continued to climb. It had already reached 117 families by 1700. Fourteen years later, its first synagogue was dedicated in the Heidereuthergasse.

As late as the second half of the eighteenth century, the law in Brandenburg made distinctions between different groups of Jews, granting them privileges in varying degrees. The "Revised General Privileges and Regulations" issued by Frederick II in 1750 distinguished six classes. Those in the category "generally privileged" (*Generalprivilegierten*) were allowed to acquire houses and property, and even citizenship in exceptional cases; above all, there was no restriction on where they could settle so long as it was in the residential area reserved for Jews. The second group of "privileged protected Jews" (*Ordentliche Schutzjuden*), by contrast, did not have the right of free settlement, and only one of their children could inherit their status. "Unprivileged protected Jews" (*Außerordentliche Schutzjuden*), in turn, were admitted because they practiced such "useful occupations" as doctor, optician, or engraver, and they were allowed to "place" one child, but only if that child owned at least 1,000 thalers. The fourth class was a collection of community officials, including rabbis. In this category were the "tolerated Jews," who required a patron's protection to stay on as residents. They could only marry a member of the higher classes. Finally, lumped together in the sixth group, were the domestic servants of the "generally privileged," household employees who were allowed to stay only until their employment contract was terminated. What applied in Brandenburg was roughly applicable in most other German territories as well. The number of Jews was to be kept as small as possible, but their economic utility maximized.

Mendelssohn and the Beginning of the Jewish Enlightenment

Moses Mendelssohn was as much affected by these discriminatory laws, as were his less prominent co-religionists. Twenty years after his arrival in Berlin, Frederick II did grant the philosopher, by now a famous man and a close friend of Lessing, the status of "unprivileged protected Jew" (außerordentlicher Schutzjude), but this grant did not include the right for his descendents to settle in the city. After Mendelssohn had made his way from Dessau to Berlin, he not only studied Talmud, but was also, secretly, learning languages, philosophy, and literature. Soon he began to write philosophical treatises on his own, the most famous of which was his 1767 work Phädon. In learned circles he achieved more acclaim than any Jew had previously received in Germany. Here, in the Age of Enlightenment, a change of attitude toward Jews was making itself felt, a new perspective associated above all with the name of Gotthold Ephraim Lessing. Already as a young man, in his one-act play The Jews (1749), Lessing had written a plea for their social integration. Thirty years later he reaffirmed this position in another drama, Nathan the Wise, which was more complex and more successful. Mendelssohn provided the model for Nathan's title character.

Mendelssohn, whose unattractive appearance (he was small and hunchbacked) served some as a confirmation of their anti-Jewish stereotypes, was now accepted as an equal in philosophical circles and acknowledged as a star in academic competitions. Even more significant was the fact that personal friendships no longer depended on what religion one professed. The friendship between Mendelssohn and Lessing is just one example; there was also mutual, warm-hearted affection between Mendelssohn and the publisher Friedrich Nicolai. Nevertheless, even among the well-intentioned, reservations about his adherence to Judaism persisted. In contrast to Spinoza, the first modern Jewish philosopher, Mendelssohn remained tied to his community. He was an advocate interceding on their behalf in perilous situations, and he adhered to Jewish religious law. The Prussian Academy, in an act of self-censorship, refused to propose him as a member; and he was repeatedly urged to let himself be baptized.

In 1769 his friend Johann Caspar Lavater, a Swiss theologian, sent Mendelssohn a letter challenging him either to refute Christianity publicly or to convert to it. In his diplomatically worded reply, Mendelssohn emphasized that Judaism was not a missionary religion and that dissuading members of other faiths from adhering to their beliefs was the last thing on his mind. For all believers there was a life after death. Religion, Mendelssohn said in hopes of ending the discussion, was a private matter and should not be the subject of public debate. Only in 1783 did he break his silence by publishing his most important work of religious philosophy, *Jerusalem, or On Religious Power and Judaism*. He did so after repeated public calls urging him to explain his religious position clearly.

Jerusalem is divided into two sections. In the first part, which builds on contemporary theories of natural law, the subject is the general relationship between state and religion. Here Mendelssohn calls for a strict separation of the two spheres, conceding no legal authority whatsoever to religious institutions, churches, or Jewish congregations. They should not have the right to demand or enforce religious duties. In the second part

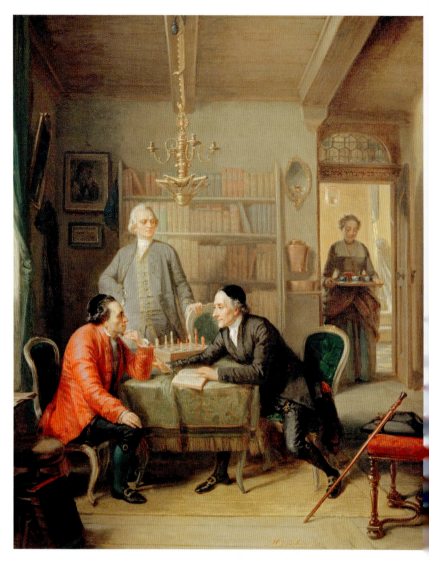

During the nineteenth century, mythologizing Moses Mendelssohn took on different guises. Here he is depicted by the painter Moritz Daniel Oppenheim playing chess with the Swiss pastor Johann Caspar Lavater, which is meant as an allusion to his dispute with Lavater. The chess game is being observed by Mendelssohn's friend Gotthold Ephraim Lessing.

of the book Mendelssohn undertakes an attempt to define Judaism as revealed legislation rather than revealed religion. In Judaism, in contrast to Christianity, there are no dogmas, no articles of faith, no theology that has to be accepted unconditionally. On the other hand, Judaism does possess legislation revealed by God to Moses on Mount Sinai, commandments and prohibitions that regulate daily life and should be followed, even if only on a voluntary basis! Salvation, accordingly, depends less on belief and more on action.

Mendelssohn was convinced that German Jews needed to become part of German society and culture. To this end, the primary requirement was that they be linguistically equipped. While he rejected the Yiddish language as jargon, he did adopt Hebrew as a vehicle of communication, and in 1758 published the first Modern Hebrew journal, *Kohelet Musar* (The Preacher of Morals). He devoted special attention to the German language, however, which he used to write most of his own works. And he also did not shy away from scolding Frederick the Great for using French instead of German. Under Mendelssohn's direction, the Pentateuch and other parts of the Hebrew Bible, along with a comprehensive commentary (*Biur*), were translated into High German, although using Hebrew letters, a concession to the fact that most German Jews did not know any other alphabet. Traditional rabbis accused Mendelssohn of profaning Holy Scripture by turning it into a textbook for the German language.

Around Mendelssohn there soon formed a circle of like-minded Jewish Enlightenment scholars, most of whom had come to Berlin from Poland and other parts of Eastern Europe. They joined him in his multifaceted enterprises. Even in the generation before these Enlightenment figures were active, change had been afoot in Jewish society. Rabbis had complained that religious laws were no longer being conscientiously observed, especially among the urban population; community leaders had chastised their followers for taking their disputes to non-Jewish courts; and guardians of morals had eyed warily the increasingly casual social interactions taking place between individual Jews and Christians. But in the first half of the eighteenth century, these were ad hoc breaches of the old order; there was as yet no effort to draw up a program for a new society. That next step would not be taken in any systematic fashion until the generation of Mendelssohn and his comrades, the so-called *Maskilim* (the Jewish term for "enlighteners"; *Haskalah*, meaning "enlightenment," is derived from the Hebrew *sekhel*, meaning "reason" or "intellect").

Now, for the first time, there was a movement to modernize and also—to the extent that this was possible within the existing framework of discriminatory laws—to integrate Jewish society. To this end educational and publishing institutions had to be created. The *Maskilim* established modern "free schools" where secular as well as religious subjects were taught. The first of these opened in Berlin in 1778. Between 1784 and 1811 (with some interruptions), the periodical *Ha-Meassef* (The Collector) appeared in Hebrew, a sign that it was addressed to a cultural elite. The journal offered its highly literate readers a wide variety of articles on Biblical exegesis and natural science, poetry, and history, as well as news reports on current Jewish life. In 1806 a German-language Enlightenment periodical, *Sulamith*, was also launched, reflecting the shift in language that had already taken place among large sections of the Jewish population.

The generation after Mendelssohn could no longer understand how adhering to Jewish religious law could be taken for granted or how it could be compatible with integration into German society. The surrounding world had also changed. Toleration and Enlightenment gave way to a new national feeling and to Romanticism. The "other," whether Jew or Frenchman, was eyed more skeptically again, and minorities were expected to conform.

David Friedländer, a student of Mendelssohn and the most important representative of Berlin's Jews at the turn of the century, made an offer in 1799 to Provost Teller of the Lutheran consistory in Berlin: Friedländer would convert to Protestantism so long as this did not require subscribing to any Christian dogmas he might have to reject as irrational. This offer was, of course, rejected. Yet most of Mendelssohn's children—with his wife Fromet Gugenheim he had ten children, of whom six survived—did not have any such scruples and converted after their father's death. One of his grandsons, the composer Felix Mendelssohn Bartholdy, was baptized as a child and composed some of the most impressive pieces of Protestant church music. For this generation what mattered most was legal and political progress in the struggle for equality, which still seemed a distant prospect even at the beginning of the nineteenth century.

This Haggadah published in Cologne in 1838 contains an appendix with musical supplements by Isaac Offenbach, the cantor of the city's Jewish community. In his introductory remarks, he alludes to the rapid cultural shift taking place in the German-Jewish community, many of whose members could not even read most of the German text so long as it was printed, as was customary, in Hebrew letters. Hence it seemed to him that an edition with a translation entirely in German was necessary. Jakob, the seventh of his nine children, personified the swift acculturation on Cantor Offenbach's mind. Under the name Jacques Offenbach he became one of the most popular operetta composers of the nineteenth century.

13. From the Ghetto to Civil Society
POLITICAL EMANCIPATION AND RELIGIOUS REFORM

IN A 1920 ESSAY about German Jewry, the philosopher Franz
Rosenzweig wrote: "What, then, holds or has held us together
since the dawn of emancipation? . . . The answer is frightening.
Since the beginning of emancipation only one thing has unified
the German Jews in a so-called 'Jewish life'; emancipation itself,
the Jewish struggle for equal rights." The struggle for emancipation so preoccupied Jews in the nineteenthth century that it
had become an end in itself. By the beginning of the twentieth
century, the Jews of Central and Western Europe (at least) had
become citizens with equal rights in their countries. But what
was left of their religious practice and their identification with a
Jewish heritage? Entry into universal society was often accompanied by the abandonment of, or at least a decline in, a particular Jewish identity. Some historians talk about an "emancipation
contract": In return for their participation in European society,
the Jews were required to remodel their Judaism, to change it
from a comprehensive outlook that had once shaped every aspect of their daily life into a denomination affecting only the
private sphere. This expectation was what lurked behind the

dictum of Count Clermont-Tonnerre in the French National Assembly of December 1789: "The Jews should be denied everything as a nation, but granted everything as individuals." In a modern society that was built on individuals rather than corporate estates, Jews could no longer continue to exist as a "state within the state" that had its own courts, its own language and distinctive clothing, and its own economic structure.

France: Complete Emancipation as a Result of Revolution

The emancipation of the Jews was a pan-European affair. The earliest theoretical writings came out of Prussia, the first cautious edicts from Austria, and France was the country affected by actual implementation. In 1781/82 an enlightened Prussian civil servant, the privy councilor Christian Wilhelm von Dohm, wrote a book entitled *On the Civic Improvement of the Jews* at the prompting of his friend Moses Mendelssohn. In this book, as in many similar writings of the time, the issue was how to make "better men and useful citizens" out of the Jews. Dohm did not see the miserable situation of the Jews as something embodied in their religion or as a consequence of inherited traits, but rather as the result of their centuries-long exclusion and persecution: He insisted ". . . that this supposed greater moral corruption of the Jews is a necessary and natural consequence of the oppressed condition in which they have been living for so many centuries." If one were to give the Jews the opportunity to prove that they could become useful citizens of their countries, then that is exactly what they would do—this was the line of argument in Dohm's book.

At almost the same time, the enlightened Austrian emperor Joseph II issued the first of his "Patents of Toleration" for his non-Catholic subjects. These edicts, issued for different provinces at different times, did not turn the Jews into citizens with equal rights, far from it. But they did rescind humiliating laws like the body tax and facilitate modern education as well as some limited autonomy for Jews.

In France, after the fourteenth-century expulsions of the Jews, the only remaining communities were a small one established in the papal territory surrounding Avignon and another near the city of Bordeaux. (Although the Jewish populations later grew considerably as a result of the incorporation of Alsace and Lorraine.) It was in France, however, that the Jews of Europe really did obtain equal rights for the first time. Emancipation grew out of general political imperatives that ensued from the revolution. If the principle of human equality (at least for men) was going to be implemented consistently, then this would have to be applicable to members of all religions. At the same time, the intellectual roots of equal rights for the Jews were less developed in France than they had been in the German states, where Lessing and other Enlightenment figures took overtly Jewish-friendly stances. Voltaire, Diderot, and other French Enlightenment thinkers, by contrast, assumed positions that were decidedly hostile to Jews. In his article about the Jews for the *Dictionnaire Philosophique*, as well as in other writings, Voltaire did not endorse Christian anti-Judaism—in fact he condemned it. Instead (and here he was entirely a man of the Enlightenment) he harked back further in time to share anti-Jewish sentiments that dated to Roman antiquity. He was less indebted to Augustine than to Tacitus, Cicero, and especially Apion. In the isolation of the Jews he detected superstition and a congenital hatred of other cultures. Even if one could cure them of their traditional religion, they still could not be integrated into society. One of the multifarious aspects of the dialectics of Enlightenment is that Voltaire, certainly no friend of the Jews, was one of the harbingers of their equality—against his own will, as it were. For it was his intellectual involvement, not least of all, that facilitated the breakthrough of a political conception that

A picture from 1802 shows Napoleon as the herald of religious freedom. Representatives of all the religions express their gratitude to the monarch illumined by heaven.

LIBERTÉ des CULTES maintenue par le Gouvernement.

distinguished between the religion of the individual and that individual's position in the state (rejecting the principle that the latter should be founded on the former).

In Paris the ideas of the *Haskalah* that had radiated out of Berlin certainly did meet with acclaim on the eve of the revolution. Count Mirabeau drew up a plea for Jewish emancipation that consisted of three parts: a biography of Mendelssohn, a popular account of Dohm's ideas about emancipation, and a discussion of the *Jew Bill* of 1753, which had granted extensive rights to the Jews in England.

It was precisely at that time that Jewish emancipation really got underway, for in 1787 the Royal Society of Arts and Sciences in Metz advertised an essay competition on the topic: "Are there means for making the Jews happier and more useful in France?" The three prize-winning essays were written by a Protestant lawyer from Nancy, a Catholic cleric (the Abbé Grégoire), and a Polish Jew (Zalkind Hourwitz). These writings, on their own, would certainly not have led to more concrete results than what the writings of Lessing and Dohm had accomplished in Prussia. But the events of the revolution set in motion a process that would separate the French path to Jewish emancipation from that of the other European states. In Prussia and other German states, individual decrees slowly granted the Jews certain rights with the intention of gradually training them so that they could become loyal citizens. In France, the process worked the other way around. The Jews became citizens of the state overnight, so to speak (in 1790 for the Sephardic Jews around Bordeaux, and in 1791 for the Ashkenazic Jews in Alsace-Lorraine), and only later did they have to prove themselves worthy of their new status. Even Napoleon undertook a thorough reexamination of whether French Jews had really deserved to become French citizens. To this end he questioned the Jewish dignitaries he had first convened in 1806 as an Assembly of Notables, and then again a year later as a "Sanhedrin" (named after the ancient Jewish court), about their attitude toward France. Finally, in 1808, he attempted to restrict the occupational freedom of Jews in a law they termed the *décret infame*. Yet the achievements of the revolution could no longer be revoked. No longer could the Jews of France be turned into second-class citizens, as they were partly to remain in Germany's various states until 1871.

Germany: Creeping Emancipation as a Result of Evolution

In the second half of the nineteenth century, the way was cleared for a decisive improvement in the legal situation of Jews in the German states. Edicts issued in Prussia (1812), Bavaria (1813), and a number of other states constituted breakthroughs in some respects, though they fell short of granting complete equality before the law. In Prussia, for example, Jews were declared to be "native residents [Einländer] and Prussian citizens" and could be elected to city councils. They were still excluded, however, from holding office at higher levels of government, and would be for many decades to come. In Bavaria, as late as 1861, there were registration (Matrikel) laws that fixed a ceiling on the number of Jews tolerated in any locality. If a family had more children than the Matrikel permitted, it had to leave the province.

With new rights came new obligations. One of the most important aspects of the quid pro quo was military service: Jews fought in the wars of liberation against Napoleon. In Austria they had been serving in the army ever since the reforms of Joseph II in the early 1780s. Even a man regarded as an authoritative figure of traditional, Halakha-abiding Jewry, Prague's Chief Rabbi Ezekiel Landau, had to approve their service, and he blessed the first conscripts. He urged them to prove themselves good soldiers "so that people will see that even our nation, oppressed until now, loves its rulers and governmental authorities and, if necessary, is willing to lay down lives." At the same time he expressed his conviction that they would adhere to Jewish dietary laws and observe the sanctity of the Sabbath.

Much of this progress was reversed in the era of political reaction that followed the Napoleonic wars. In the negotiations over the Acts of the Vienna Congress of 1815, one small word made a big difference. At dispute was whether Jews should be granted those rights accorded "by the individual Confederate States" or those conferred "in the individual Confederate States." Jewish representatives called for the word "in" because this included the period of foreign rule under Napoleon when the rights of citizenship proclaimed by the French Revolution had been extended to Jews, whereas "by" was interpreted to mean that the rights now had to be issued by the states that had

The painter Moritz Daniel Oppenheim (a native of Hanau in Hesse) made portraits of Jews during the period when they were integrated into society. His paintings show how they continued to adhere to their religion while simultaneously becoming part of German society and culture. His 1833/34 *Return of the Volunteer* portrays the patriotism of German Jews by depicting a Jewish hussar returning from the Wars of Liberation against Napoleon to a traditional parental home on the Sabbath.

just recovered their sovereignty after French occupation. The more restrictive version triumphed, with the result that much of what was achieved under Napoleonic rule was undone and that some cities, like Lübeck and Bremen, completely shut their gates to Jews once again. But there were also setbacks in Prussia: The Edict of 1812 was kept in place, to be sure, but it was not extended to Prussia's new territories. And it was in those very territories, especially in Posen, that the majority of Prussian Jews now lived.

The Age of Restoration (1815–48) was another unfortunate time for Jews in the various German states. The era was ushered in by violent anti-Jewish riots that began in Würzburg on August 2, 1819, and then extended across major portions of the German states until they reached Copenhagen and Amsterdam. The riots showed that broad sections of the population did not want to share the privileges previously granted only to Christian residents with the Jews, who were jealously eyed as "upstarts" (*Aufsteiger*) in the economy and "neophytes" (*Einsteiger*) in society and were blamed for economic distress in 1816 and 1817. The fact that Napoleonic troops had liberated Jews from Germany's ghettos made them allies of the hated French in popular opinion. In addition, there were traditional, religiously motivated anti-Jewish stereotypes mixed in with elements of a more modern antisemitism. The 1819 incidents were called "Hep Hep Riots" (based on the battle cry that accompanied the attacks), although it is not clear whether this was meant to be an abbreviation for *Hierosolyma est perdita* (Jerusalem is lost), mimicry of some goat-like noise (alluding to the beards of the Jews), or an abbreviation for the word *Hebräer* (Hebrews). These kinds of aggression-charged riots would be repeated in the course of the nineteenth century whenever conditions of political instability prevailed, as for example in 1830 and 1848.

The ideal of the Christian state also solidified in Prussia during the Age of Restoration. Its best-known theoretician, ironically, was himself a converted Jew, Friedrich Julius Stahl, who taught law at the University of Erlangen. Usually it was people from the highest or lowest social strata who opted for baptism, which they hoped would open the way to advancement of one kind or another. Prominent figures, such as most of Moses Mendelssohn's children, were among the converts.

Henriette Herz conducted one of the earliest salons in Berlin literary society. She was married to the Jewish physician and Kant student Marcus Herz and had herself been baptized as a Protestant after the death of her mother.

Career motives were often the decisive ones when it came to baptism, as was the case for the parents of Karl Marx and Felix Mendelssohn Bartholdy or for Heinrich Heine, who sought a university career. For him baptism was merely an *"entrée billet* into European culture." A chapter all to itself is the story of the literary salons run by those women, mostly of Jewish origin, who were the center of attention in Berlin intellectual society at the beginning of the nineteenth century. The Humboldt brothers, the author Jean Paul, and the theologian Friedrich Schleiermacher socialized in the salon of Henriette Herz, who had herself baptized, as did the wife of the diplomat Karl August Varnhagen von Ense, the writer Rahel Levin, whose salon was later frequented by other converted Jews such as Heine, Ludwig Börne, and Eduard Gans. The salons were early meeting places for Jews and Christians, women and men. But while they played a rather significant role in the intellectual emancipation of women, the encounter between Jews and Christians often ended in conversion to Christianity. This can be seen in the case of Dorothea Veit, the daughter of the philosopher Moses Mendelssohn, who met her future (second) husband Friedrich Schlegel in the salon of Henriette Herz and converted, first to Protestantism, then to Catholicism.

Most Jews who, though not ready to discard their Judaism, were quite prepared to acculturate, i.e., to become German and remain Jews at the same time, even though their continued adherence to Judaism implied a significant redefinition of its content. The Jews' transformation from subjects to citizens in the German states gradually reshaped their self-image. As subjects of rulers who had frequently not been very friendly toward them, Jews' loyalty derived, as a rule, from considerations of expediency and was calculated to ensure their security in a state experienced as alien. As prospective citizens, by contrast, Jews could identity with the state in which they lived as if with their own fatherland. They increasingly viewed themselves as part of the German nation, while their Jewish identity was more and more restricted to the private sphere of religious belief. The Hamburg notary Gabriel Riesser, who would later become vice president of the Frankfurt National Assembly in 1848, could assert without fear of contradiction: "The nationality of the Jews lives only in our memories . . . . In reality, it has died."

Rights, admittedly, took a longer time coming than did obligations. In Prussia, for example, there was no opportunity for a Jew to become an officer. The only exception proving that rule was an officer named Meno Burg. Things were different in Austria where there were Jewish officers and reserve officers, as well as Jews elevated into the nobility. Even in Bavaria a few Jews became officers without having to be baptized. Civil service appointments, however, were as a rule still impossible for Jews during the first half of the nineteenth century, especially appointments to higher offices, such as that of a judge or professor. Prior to 1848 there were no Jewish political officeholders above the local level. Jews could not be elected to provincial parliaments; a cabinet position in any provincial government was virtually unthinkable. Here, too, there was one exception proving the rule prior to 1918: the Finance Minister of Baden, Moritz Elstätter.

The revolutionary events of 1848 were therefore watched with high hopes by the Jews—and now from two perspectives: As one of the most prominent Jewish participants, the Königsberg liberal Johann Jacoby, put it: "As I myself am both German and Jewish at the same time, the Jew in me cannot become free without the German; nor the German free without the Jew." An impressive symbol of this coincidence of identities was the funeral service in Vienna on March 17, 1848. Among the five victims of the battles at the barricades, two were Jews; during the memorial service, therefore, a Catholic priest, a Protestant pastor, and a Jewish rabbi stood peaceably alongside each other. Yet here, too, the progress proved short-lived. The revolution itself, especially in the rural areas of southern Germany, was accompanied by waves of anti-Jewish violence. And, as far as legal developments were concerned, although Jews were now promised equality before the law for the first time, in Germany too the failure of the entire revolution would undo these gains before they could even be put into practice.

Jews could now no longer be certain whether the events of March 1848 had really made them accepted as equals, or whether they had merely been tolerated, even by former fighters at the barricades. Richard Wagner, for example declared: "When we strove for emancipation of the Jews . . . we were more the champions of an abstract principle than of a concrete cause: just as all our Liberalism was a not very lucid mental sport—we championed the freedom of the Folk without knowledge of that Folk itself, nay, with a dislike of any genuine contact with it—so our eagerness to level up the rights of Jews was far rather stimulated by a general idea than by any real sympathy; for, with all our speaking and writing in favor of the Jews' emancipation, we always felt instinctively repelled by any actual, operative contact with them."

After 1848 there was once more a period of reaction, but this time more short-lived. After the reactionary interlude, legal equality had to be implemented east of the Rhine—and for the same reasons that brought it to France a century earlier. It had become an imperative for society as a whole. The emancipation laws that were now passed in individual German states, as in Baden in 1862 and Württemberg in 1864, were enacted not so much in order to reward whatever Jewish acculturation had transpired in the interim as to fulfill the principle requiring equality before the law for all citizens. These two southwestern German states were followed in 1867 by Austria-Hungary, and two years later by the states that had joined together in the North German Confederation. In 1871, finally, the constitution of the new German Empire confirmed equality before the law as a principle applying to members of all religious communities.

Religious Reforms

For the Jews of Central and Western Europe, it was not only the legal framework that changed over the course of the nineteenth

century, but their entire way of life. Within two to three generations, an almost exclusively rural population of peddlers,
pawnbrokers, and livestock dealers became an urban bourgeoisie engaged, above all, in trade and commerce, and cultivating a
lifestyle in which religiosity increasingly gave way to secularization. These trends affected both religious reformers, the ones
who created the movement of Liberal Judaism, and the traditionalists who, despite their integration into the larger society,
continued adhering to religious law and described themselves
as neo-Orthodox.

The reformers, or Liberal Jews, no longer viewed the entire rabbinic tradition of the Talmud and its interpretations
as having a divine origin, and they also rejected as outmoded
key commandments such as the dietary regulations and laws
on Sabbath observance. Instead, their chief concern was with
the moral obligations of Jewish teaching, as well as with aes-
thetic changes in worship services at the synagogue, which they
sometimes called a "temple" in order to show that their Temple
no longer stood in Jerusalem, but in Hamburg or Berlin. Outwardly, synagogues were now supposed to breathe the spirit of
emancipation. Imposing architecture was wanted, and a central
location. Architecturally, a "Moorish" style was often chosen.
There were also some changes in what went on inside the synagogue. Prayers were increasingly spoken in German, references
to a return to Zion would disappear completely, rabbis dressed
like Protestant clerics, and the pulpit where readings from the
Torah took place was moved from the middle of the room eastward, closer to the ark where Torah scrolls are housed between
recitations. A confirmation ceremony for twelve-or thirteen-
year-old girls was introduced, often held in conjunction with
the confirmation rites of thirteen-year-old boys.

A very important innovation was the introduction to the
synagogue of the organ; the first one built for synagogue use
was made in 1810 by Israel Jacobson in the northern German

town of Seesen. Organ music was inconceivable in a traditional service. First of all, sorrow over the destruction of the Temple in Jerusalem meant that no instrumental music was allowed in the synagogue; secondly, introducing the organ was seen as copying a Christian service; and thirdly, an organ could not be played on the Sabbath anyway, since this counted as work.

The most important advocate of Liberal Judaism was Abraham Geiger, who was active as a rabbi in several cities, first in Wiesbaden, later in Breslau, and finally in Frankfurt and Berlin. Geiger was also known as a scholar of Islam because of his book *Was hat Mohammed aus dem Judenthume aufgenommen?* (What Did Muhammad Adopt from Judaism?, translated into English under the title *Judaism and Islam*). His view was that Judaism was constantly evolving in a way that would quite naturally lead to changes in religious practice, although he personally adhered to the dietary laws and many other traditional rules. More radical advocates of the reform movement demanded accommodations to the Christian environment that went even further: abolition of circumcision for newborn boys, and moving the day of rest from Saturday to Sunday. In the long run, this more sweeping trend lost out; it went too far in blurring distinctions between Judaism and the Christian denominations.

At bottom, even Orthodoxy was a development of the nineteenth century, a reaction to the innovations of the reformers. The great name most closely associated with Orthodoxy was Samson Raphael Hirsch, who ended up working in Frankfurt am Main. Like Geiger, he too had little in common with the traditionalists in Eastern Europe. He did not shut himself off from secular education, but instead propagated a new approach known as *torah im derekh eretz* (literally "Torah with the way of the world"), which advised that one should live according to Jewish religious law, but nonetheless take part in the broader culture. Orthodox rabbis also adapted to their environment by the way they dressed, by introducing regular sermons in the vernacular, and by deleting certain prayers. Frequently they were not only scholars of Judaism, but also connoisseurs of the German classics who instructed their students in Talmud in the morning and in philosophy and literature in the afternoon. For Orthodox as for Liberal synagogues, there were new rules prescribing what an orderly worship service should look like, with prayer spoken by the individual receding into the background and precedence given to prayer by the cantor, often enhanced by a male choir.

Only on one point were the neo-Orthodox adamant: Everything that was part of Jewish religious law had to be regarded as the word of God. No emendations were permissible. Dietary regulations and the laws of Sabbath observance in particular must be followed strictly, holidays were to be celebrated without reservation, and all prayers must be spoken in Hebrew. There was a rupture within Orthodoxy in the second half of the nineteenth century when Samson Raphael Hirsch called for withdrawal from communities increasingly dominated by the Liberal movement. It was unconscionable, Hirsch argued, for the taxes of the Orthodox to be used to fund practices going against Jewish law, such as playing the organ during worship services. With his *Israelitische Religionsgesellschaft* (Israelite Religious Society), Hirsch aimed at leaving the broader framework of the officially sanctioned community, and in 1876 this move was facilitated by the Prussian Diet, which passed a law allowing two different Jewish communities to exist in the same locality. One section of the Orthodox, however, went against Hirsch. In their view, the principle of unity (*Klal Yisrael*) had priority over all special interests. Under the leadership of the Würzburg rabbi Seligmann Baer Bamberger, this movement took shape as "Community Orthodoxy" (*Gemeindeorthodoxie*), which adhered just as strictly to religious observance as Hirsch's "Secessionist Orthodoxy" (*Austrittsorthodoxie*) but did not want to separate from the rest of the Jewish community. As a result of this divergence of opinion, many German cities now had three types of synagogues, each with its respective rabbi: those of the Liberal reformers, those staying within "Community Orthodoxy," and those congregations affiliating with the separatist movement. As a fourth group one might add the radical "Reform Temple" in Berlin, where services were held on Sunday.

Between the Reformers and the Orthodox a moderate centrist group took shape that called itself "Positive-Historical" and is usually designated in the United States today as "Conservative" (or, in Israel and a few other countries, as *Masorti*, meaning "traditional"). Its adherents wanted to preserve more than the reformers did and, in the person of their leading figure, the Dresden rabbi Zacharias Frankel, they opposed discarding Hebrew as the language of prayer and other innovations. They were the first movement to succeed in establishing a modern rabbinical seminary, the "Jewish Theological Seminary" founded in Breslau in 1854. Here rabbis were trained using modern scholarly methods that were completely different from the methods employed in traditional Talmud schools. In addition, as a rule, the Seminary's prospective rabbis also pursued the parallel track of getting a doctorate at the university. This gave rise to the phenomenon of the *Doktor-Rabbiner*. With considerable support from Abraham Geiger, the Liberals founded the *Hochschule für die Wissenschaft des Judentums* (Higher Institute for Jewish Studies) in Berlin in 1871, and two years later they were followed by the Orthodox, also in Berlin, where Rabbi Esriel Hildesheimer (a native of the Orthodox bastion of Halberstadt) started the rabbinical seminary later associated with his name. Additional rabbinical seminaries were founded in Padua, Budapest, Vienna, London, Metz, and Paris.

Wissenschaft des Judentums

Wissenschaft des Judentums—modern Jewish studies (literally, the "science" or "scholarship" of Judaism)—was the product of

The "New Synagogue" on Berlin's Oranienburger Strasse, dedicated in 1866, was built in a "Moorish style" intended to make Berlin's Jews imagine the "golden" era of the Spanish-Jewish Middle Ages as a model for successful symbiosis between Jews and the society around them. Many synagogues in Germany were built in this style, which also alluded to the Jews' Oriental ancestry.

an association of young Jewish students at the University of Berlin who wanted to absorb Judaism's history and culture, especially its writings and documents, before these fell into oblivion. With the founding of the *Verein für Cultur und Wissenschaft der Juden* (Association for Jewish Culture and Research) in 1819, history itself became a kind of holy source. Through knowledge of their own history and culture, a new Jewish identity would take shape, especially among secularized Jews. *Wissenschaft des Judentums* was also meant to carry forward the struggle for emancipation: "A time will come when nobody in Europe will ask any longer who is a Jew and who a Christian," as the first president of the association, the lawyer Eduard Gans, put it.

This vision was still far from reality in Christian Prussia. The Association soon disbanded, and Gans, like his fellow-member Heinrich Heine, had himself baptized. Some of its members, however, became forerunners of a new kind of scholarship. Leopold Zunz composed numerous works on Jewish literature, and Isaak Markus Jost had a go at being the first Jewish author of a multi-volume *History of the Israelites* (1820–47). Jost's history was, admittedly, overshadowed in the next generation by the work of Heinrich Graetz. Between 1853 and 1876, Graetz brought out the eleven volumes of his *History of the Jews*, regarded to this day as a classic of nineteenth-century Jewish history writing. Graetz became the most widely read historian of Jewish history, especially with his three-volume *Popular History of the Jews* (1888). Within the space of just a few generations, lively research activity was underway, especially in German-speaking Europe and in the fields of Jewish history and literature. Yet the establishment of a teaching position in Jewish studies at a German university was not forthcoming. For all that, scholarly activity on the Jewish past did flourish, not only in Germany but in other European countries as well, where it remained as in Germany almost the exclusive purview of the Jews themselves and outside the elite academic establishment. It is remarkable how Hungarian and Italian, English and French Jews all composed national histories of their own, each placing their own community at the center of Jewish history and attempting to portray the circumstances in their respective countries as particularly fruitful for the development of Jewish life. History writing became a veritable mirror of the new Jewish identities that took shape in the course of emancipation.

By the end of the nineteenth century, the Jewish community of Europe looked very different. Whereas the majority of Jews in the East, in the three multinational empires of the Romanovs, Habsburgs, and Ottomans, still lived under relatively traditional conditions, the Jews of the West had now become German, French, or Italian citizens of the Jewish persuasion. Their Judaism was officially defined as religion, and all references to Jewish nationality were now removed. The birth of a newfangled, racially defined antisemitism in the second half of the nineteenth century, however, would put a quick end to the dream of emancipation.

סדר

הגדה של פסח

מה נשתנה הלילה הזה מכל הלילות?

New York,

Truck u. Verlag der H. Frank's Buchdruckerei, 205 Houston St.

1851.

The title page of this 1851 Haggadah shows an elegantly clothed father and son. While the place of publication is New York, the print shop is indicated in German, which points to the German background of most American Jews in those years. A third cultural component comes from the Passover question posed in Hebrew: "Why is this night different from all other nights?"

14. From Posen to New Orleans
STARTING OVER IN AMERICA

"**My unbearable sorrow,** and in order to escape poverty and shame and not be dependent on the goodwill of the family, drove me to the decision to emigrate to America. My second wife and children remained amply provided for in the parental home and business, [and] my oldest child I brought to my parents. At the end of August 1852 I told my wife that I would be traveling to my old familiar region—Danzig, Marienwerder—in order to select a more favorable place of sustenance. I took with me only twenty-five thalers of travel money and the most essential laundry, and I did not let my wife notice anything about my travel plan. I did not travel to Danzig, but to Hamburg, had to leave my wife and two children in the cradle with an agitated heart and bitter tears. My cash wasn't enough for a ship's ticket, [so] I sold my silver watch and gold ring, departed mid-September by sailboat, for twenty-eight thalers. After forty-four harrowing days we landed in New York." (Monika Richarz, ed., *Jüdisches Leben in Deutschland. Selbstzeugnisse zur Sozialgeschichte, 1780–1871* [Stuttgart: Deutsche Verlags-Anstalt, 1976] 473.)

The Migration of Rural Jewry

The grain dealer Isaak Bernstein, from a poor family in the province of Posen, was one of about 250,000 Jewish immigrants who left Central Europe for America between 1840 and 1910. Over the next six years he sought his fortune in different occupations, wandering from New York to Savannah, and from New Orleans to Bedford, Massachusetts. While he ultimately returned to his wife and children in Europe, most other emigrants brought their families over to the New World. They were part of a much larger German-speaking wave of immigration. Like their Christian neighbors, they were fleeing political repression, legal discrimination, and economic distress. But whereas most of the Christian emigrants from Germany were of the middle class and came with their families, the typical Jewish emigrant was young, poor, and unmarried. There were also differences in the geographic origins of the two groups. In percentage terms there were more Jews than Christians emigrating from Bavaria, for example, where discriminatory registration (matriculation) laws limited the number of Jews at any locality. From Württemberg, too, the percentage of emigrating Jews was three times as high as that of Christians in the 1860s, in spite of the emancipation that had just taken place. Villages were left half empty, and some rural Jewish communities disappeared entirely within a matter of years, as a result of dual out-migration to cities and across the ocean. The 537 Jews who lived in Jebenhausen in Württemberg made up nearly half of the total population in 1838; by 1871 only 127 Jews still lived in the town, and by the end of the century only 9 were all that was left.

The Beginnings of American Jewry

As late as 1820, over one hundred and fifty years after the first Dutch Jews from Recife landed in New Amsterdam, there were barely more than 3,000 Jews in the United States. They were spread across eight communities along the Atlantic coast. Sixty years later the number had reached 250,000 in over 300 communities, scattered over all parts of the country. There were twenty congregations in New York alone.

At the beginning of the nineteenth century American Jewish congregations had neither a rabbi nor a Jewish periodical. As a result of many interfaith marriages and a weak organizational structure, there were clear signs that American Judaism was on the verge of disintegration. The communities' core was Sephardic in origin, but soon the majority of members were of Ashkenazic origin. The only spiritual leader of the community in the eighteenth century, Gershom Mendes Seixas, called himself the "Minister" of the congregation Shearith Israel in New York (where Seixas served in the decade before the War of Independence, before fleeing New York in 1776 for Connecticut and later Philadelphia's Mikveh Israel congregation, then returning to Shearith Israel in 1784). At New York's oldest synagogue, both before and after independence, Seixas functioned as prayer leader, preacher, and teacher. He was not a great scholar—the surviving documents we have by his hand show that his Hebrew was often faulty—and yet Seixas was an influential man outside the Jewish community as well as within. He was the recipient of various honors and became a trustee of Columbia College. This says something about the status of Jews in American society. Even before the Jews of France, they had received equal rights before the law, thanks to the American Constitution and the Bill of Rights, which prevented religious discrimination in public office holding and guaranteed the free exercise of religion.

Even under British rule, the Jews of America had been accorded equal treatment with the rest of the population by the Plantation Act of 1740. After the United States became independent in 1776, this equality before the law (at least for white males) would be confirmed within the framework of a broader policy of tolerance. Accordingly, Article VI of the Constitution, drawn up in August 1787, decoupled holding public office from any religious precondition: "No religious test shall ever be required as a qualification to any office or public trust under the United States." Individual states, however, could discriminate against their Jewish inhabitants. Thus, Maryland limited Jewish office-holding in the state until 1826, and New Hampshire until 1877.

President Washington's letter of greeting to the Jewish congregation in Newport on the occasion of a visit to the city was a benevolent confirmation of this principle: "May the Children of the Stock of Abraham, who dwell in this land, continue to merit and enjoy the good will of the other Inhabitants; while every one shall sit under his own vine and fig tree, and there shall be none to make him afraid."

From the outset of their immigration to the New World, Jews associated America with the dream of liberation from bondage. Some had fled from the Spanish and Portuguese, others from discriminatory laws in the German states, and later the chief motivation would be escaping the pogroms in the lands under Czarist rule. From time to time, messianic expectations about the redemption of the Jews would be mixed in with ideas about reestablishing a sovereign state. Thus, "in the fiftieth year of American independence" (1825), Mordecai Manuel Noah, High Sheriff in New York, issued a proclamation founding a place of refuge for all Jews, "'a land of milk and honey,' where Israel may repose in peace, under his 'vine and fig tree.'" This haven was not located along the banks of the Jordan, but in the vicinity of Niagara Falls on Grand Island. Noah laid a symbolic cornerstone for his project on September 15, 1825, at St. Paul's church in Buffalo, which lacked a synagogue. The international press and the Jewish world certainly took notice of his plan, but it was rejected from the outset as an unrealistic adventure. He waited

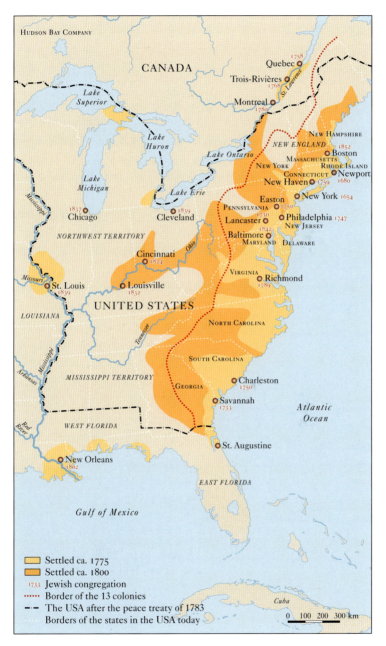

HUDSON BAY COMPANY

CANADA

Lake Superior

Lake Huron

Lake Michigan

Lake Ontario

Lake Erie

Quebec 1758

Trois-Rivières 1768

St. Lawrence

Montreal 1780

NEW HAMPSHIRE

NEW ENGLAND 1852

Boston

MASSACHUSETTS

NEW YORK

RHODE ISLAND

CONNECTICUT Newport

New Haven 1759 1680

New York 1654

Easton 1759

PENNSYLVANIA 1730

Lancaster Philadelphia 1747

1842 NEW JERSEY

Baltimore

MARYLAND DELAWARE

Mississippi

1837 Chicago

1839 Cleveland

NORTHWEST TERRITORY

Ohio

Cincinnati 1824

Missouri

St. Louis 1839

Louisville 1832

UNITED STATES

LOUISIANA

VIRGINIA Richmond 1789

Tennessee

NORTH CAROLINA

SOUTH CAROLINA

Mississippi

Arkansas

MISSISSIPPI TERRITORY

GEORGIA

Charleston 1750

Savannah 1733

Red River

WEST FLORIDA

St. Augustine

Atlantic Ocean

New Orleans 1802

EAST FLORIDA

Gulf of Mexico

Cuba

Settled ca. 1775
Settled ca. 1800
1733 Jewish congregation
Border of the 13 colonies
The USA after the peace treaty of 1783
Borders of the states in the USA today

0 100 200 300 km

The settlement of North America, seventeenth to nineteenth century.

in vain for Jews to flock to Grand Island and later became an advocate of Jewish restoration to Zion.

Reform Plans

At this early time the Jewish community in the United States was still very small. Only in the second third of the nineteenth century did the picture begin to change, as a result of massive immigration from Central Europe. A self-confident demeanor began to be discernible in America's Jews, for example vis-à-vis Christian missionaries, who were especially interested in converting poor Jewish immigrants and had, to this end, established the American Society for Meliorating the Condition of the Jews in 1820. The Jewish community reacted by publishing the periodical *The Jew* (1823–25) and founding free schools for poor Jewish children. Rebecca Gratz played an outstanding role in these endeavors. She saw to it that Jewish girls also got an education and, in addition to starting Jewish Sunday schools, created the first Jewish welfare organization outside a synagogue, the Female Hebrew Benevolent Society in Philadelphia, as early as 1819.

Religious reforms were also undertaken in an effort to make the practice of Judaism more attractive in a changing world. An initial breakthrough with respect to religious observance was the series of reforms inaugurated in 1824 by young people who broke away from Congregation Beth Elohim in Charleston. By introducing English prayers and sermons as well as shortening the service, reformers attempted to tackle the general problem of religious apathy. American Reform Judaism gradually developed, starting in the 1840s. In 1841 the first organ was installed in Charleston. At the dedication of the new synagogue building, the words spoken by Cantor Gustav Poznanski gave clear expression to the new Jewish-American self-confidence: "This synagogue is our temple, this city our Jerusalem, this happy land our Palestine." Prior to 1850 there were only three Reform congregations: Beth Elohim in Charleston, Har Sinai in Baltimore, and Emanu-El in New York. In contrast to the Old World, where traditionally there was just one overarching Jewish community in each locality, in the New World the community structure that crystallized was made up of several congregations acting independently of each other. This opened the gates to religious pluralism. Reform congregations in the United States frequently introduced mixed seating for men and women, but otherwise they were closely aligned with trends in the German states. Their first rabbis came from Germany, and they spoke and preached in German. Rabbis were poorly paid and dependent on the good graces of a lay administration. They were no longer required to clarify legal questions; instead, they increasingly fulfilled the functions of preacher and pastor.

Three factors became decisive for the continued success of the Reform movement: upward mobility, Americanization, and especially the emergence of an energetic personality whose leadership qualities would help organize Reform Judaism at every level of American society. This figure turned out to be the Bohemian native Isaac Mayer Wise, who had already introduced reforms into his congregation in Albany in 1850 and was chosen in 1854 as a moderate reformer to serve as the rabbi of Congregation B'nai Yeshurun in Cincinnati. He published the English-language journal *The Israelite* (later *American Israelite*) and a supplement, *Die Deborah*. In 1856 he saw to the publication of his first prayer book for Jewish-American congregations, *Minhag Amerika* (The American Rite). The decisive phase in the creation of the organizational Reform structures that have persisted to this day began in the 1870s: In 1873 the Union of American Hebrew Congregations (which changed its name to the Union for Reform Judaism in 2003) was formed, followed in 1875 by the Hebrew Union College in Cincinnati for the training of rabbis. In 1889 came the Central Conference of American Rabbis.

Wise had hoped that these institutions would create a new American Judaism capable of avoiding the European rift between Orthodoxy and Reform. But traditional Jews, a minority in America, could not accept the Reform proposals. One of their earliest voices was the Westphalian native Isaac Leeser, who was active in Philadelphia's Sephardic congregation as a cantor, undertook the first popular English translation of the Hebrew Bible, and edited *The Occident*, the first English-language Jewish journal with more than regional importance in the United States. But at a conference Wise convened in Cleveland in 1855, where his aim was to unite all the trends in American Judaism, the upper hand was retained by rabbis who deviated from orthodox interpretations about the divine origin of the Torah and the binding character of the Talmud. And so it came to a rupture between Wise and Leeser's Orthodox group.

There was dissent at the other end of the religious spectrum as well. For those following a more radical path under the leadership of Rabbi David Einhorn of Baltimore (formerly the chief rabbi of the Grand Duchy of Mecklenburg-Schwerin), Wise's reforms did not go far enough. Einhorn's group introduced worship services on Sunday and advocated social reforms. For them, the rights of workers, women's suffrage, and promoting world peace were at the center of a modern Jewish theology. Others went even further and founded the "Society for Ethical Culture." Felix Adler, son of the rabbi at the elegant Temple Emanu-El in New York, stood at the head of this movement, which saw itself not as a part of organized Judaism, but rather of a larger social justice movement directed against the kind of capitalist exploitation that was becoming increasingly conspicuous in Gilded Age America.

Reform Judaism, which established itself as the most important strain among American Jews, passed the "Pittsburgh Platform" in 1885 as a set of guidelines touching on all areas of both religious and non-religious life. Kaufmann Kohler, a native of

Fürth and rabbi of Congregation Beth El in New York, was the *spiritus rector* behind these guidelines, which he later attempted to implement as president of Hebrew Union College. Only the moral laws of the Bible should remain obligatory, according to the Platform. By contrast, whatever stood in opposition to modern civilization could be modified. Thus, dietary laws and regulations about clothing were no longer binding. According to the Pittsburgh Program's principles, a return to Zion was no longer to be expected as the modern age had already seen the realization of messianic ideals. The Jews no longer formed a nation, but were instead a religious community that was constantly evolving in conjunction with the postulates of all monotheistic religions.

Peddlers and Bankers

Although the east coast remained the center of America's Jewish population (in 1860 approximately 40,000 of America's 150,000 Jews lived in New York, an additional 8,000 in the next largest centers of Philadelphia and Baltimore), new centers emerged in the west and the south. Around 1860, for example, about 5,000 to 8,000 Jews settled in Cincinnati and New Orleans, and about as many in San Francisco.

The United States was regarded as a land of individualists. It offered opportunities that were impossible in the Old World, with its social and legal obstacles. For most Jewish immigrants, the dream of rising from dishwasher to millionaire or from peddler to banker remained far from reality. Yet this image often shaped the way subsequent observers perceived the entire wave of immigration. The fortunes of Joseph Seligmann stand as one highly extreme example. In the 1840s eight brothers and three sisters of this native Franconian followed their sibling, who had already left his hometown of Baiersdorf in 1837, to the United States. Most of the Seligmans (the second "n" of the

Jewish settlers in Montana, around 1890.

surname was eventually dropped in America) earned their living as peddlers. With the money they saved, the brothers first founded a textile factory, and then later a bank. Their great opportunity presented itself during the Civil War, when they supplied Union troops with all kinds of goods. By the end of the war the federal government owed them a million dollars. Other examples are those of Simon Guggenheim, the tailor who emigrated from the Swiss village of Lengnau, and whose family would soon become part of America's financial aristocracy, as well as the Bavarian native Benjamin Bloomingdale. To this day the Guggenheim museums and the Bloomingdale's department stores preserve these families' names. Equally legendary is the rise of the jeans king Levi Strauss from out of Franconian Buttenheim: He, too, started out as a peddler, followed the Gold Rush to San Francisco, where he first manufactured some sturdy working clothes using tarpaulin and later, together with his partner Jacob Davis (an immigrant from Riga), registered a patent using denim, the indigo-dyed blue cotton fabric.

Employees of the jeans factory Levi Strauss & Co. in front of the company headquarters in San Francisco, Battery Street 14–16. The building was destroyed during the San Francisco earthquake of 1906.

One could produce a whole string of such success stories. As part of the overall picture, however, they remain exceptions to a far less spectacular story of upward mobility into the ranks of the middle class. In Boston during the 1850s, for example, most Jewish taxpayers were in the lowest income category, earning less than 200 dollars, while no Jews at all were in the highest tax bracket with an income of over 10,000 dollars, even though 13 percent of the total population was in that upper range.

Rejection in the New Homeland

By and large, emigration to America resulted in an undeniable social improvement for the individual. Even rising into the lower middle class was a major triumph for many immigrants, and their children were often able to climb even further up the social ladder. Yet even in the New World Jews were not immune to setbacks that must have reminded them of the anti-Jewish climate of the Old World. On December 17, 1862, one of the heroes of the American Civil War, General Ulysses Grant, issued a directive (General Order No. 11) in which he accused Jews in general of violating trade laws and ordered their expulsion from

Tennessee, Mississippi, and Kentucky. Even when President Lincoln rescinded this order and Grant distanced himself from the measure, it still seemed as if the threat of expulsion hovered ominously over the Jews in this secure new homeland of the United States.

A decade and a half later, at the swanky resort town of Saratoga Springs, there was a much-discussed incident involving the banker Joseph Seligman, by now the most prominent Jew in America. In 1877, as every year, Seligman and his entourage traveled in his private railroad car to vacation there with the New York finance aristocracy. When he asked to move into his rooms in the Grand Union Hotel, he was informed that he did not have a reservation. The wealthy circles of the Protestant Anglo-Saxon establishment would tolerate no Jews, and frequently also no Catholics, joining their social circles. Posh hotels and clubs remained closed to them. Christian neighbors moved away when too many Jews settled in the better residential districts, with the result that Jewish quarters emerged without any formal planning. In the first half of the twentieth century, the most prestigious universities introduced quotas in order to reduce the number of Jewish students. But while the social exclusion of Jews from elite circles was palpable, political antisemitism never rose to the level of genuine peril. Nothing is more telling than the fact that Ulysses Grant, now President of the United States a decade after his unfortunate order, offered Joseph Seligman a cabinet position in his administration. Seligman declined the offer and remained a banker. It would appear, then, that in spite of their social ostracism, the highest political positions in the country were already open to Jews. (It would, however, not be until 1905 and the first elected term of Theodore Roosevelt that Oscar S. Straus would become the first Jew to hold a cabinet post in an American administration.) At the local level it was not rare to see Jews holding public office, and in several cities they were elected as mayors.

One way Jews reacted to social exclusion from wealthy Protestant circles was, as in Europe, by forming their own clubs and organizations. In 1843, when a dozen young Jews were denied membership in the Odd Fellows Lodge (which already included numerous other Jews among its ranks), they created their own charitable organization, the Order of B'nai B'rith. It rapidly spread to include many local groups, and by the end of the century it represented the most important secular organization of American Jews. One of its most urgent missions was to introduce immigrants to American society.

By the end of the nineteenth century, "German" Jews (many of whom came from Poland, Bohemia, and Hungary) had become acclimated to America. German sermons in the synagogues gave way to English texts, the Reform movement had developed its own ideology and practices, and the peddlers had become merchants, with shops at fixed addresses, or even lawyers and doctors. The United States was their homeland and the home of their children. This process had not yet drawn to a close when the next, even larger wave of Jewish immigration began. East European Jews, many of whom were now arriving in flight from Czarist Russia, would regard German Jews as old, established residents of America.

הגדה של פסח.

יְמֵי חַיֶּיךָ. הָעוֹלָם הַזֶּה. כֹּל יְמֵי חַיֶּיךָ. לְהָבִיא
לִימוֹת הַמָּשִׁיחַ:

בָּרוּךְ הַמָּקוֹם בָּרוּךְ הוּא. בָּרוּךְ שֶׁנָּתַן תּוֹרָה

denotes this time only; but ALL the days of thy life, denotes
even at the time of the Messiah.

    Blessed be the Omnipresent; blessed is he, blessed is he who
hath given the law to his people Israel, blessed be he: the

This Haggadah from Chicago (1883, first printed in 1879) illustrates the progressive assimilation of American Jews. A traditionally clothed father shares the table with his wife and the four sons mentioned in the Seder service. On the right edge of the picture, the ill-mannered son from the Haggadah story is shown smoking provocatively during the festivities, which may be a reference to the gap between the different generations of immigrants.

15. From the Shtetl to the Lower East Side
EAST EUROPEAN JEWISH DREAMS AND AMERICAN REALITIES

"**WHY SHOULD NOT WE TOO** have a chance to get away from this dark land? Has not every heart the same ... longing to live and laugh and breathe like a free human being? ... We'll sell everything we got—we'll go to America.... White bread and meat we'll eat every day—in America!" (*American Jewish Fiction*, ed. Gerald Shapiro [Lincoln: University of Nebraska Press, 1998], 19–20).

Like the heroine in her 1920 short story "How I Found America," Anzia Yezierska emigrated at the turn of the century, at the age of fifteen, from a shtetl in the old world to the country that East European Jews called the *Goldene Medine* (the Golden Land). Before the family of Yezierska's heroine sells all its worldly possessions, she reads a letter from the water carrier Gedalyeh Mindel, who wants to bring his wife over to America. As a street hawker he is making a profit of two dollars a day, an inconceivable sum in the minds of that family, and when he becomes a citizen, his vote at election time will count as much "as Mr. Rockefeller, the greatest millionaire."

But the best thing is: "There is no Czar in America." On the voyage across the Atlantic, people try to envisage what it will be like over there: "In America you can say what you feel—you can voice your thoughts in the open streets without fear of a Cossack. . . . In America is a home for everybody. The land is your land. Not like in Russia where you feel yourself a stranger in the village where you were born and raised—the village in which your father and grandfather lie buried." No Czar, no Cossacks, no pogroms—this alone was a golden prospect for the emigrants. Reason enough to leave the place in which parents and grandparents had lived and were buried. In 1900, when Yezierska and her other siblings followed an older brother who had already emigrated ten years earlier, she became part of the largest wave of migration in all of Jewish history.

Under the Czars

It was only a good century earlier that the Jews had come under the rule of the czars. The partition of Poland, initiated in 1772, was concluded in 1795 when the former Poland was divided up between the great powers of Russia, Austria, and Prussia. Each would now develop its own policy with respect to the Jews. Whereas there were pre-existing Jewish communities in Austria, which received Galicia, and in Prussia, which was awarded West Prussia and Posen, Jewish communities had not been officially tolerated in the Czarist Empire heretofore. But now, with central and eastern Poland as well as Lithuania among its new domains, Czarist Russia had not only received the lion's share of the Polish state; at a single stroke it also had incorporated the largest Jewish community in the world, numbering around three quarters of a million people.

Russian policy reflected its insecurity and lack of experience in dealing with the Jewish minority. The policy alternated between magnanimously granting civil rights and brutally denying the very same rights. The policy of the German-born Catherine II was initially animated by the ideas of the Enlightenment. The Czarina, who reigned between 1762 and 1796, wanted to turn the Jews into good citizens of the state and believed, entirely in the spirit of Dohm in Prussia or Joseph II in Austria, that this outcome could be achieved by the right kind of education policy. Thus, in the wake of the first Polish partition in 1772, no special rights were accorded to Jews. They were treated like the rest of the population. Czarist officials had trouble, however, fitting them into the rigid categories of the Russian social system. They were neither part of the nobility nor free peasants or serfs. Catherine placed them in the category of urban residents, which admittedly corresponded only partly to the truth, since so many of them lived in the countryside. But city people had to live in cities. This classification therefore had the originally unintended effect of opening the door for Jews to be expelled from the countryside. In 1808 and again in 1823 the government really did try deporting the Jewish village population into the cities, but both of these attempts proved unfeasible.

More important was a decree Catherine issued in 1791— probably out of consideration for Moscow's merchants, who were afraid of competition—banning Jews from settling in the interior of the empire. Instead, they were required to remain in the provinces that had once belonged to Poland, as well as in the newly acquired territories of the Black Sea region. This territory, known as the "Pale of Settlement," thus became almost the only region where Jews could legally live inside the Czarist Empire. At the same time as the Jews' opportunities for settlement were restricted, attempts were made to formulate a policy of assimilation. The Jewish "Statute of 1804" made it clear that Jews had to go through a process of education before they could become emancipated. The statute was meant to facilitate their access to modern educational institutions, from elementary school to the university, and to alter their

The Jewish Pale of Settlement in Russia. The data on the number of Jews and their percentage of the population in the individual regions refer to the year 1897.

occupational structures without forcing them to abandon their religion. In some respects it recalled similar measures in more Western countries: Jews were supposed to acquire surnames and use non-Jewish "standard languages" in official documents, while their rabbis were to be placed under special supervision, just as was the case with representatives of other state religions in Russia. In other respects, the statute took account of conditions peculiar to Eastern Europe: Owing to what was viewed as their particularly damaging influence on the peasantry, Jewish publicans (that typically East European line of work for Jews) were the targets of a policy that aimed at removing them completely, if possible, from the business of running taverns.

Subsequent measures went a step further. The policy of Czar Alexander I (1801–1824), which wavered between enlightenment and despotism, gave way to the hard line of Nicholas I (1825–1855). At the end of the educational process set up for Jews, the way would be clear to abolish Jewish community autonomy and (ideally, according to the hardliners) convert Jews to the Orthodox Church. The best means to these ends was the lengthy term of military recruitment Czarist officials imposed on "cantonists": Often twelve year-old boys were snatched away from their families with the help of Jewish community officials in order to fulfill the quota of draftees and were given pre-military training that could lead to twenty-five years of military service. During this lengthy period they had no opportunity to live according to Jewish law. Not surprisingly a large number of the children thus forcibly recruited—approximately 50,000—ultimately did land in the bosom of the Orthodox Church. Jewish communities were anxious to fulfill their obligation toward the government and sent *chappers* ("bailiffs," from the Yiddish word for "grabbers") to meet recruitment targets. This led to tensions within the Jewish communities and to the undermining of communal authority. It is remarkable how much resistance these measures aimed at forced assimilation encountered. Parents hid their children or sent them to live with distant relatives so that they might not be drafted; some young men preferred to maim themselves rather than be forcibly alienated from Judaism. The dissolution of the *Kahal* (the autonomous Jewish community administration) decreed in 1844 proved impossible to implement in practice. During the reign of Czar Alexander II (1855–1881) dramatic improvements were made to many sectors of Jewish life, as part of broader reforms in Russian society. Although there were high hopes for emancipation in the Western style, many restrictions pertained. For example, Jews could occupy no more than a third of all the seats on a city council (even when they formed a majority of the population), and they were not allowed to hold the office of municipal leader.

Between Religious Renewal and Secularization

The small minority of those influenced by Enlightenment ideas found themselves in a dilemma. On the one hand, they were convinced that the Jewish community had to change, they mocked the "superstitious" traditions of the Hasidim, called for a secular education in addition to Talmud study, preached the use of non-Jewish languages, and advocated a new occupational structure for Jews. On the other hand, they did not want to become stooges for a government that used many of these measures simply as a pretext for turning orthodox Jews into Orthodox Christians.

Extremely important for the intellectual and religious life of non-Hasidic Jews was the establishment of a new type of yeshiva (Talmud school) in Lithuania. In 1803, one of the students of the Vilna Gaon, Rabbi Chaim of Volozhin, founded the most famous of these, the Yeshiva of Volozhin, which attracted students from all parts of the country and lent them financial support. Scholars from Volozhin were long accepted as the highest authorities on matters of legal interpretation and personal conduct. Here a clear and rational understanding of the text was promoted, and there emerged a stratum of highly educated laymen who often formed the intellectual elite in their localities and were among the biggest supporters of rabbinical Judaism in its disputes both with the Hasidim and with Enlightenment figures. Additional yeshivas modeled after Volozhin were founded in Mir, and later in Telz (Telšiai), and Slobodka.

Israel Salanter, born in Kovno in 1810, attempted to counter increasing secularization at the hands of the *Maskilim* (the enlighteners) by founding the *Musar* movement. Literally, the word means "morals" or "ethics," and Salanter and his students made ethics central to their interpretations of religious laws. They saw self-examination and repentance as alternatives to both the emotionality of the Hasidim and the pure reason of the "enlightenment proponents." Salanter also attempted to establish a balance between the Hasidim and their Orthodox opponents by criticizing both: "'Why do I need a book for religious instruction when I have my rebbe?' asks the Hasid, and the *Misnaged* counters: 'I have a book for religious instruction, so why do I need a rabbi?'"

The *Maskilim* took a giant step further, even if not all of them behaved as enthusiastically toward the government as did Isaac Baer Levinsohn, whose 1828 call for occupational restructuring and educational reform (*Te'udah be-Yisrael*, "Testimony in Israel") was dedicated to Czar Nicholas. They have left behind some moving statements documenting their doubts about the faith of their childhood. Much later, Moshe Leib Lilienblum, one of the most important Hebrew writers of the second half of the nineteenth century, wrote the following in the autobiography he composed in 1876 at the age of thirty-three: "That Day of Atonement I was as if struck by thunder. . . . The cantor chanted the prayer, 'Here am I, poor in good deeds.' The congregation trembled at his voice. I saw everyone lifting hands and heart to God, while I—where was my God? I covered my face with the prayer shawl and dissolved in tears." At first, Lilienblum tried to repress these evil thoughts and find his way back by studying Talmud, founding a yeshiva, and teaching schoolchildren. Yet soon word got around that he was reading secular books and cultivating heretical thoughts. He was denounced and persecuted and eventually turned to Hebrew literature as well as to the ideas of socialism and Zionism.

In addition to acquiring an all-round education and learning non-Jewish languages, the cultivation of the Hebrew language was one of the most important aims of the East European

Maskilim. Thus, starting about mid-century, Hebrew novels and periodicals began to appear. There were journals like *ha-melits* (The Advocate), founded in 1860 by Alexander Zederbaum and later edited by the poet Judah Leib Gordon, *ha-shahar* (The Dawn), created in 1868 by Peretz Smolenskin, or *ha-shiloah*, founded in 1896 by Ahad Ha'am (and named after the Biblical reservoir in Jerusalem). This dissemination of new ideas among the Hebrew-reading population, for whom the Lithuanian-born journalist Eliezer Ben-Yehuda compiled the first Modern Hebrew dictionary, took on immense importance with the advent of political and cultural Zionism during the last two decades of the century.

Odessa was a focal point for Eastern Europe's Jewish intellectuals. The metropolis that had risen to become a port and commercial city in recently conquered southern Russia was home to people of many different nations and religions. Along with Russians and Ukrainians, Greeks and Armenians lived there, as did Jews in large numbers. At the end of the nineteenth century they made up close to 140,000 of its 400,000 inhabitants, including two thirds of the doctors in the city, two thirds of the bankers, and over half the lawyers. One third of all the Jews, however, belonged to the proletariat, as industrial workers or day laborers. The city attracted many *Maskilim* from other parts of the country and, together with St. Petersburg, became the site where a new imperial Russian-Jewish identity was tested. As of the turn of the century, Odessa also played a decisive role in the formation of Hebraism and the Zionist movement. It was home both to Hebrew-speaking endeavors and to the first Russian-language Jewish journal (*Razsvet*, "Dawn," 1860).

For the great majority of Jews in the Czarist Empire, however, neither the Hebrew route nor the one leading into Russian culture was relevant. While one should take into account increasing Russification and Polonization even in smaller towns, the Jewish masses of Eastern Europe remained true to the Jewish

In 1878 Maurycy Gottlieb depicted a Yom Kippur service in his Galician home of Drohobycz. In the midst of those at prayer, he seems to be having doubts about his faith, much like many Enlightenment figures who had been confronted with secular knowledge. At the age of fifteen Gottlieb had studied at the Viennese Art Academy and was a student of the Cracow painter Jan Matejko. He died only one year after this portrait, at the age of twenty-three. On the Torah cover there is a premonition of his death in writing: "Donated in memory of the deceased and revered teacher Moshe Gottlieb, of blessed memory, 1878."

religion and continued to communicate largely in Yiddish. As late as 1897, 97 percent of all Jews surveyed in Russia gave Yiddish as their mother tongue. So it was hardly surprising that Jewish writers increasingly availed themselves of the Yiddish language. On Mendele Moykher-Sforim (Sholem Yankev Abramovitch) was bestowed the honorary title of "grandfather" (zeyde) of Yiddish literature. At first he also published in Hebrew, but in 1863 in Odessa, he founded the first Yiddish periodical, *Kol mevaser* (Voice of the Herald). He justified his turn to Yiddish in this way:

> Here I am, observing the ways of our people and attempting to write for them stories from Jewish sources in the holy tongue, yet most of them do not even know this tongue. Their language is Yiddish. And what life is there for a writer, what profit in his labor, if he is of no use to his people? The question, "For whom do I toil?" has not ceased to trouble me. The Yiddish language in my day was an empty vessel, containing nothing but slang and trite, meaningless phrases.... The women and the poor would read Yiddish without understanding it, while the rest of the people, even if they didn't know how to read in another language, were ashamed to be caught reading Yiddish, lest this private folly of theirs become public knowledge.

Later, Yitzhok Leibush Peretz and Sholem Aleichem would contribute toward elevating Yiddish to the rank of a literary language. They were not interested in becoming conveyers of an elitist culture; they aimed instead to be understood by a wide public, and this was only possible in Yiddish. The Yiddish language united Jews in the Czarist Empire with Jews living in other parts of Eastern Europe. In spite of all the political and legal differences between one region and another, East European Jews had common cultural ties extending from Romania and Hungary in the south, across Slovakia and Galicia, and all the way north to Belorussia and Lithuania.

In the Habsburg Empire

At the end of the nineteenth century, the Habsburg Empire contained the second largest Jewish community in the world, with around two million Jews. In Galicia the Jewish population grew from about 200,000 at the time of the Polish partitions to over 800,000 by the end of the nineteenth century. In this region, where the majority of inhabitants were Catholic Poles and Orthodox Ukrainians, the Jewish share of the population remained relatively constant at just over 10 percent. In some cities like Brody they represented up to 90 percent of the residents, and even in the center of Lemberg (Lvov) they made up over a third of the inhabitants. Galicia was part of the world of East European Jewry, but at the same time it was heavily influenced by the ideas of Enlightenment and integration that prevailed in Vienna. Here the traditional Jewish way of life collided quite virulently with efforts at religious and cultural reform.

On the one hand, the Hasidic legacy was especially strong in this region. Almost all religious Jews felt connected with one of the many Hasidic dynasties whose leaders literally held court in some of the smaller towns like Belz, Zanz, or Sadagora, and whose residences became pilgrimage sites for the faithful. On the other hand, the *Haskalah*, or Jewish Enlightenment, did gain a foothold in nineteenth-century Galicia, especially in the larger cities. Its origins were in the circle of Moses Mendelssohn, on the one hand, and in the educational policy of Emperor Joseph II, on the other. Jewish Enlightenment figures like the Bohemian native Herz Homberg, who was one of Moses Mendelssohn's collaborators, started out promoting a particularly rigorous reform policy. Children should be taught not only German, according to Homberg, but also a new doctrinal form of Judaism in a style that emulated the Protestants' catechisms. This meant reducing the culture of everyday Jewish life to certain matters of faith along with the transmission of patriotism fixated on the emperor and the state. The school system introduced by Homberg was already abolished by 1806. An examination in German on the basis of the hated catechisms, however, remained a precondition for an officially sanctioned marriage, and couples frequently tried to find a way around it.

Taxation of kosher meat and Sabbath candles increasingly became a financial burden on a Jewish population that was becoming impoverished.

After the failure of Homberg's school reforms, a number of prominent *Maskilim* undertook new attempts at educational reform. In 1813 Joseph Perl founded the *Israelitische Freyschule* (Israelite Free School) in Tarnopol. Perl was one of the most vociferous opponents of the Hasidic movement, which he made fun of in his satirical polemics. Another member of the *Maskilim* who took up the cause against Hasidism was Mendel Lefin, whose Yiddish and Hebrew writings called for a rational doctrine of Judaism. Thus, he published a Modern Hebrew edition of Maimonides' *Guide to the Perplexed*. Maimonides was the favorite Jewish philosopher of the *Maskilim* and became their model for more than an entire generation. Salomon Maimon adopted his name in order to show that he was modeling himself after the great scholar. And in a book, *The Guide to the Perplexed for Our Time*, whose title echoes that of Maimonides' great work, Nachman Krochmal developed a philosophy of history that also had an impact on *Wissenschaft des Judentums* and was posthumously published by Leopold Zunz, the most important representative of modern Jewish scholarship in Germany.

By contrast, most East European *Maskilim* eschewed ideas of organized religious reform on the German model. Such ideas were usually imported by rabbis from German-speaking Europe, such as Rabbi Abraham Kohn, who was born in western Bohemia and worked for a decade in the Vorarlberg town of Hohenems (near Austria's border with Switzerland). He introduced German-language sermons, an orderly worship service, and a choir into his new congregation in Galician Lemberg. These innovations, which even the Orthodox had adopted in Germany, met with such fierce resistance among the Jews of Lemberg that some of them tore their clothes as a sign of mourning over their "desecrated" synagogue, just as one might at a funeral. Kohn also provoked his congregation's traditional majority by replacing the bar mitzvah with a confirmation ceremony for young boys and girls, on the Protestant model. Though his reforms were moderate compared to what had been introduced in regions further west, Kohn nonetheless managed to make himself so hated among the Hasidic population that he fell the victim to a fatal, and still not entirely explained, poisoning in 1848.

1848 was a year of transitory hopes for the Jews in eastern Central Europe as the short-lived revolution gave rise to expectations of emancipation, even in the Habsburg Empire. In the cities Jews from the bourgeois strata often joined revolutionary Bohemians, Hungarians, or Poles on the barricades in their common struggle against the authoritarian imperial state and against the suppression of national minorities. But equality would be a long time coming to Galicia. At the local and regional level Jews attained recognition more quickly. Thus, in 1874 there were already seventy-one Jews in regional parliaments, five (of 155) Jewish deputies in the Galician Sejm, ten Jewish mayors, and 261 Jewish city councilors distributed across the entire region. The legal situation in Hungary was improving in the same period. To be sure, owing to the Jews' high level of participation in the revolutionary events of 1848, a heavy monetary fine had been imposed on their communities, and even in the 1850s they still had to put up with various kinds of legal discrimination, such as a prohibition on acquiring land and the requirement that they take a special examination before marrying. But in 1859/60 most of these legal requirements were abolished and, after the Austro-Hungarian Compromise (*Ausgleich*) of 1867, full rights were also conferred on Hungarian Jews. Between 1850 and 1869, especially as a result of immigration from Galicia, their numbers grew from 340,000 to 540,000. On the eve of the First World War, the Hungarian-Jewish community numbered over 900,000 members, and in Budapest nearly a quarter of the inhabitants were Jews. They made up about half of all merchants, lawyers, and physicians in the country.

At the same time, Hungarian Jews were a very heterogeneous community. The Jews of the upland region, on the border to Austria and Moravia, spoke German or Yiddish; the most traditional communities were in the northeast (lowlands) and had close linguistic, cultural, and religious ties to Galician Jewry; while Jews in central Hungary and especially in the capital of Budapest usually spoke Hungarian and felt like Hungarians. There were also crucial differences with regard to religion. Thus, parts of Hungary remained a bastion of Orthodoxy, following the teachings of the *Hatam Sofer* (Ashkenazic pronunciation: *Hasam Sofer*, meaning "Seal of the Scribe"), Rabbi Moses Schreiber from Pressburg (Bratislava), whose well-known motto was: "Anything new is forbidden by Torah" (*hadash asur min hatorah*). The *Hatam Sofer* led an especially fierce struggle against any attempt at reform and against those who called into question the divine origin of the Talmud. Like many of his predecessors, he was entirely open to acquiring worldly knowledge so long as it served the higher purpose of religious study or earning a living. Emancipation, by contrast, was something he viewed skeptically, since he suspected that it was linked with the dissolution of the traditional Jewish world. Even in the second half of the nineteenth century, this outlook found an echo among Orthodox Hungarian rabbis, most prominently Akiba Schlesinger. Schlesinger was against Jews imitating the customs of their non-Jewish neighbors, as far as language, their choice of names, and their clothing were concerned, and in so doing he rejected the entire project of emancipation as a danger to the future of the Jews.

In northeastern Hungary there were Hasidic bastions with their own dynasties in Sighet and Munkacz. But the religious reform movement did quickly establish a foothold. Its spokesmen, usually called Neologs, were less radical than in Germany. Their conflict with Orthodoxy, however, was so intense that the government summoned a Jewish Congress in 1868, at which Neologs and the Orthodox collided without being able to reach any accord. As in Germany, the Orthodox got their way and were able to found their own separatist congregations. In addition to these two groups, a third refused to join either camp and tried instead to maintain its status before the Congress, so that its affiliates were called "status quo congregations."

The legal status of the Jews of Romania was closer to that of Jews in the Czarist Empire than to that of Jews under the Habsburgs. They remained restricted in their choice of gainful employment and in their opportunities for owning land. Although Jewish intellectuals had played some role in the Romanian independence struggle, and King Carol I (Karl von Hohenzollern-Sigmaringen), whose reign began in 1866, advocated granting them civil rights, a population that opposed Jewish emancipation succeeded in preventing steps in this direction. As a result, with just a few exceptions, only Christians could become citizens. While the emancipation of the Jews was one of the provisions granted in neighboring Austria-Hungary by the Compromise of 1867, Romanian Jews were in that same year driven out of villages. A majority of Romanian Jews lived in the cities, where they constituted a large share of the population. In Iași (Jassy), they formed 40 percent of the population, and at least 15 percent in Bucharest. In 1868 in the city of Galați there were serious anti-Jewish pogroms, which were repeated a few years later in other cities. The situation of the Jews in Romania aroused international furor and led to the matter being taken up at the Berlin Congress of 1878. Like Bulgaria and Serbia, Romania also had to declare that it would grant all its citizens equal rights. While the first two states implemented this policy (although the Serbian parliament only assented in 1889), the Romanian government ignored the resolution. Because of the discussion that took place at the Berlin Congress, the emancipation of the Jews was stated as an international principle. This did not, however, help Romania's Jews. By the end of the century, at around 300,000, they were one of Europe's largest Jewish communities, but only a few hundred were granted their civil rights.

In Serbia the Jewish population, at about 5,000, was quite small, and in Croatia and Bosnia each there lived just about 10,000. The latter, like most of Bulgaria's nearly 30,000 Jews, were largely Sephardic and spoke Judeo-Spanish.

Pogroms

In the meantime, the conditions of Jewish life in the Czarist Empire had dramatically worsened with the murder of Czar Alexander II on March 1, 1881. What happened after the assassination clearly shows several factors interacting in the face of this threatening situation. Easter and Passover coincided that year. The accusation of deicide was intermingled with medieval legends of Jewish ritual murder. Added to this, the fact that a Jewish woman was in the circle of the assassins led reactionaries to insinuate that the Jewish population as a whole sympathized with the revolutionaries. The anti-Jewish riots that followed, called "pogroms" in Russian, did not prove inconvenient for the government, since the Jews could be used as a lightning rod deflecting flare-ups of social unrest. More importantly, the previous policy of "selective integration," which had led to significant sociocultural changes among Russian Jews and the rise of a Russified Jewish elite (especially in St. Petersburg), now gave way to more restrictive measures. While earlier Czars had believed that Jews were "corrigible" by means of education and Russification, the last two Czars, Alexander III and Nicholas II, saw in the Jews a kind of social cancer. The assimilated Jews were even worse in their eyes than the traditional ones, since the former were regarded as a major source of social unrest.

The pogroms of 1881 first erupted on April 15 in Yelisavet-grad and rapidly spread to between 200 and 250 cities other cities. These were not the first violent acts to affect Jews in the Czarist Empire. In 1859 and 1871 the Jews of Odessa had already been visited by a wave of physical violence. But after 1881 one pogrom followed another with increasing frequency. On top of the economically and legally precarious situation facing the Jews, who remained confined to the Pale of Settlement, fear of physical violence was now added. The worst violence erupted, after twenty years of accelerated social change and the development of a new anti-Jewish discourse, on April 3, 1903 (again at Easter time) in the city of Kishinev and lasted three days. One week earlier, a journalist's pamphlet had stirred up the masses by drawing a connection between the old ritual murder legend and some new conspiracy theories. The result was 50 dead and over 500 injured, with 2,000 Jews losing their homes. Houses and businesses were destroyed and ransacked. The Russian army and police could have put a quick stop to the violence, but they deliberately stayed on the sidelines. Better to let the masses, politically and economically frustrated, take things out on the Jews than vent their anger on the authority of the state. It was by no means only Russians who were part of the violent mob. Just as part of the local Greek population fell on the Jews in Odessa, so the Romanian population in Kishinev took an active role in the plundering and killing.

The pogrom in Kishinev gave rise to a wave of international protests. It inspired Chaim Nachman Bialik, who would later become the Hebrew national poet, to write his most famous poem, "In the City of Slaughter." The poem was not content with bewailing the terror; it also lamented the passivity of the Jewish victims, and so provided impetus for the Zionist idea that Jews would only be secure in their own state.

For the first time, activists and intellectuals from the Russian opposition joined in the cry of protest against this anti-Jewish violence and blamed the government for what happened. Leo Tolstoy, who had remained silent in the face of the pogroms of the 1880s, now expressed abhorrence at how the government and the Church were leaving the people in a state of ignorance and fanaticism. Conspiracy theories were gaining popularity in the Czarist Empire, especially allegations (still heard to this day) about a plan for global domination by the Jews, as reported in the "Protocols of the Elders of Zion." This fraudulent document first appeared in Russia in 1903, in an abridged form, in the journal *Znamya* (The Banner). It was most likely the translation of a French text now lost. Its publisher was the fanatical antisemite Pavolatchi Krushevan, who had already helped stage the Kishinev pogrom. The *Urtext* used as the basis for most subsequent translations and revisions of this forgery was a version published in 1905 by the religious fanatic Sergey Nilus. The motive of the authors, who were from circles associated with the Russian secret police in Paris, was to push the Czar and influential politicians toward an openly antisemitic policy. The Protocols were later translated into numerous languages and disseminated in English by the automobile manufacturer Henry Ford.

Even after the bloodbath of Kishinev, conspiracy theories and ritual murder legends remained staples of popular opinion in Eastern Europe. The death of a Christian child in Kiev in 1911 led to the arrest of a Jewish brick factory employee named Mendel Beilis. He was subjected to a lengthy trial even though the authorities knew the identity of the real guilty parties. Over and over again, the prosecution, supported by the Justice Minister with the interposition of Czar Nicholas II, kept mounting new arguments and trying to pillory the Jewish religion as a whole. Beilis was finally acquitted, though no clear statement exonerating Judaism was forthcoming.

In his painting *After the Pogrom* (around 1910), the Polish-Jewish painter Maurice Minkowski captured a Jewish population that had become homeless and was fleeing violence. In despair, many chose to cross the Atlantic.

In other countries throughout Central and Eastern Europe, too, the ritual murder legend gained popularity. There are seventy known cases of Jews accused of ritual murder from the last decade of the nineteenth century alone. The most notorious of these blood libel accusations happened in the Hungarian village of Tiszaeszlar and in northern Bohemia where the itinerant Jewish cobbler Leopold Hilsner was sentenced to death for murdering a girl but later had his sentence commuted to life in prison. He remained in prison from 1899 until a pardon was granted in 1916. In 1961, the brother of the murdered girl confessed on his deathbed that he had murdered his sister. In Germany, too, this medieval legend was revived. The most famous cases took place in 1891 in Xanten in the Rhineland, and in 1900 in Konitz in western Prussia. Although there were acquittals in both cases, the houses and livelihoods of the accused were destroyed. In the Konitz region, antisemitic riots persisted for years. In both cases, the ritual murder legends were embroidered with anti-Jewish slanders about kosher slaughtering.

Further east, in the Czarist Empire, it was not only the material situation of the Jews that worsened after 1881, but also their legal status. An 1883 "High Commission for the Revision of the Current Laws concerning the Jews" in the empire, also called the Pahlen Commission after its chairman, recommended granting gradual equality to the Jewish minority vis-à-vis the rest of the population. But Czar Alexander III (1881–1894) refused to follow the commission's advice and advocated maintaining the legal restrictions. New laws now limited the number of Jews at universities and high schools, prevented Jews from taking up the legal profession, prohibited new settlements, and deprived Jews of voting rights in local elections. In 1891 a large number of Jews who had previously gotten permission to settle in the capital were expelled from the city and administrative district of Moscow. Only after the Revolution of 1905 did Jews, along with many other Russians, get the right to vote, and in 1915 the Pale of Settlement was abolished owing to the military exigencies of the First World War. Heretofore Jews had only been allowed to settle outside the Pale in exceptional cases—for example, if they were merchants, artisans, soldiers in the highest tax bracket, or high school graduates.

These legal restrictions went hand in hand with an increasing economic polarization of Eastern Europe's Jews. In the cities a business elite developed, which included leading industrialists like the textile manufacturer Poznański in Łódź or the "railroad kings" Poliakov and Bloch. This elite also included the small community of prosperous merchants, academics, and artisans who obtained the right to settle in St. Petersburg. They numbered some 20,000 people (or 1.5 percent of the population) by the end of the century. In 1863 several Jewish philanthropists and Enlightenment figures in the city, centered around the bankers Leon Rosenthal and Baron Joseph Günzburg, founded the "Society for the Promotion of Culture Among the Jews of Russia," which supported educational reform, occupational restructuring, and the promotion of the Russian (but also Hebrew and German) language and culture. The Society awarded numerous scholarships to students who were envisioned as future champions of social reform and Russification. While this financial and educational aristocracy was growing in the big cities, the middle classes were rapidly becoming impoverished. The picture of the shtetl was increasingly one of small craftsmen, peddlers, and *Luftmenschen* (people without training or a steady occupation). In many places the latter formed one third to a half of the Jewish population.

In 1897, over five million Jews lived in the Czarist Empire, about 5 percent of the country's total population and half of all Jews worldwide. Over 90 percent remained in the Pale of Settlement, where they made up 11.5 percent of the total population. In Poland, Belorussia, and the Ukraine there were many typically Jewish shtetls in which they formed the majority; thus, in Berdichev Jews were 87.5 percent of the population, in Plinsk 80 percent, in Białystok 66 percent. More and more Jews were drawn to the big cities in search of opportunities for a livelihood. On the eve of the First World War, Warsaw had 337,000 Jews, who made up almost 40 percent of the population, in Łódź they represented 36 percent of the city's 480,000 inhabitants, and Odessa's 150,000 Jews formed a third of all the townspeople. Even St. Petersburg, officially closed to Jews, was home to 35,000. In the major cities most Jews lived in their own neighborhoods and socialized among themselves.

A Modern Exodus

On August 11, 1881, a group of the most influential and prosperous Jews in the Czarist Empire gathered in the St. Petersburg home of Baron Horace Günzburg in order to show how upset they were at the prospect of a mass exodus of Russian Jews. The Russian government would have an easy job of it if this happened, these community leaders worried; all it would have to do was give the Jews enough provocation and they would leave the country. Günzburg and his colleagues, however, dreamed of a Russian-Jewish future that, as in Western Europe, would be shaped by the principles of integration and acculturation. These Jewish notables received support from Orthodox rabbis who saw flight to the West as a move in the dangerous direction of assimilation.

Both these sides of Russian Jewry were, however, powerless to prevent the stream of eager emigrants who, ever since the assassination of Alexander II and the ensuing pogroms, had been looking toward the West, and especially toward the other side of the Atlantic, as a way out of violence, economic distress, and legalized oppression. All in all, over two million Jews left the Czarist Empire between 1881 and the First World War. They were joined by several hundred thousands from the Habsburg Empire and 75,000 from Romania, where one out of four Jews left the homeland. Frequently they spent several days on trains in order to reach the ports of Hamburg, Bremerhaven, or Rotterdam. They had scraped together the necessary rubles for third-class passage. In order to ease the arduous journey to the point of embarkation, German and Austrian Jews founded relief agencies that provided the émigrés with food and lodgings while they were underway. Some of these "benefactors" may have been motivated by a desire to move the impoverished East European masses along as quickly as possible, so that their German co-religionists, who had only recently been emancipated, would not be confused with these unassimilated Easterners. Whatever their motives, their actions proved to be extremely fortunate for the emigrants, in some cases even lifesaving.

A small portion of the emigrants from the East remained in Europe. At least 80 percent of the 250,000 Jews in Great

Britain prior to the First World War had arrived from Eastern Europe over the last three decades, and in France the new immigrants made up half of the nearly 150,000 in that country's Jewish community. Some 70,000 Jews from the East remained in the German empire prior to the First World War, but there they made up only about 15 percent of all Jews. The great majority, however, wanted to leave Europe behind them. Some were drawn to Australia, South Africa, South America, and Canada. Eighty-five percent had a single goal in sight: the "Goldene Medine" (the golden land), the United States of America.

And just as most East European Jews chose to settle in London and Paris when they remained in Western Europe, in Sydney and Melbourne when they emigrated to Australia, and in Buenos Aires and Montevideo or São Paulo and Rio de Janeiro in South America, in the United States they were drawn to the metropolis of New York. At the outbreak of the First World War, over three million Jews lived in the United States, nearly half of them in New York City. This gave the city five times as many Jewish inhabitants as Warsaw, which had the second largest Jewish population in the world. It was the Lower East Side of Manhattan with its dark, damp, and overcrowded housing blocks in the vicinity of the port of arrival, that became the temporary home for several generations of city dwellers. Major Jewish centers also sprang up in Chicago and Philadelphia, whose 285,000 and 240,000 Jews, respectively, turned them into the third-and fourth-largest Jewish communities in the world at the turn of the century. Here Jews were more numerous than in such major Jewish centers as Vienna, Berlin, and Budapest.

The Jewish communities that had already been established in America for one to two generations set themselves the task of supporting the new immigrants. At the same time, East European Jews began to help themselves. In 1881 they established the Hebrew Immigrant Aid Society (HIAS), which provided new

A humoristic Yiddish greeting card for the Jewish New Year (around 1914)—
"good for one 120-year round trip in the stream of life"—alludes to ships
taking emigrants to America with its depiction of the Statue of Liberty on
the lower edge of the picture.

immigrants with clothing, shelter, and food. The newcomers also created their own mutual aid societies based on town or region of origin, called *landsmanshaftn* in Yiddish. Almost every city and village from which Jews had emigrated had its own *landsmanshaft* in the new metropolis. The first of these institutions was the Bialystok Mutual Aid Society founded in 1886.

The greatest assistance immigrants could manage to give to themselves, and especially to their children, was to pave the way for upward mobility through education. Already in the nineteenth century, many secularized Jews had exchanged a traditional religious education for an academic one. The tradition of learning, whether secular or religious, was also pronounced among American Jews. Here the doors of public schools and public universities were open to them. As early as 1905 they formed over half of all students at City College in New York, and in 1910 nearly a quarter of the medical students at American universities. A large share of the instructors, especially female teachers, in New York's public schools were the children of Jewish immigrants. Meanwhile, the guardians of religious tradition back in Eastern Europe feared that the emigrants would assimilate too quickly to their environment and no longer live according to the rules of the Jewish religion. Some, like the illustrious scholar Israel Meir ha-Kohen, even prohibited emigration to America. In fact, some emigrants did transform themselves from religious traditionalists into freethinkers, socialists, and anarchists, some shortly after their arrival or even during the voyage across the Atlantic. The majority, however, tried to harmonize religion with their new life. The Jewish Theological Seminary was founded in 1886 in order to train rabbis who would later call themselves Conservative and occupy a position between Orthodoxy and the Reform movement, while the Isaac Elchanan Yeshiva, which later grew into Yeshiva University, epitomized an Orthodoxy open to its modern surroundings. These institutions laid the cornerstone for a comprehensive higher education that was both Jewish and secular.

Attempts to appoint a chief rabbi in the major cities failed, as did efforts at forming an all-encompassing community for the entire Jewish population in a single locality. Religious congregations were voluntary combinations, and even the supervision of kosher meat was left to private competition. Each private food producer engaged a rabbi, whose authority was either recognized or contested by customers.

On the Lower East Side

The Lower East Side, populated by people uprooted from the entrenched world of the shtetl and forced into trying living conditions, was an ideal breeding ground for prostitution and crime. But these same circumstances also favored a cultural efflorescence that followed up on Old World achievements. Over a dozen Yiddish theaters were founded, and while many of their plays were critical or even dismissive of the Jewish religion, they nonetheless drew their subjects from the storehouse of Jewish traditions. In addition to Yiddish classics like the plays of Sholem Aleichem und Y. L. Peretz, Yiddish adaptations of Western classics, from Shakespeare to Ibsen and Molière to Schiller, were also staged.

Yiddish writers tried their luck in the world of the East European Jews transplanted to America. The most popular, Sholem Aleichem, spent the last two years of his life in New York, but he never warmed to the New World. On the eve of the First World War, another popular Yiddish writer, Sholem Asch, arrived in New York. Asch, who opened up Yiddish literature to subjects much broader than those of the shtetl and became the first Yiddish writer to achieve international renown, also did not feel at home in the New World and temporarily moved back to Poland in the 1920s.

There was then no lack of attempts, even in America, to pass on the heritage of the Yiddish language to the next generation. Over 16,000 schoolchildren were enrolled in two hundred Yiddish schools. These were secular, and frequently even strictly anti-religious, and they were usually run by socialist organizations like the *Arbeter-Ring* (the Workmen's Circle). Yet for those born in America, Yiddish was only an obstacle on the path into English-speaking society. The rich blossoming of Yiddish culture would slowly wither during the interwar years, and as a mass phenomenon it remained confined to the immigrants themselves.

Little by little, the kind of modern Jewish scholarship that originated in Germany with *Wissenschaft des Judentums* also found new centers in American academe. Professorships in Hebrew were established at some universities, Philadelphia's Dropsie College specialized in Jewish studies, and when Solomon Schechter arrived in New York from Cambridge University in 1902, the Jewish Theological Seminary acquired a scholar with an international reputation at the peak of his career. The crowning achievement of Jewish scholarship in the New World, however, was the twelve-volume *Jewish Encyclopedia* published in New York between 1901 and 1906, the first comprehensive encyclopedia of Judaism.

About 150 Yiddish newspapers and periodicals appeared in the decades following the great immigration. *Forverts*, founded by Abraham Cahan in 1897, had a circulation of 200,000 during the First World War, which made it not only the largest Yiddish daily newspaper but one of the highest-circulation newspapers in America altogether. Cahan attempted to harmonize socialist ideas with Jewish traditions. Thus, even before his tenure at the *Forverts*, he had published a column in another Yiddish paper with the title "The Proletarian Preacher," in which he drew socialist messages from scriptural passages. Moses was portrayed as the first strike leader when he called on the Israelite slaves to

The Jewish Lower East Side: View of Hester Street with pushcart peddlers, around 1900.

refuse the workload demanded by Pharaoh. In the most popular *Forverts* column, "A Bintel Brif" (A Bundle of Letters), readers addressed their everyday problems to the editor, who both published the questions and provided answers. How should one behave toward an employer who maltreats his workers? What should a woman do who has followed her husband to America only to discover that he is now living with another woman? What language should one speak with one's children? The array of problems for which readers wanted solutions embraced

New York textile workers from different countries went on strike against poor working conditions and starvation wages in 1913. Here they are invoking a spirit of unity at a demonstration.

almost all areas of life. The newspaper's social democratic attitude reflected the prevailing political mood among Jewish immigrants, who often lost their illusions about the *Goldene Medine* soon after arriving in America. Most of them found poorly paid work in the clothing industry, the branch of employment that accommodated almost half of urban industrial workers. Unskilled workers were often crowded in so-called sweatshops, private houses where work was farmed out. They toiled long hours under miserable sanitary conditions, though they often did manage to keep the Sabbath free. Among the sweatshop workers there were 60,000 children in New York alone.

Many workers joined socialist organizations and trade unions. Meyer London, who had come to New York at the age of sixteen and studied law at New York University, became the first socialist from New York elected to Congress. Morris Hillquit, who ran five times for Congress unsuccessfully, founded the United Hebrew Trades in 1888, but in the long run this attempt to found a coalition of Jewish unions failed, and his organizations became affiliated with the American Federation of Labor (AFL), which was headed by Samuel Gompers, a London-born descendent of Dutch Jews. Gompers also played a critical role in the formation of the International Ladies' Garment Workers' Union in 1900. Jewish women formed the vast majority of its membership, which grew to 20,000 by 1909. They protested against inhumane working conditions in factories with a 60 to 70-hour workweek, and in September 1909 they organized the first strike of female workers, which began in the largest firm, the Triangle Shirtwaist Company. One and a half years later, on March 25, 1911, miserable sanitary installations there triggered a fire that cost the lives of 147 women and 21 men. The Triangle fire was the cause of an even more intense struggle by the unions for the rights of the mostly Jewish workers in this sector. It was, by and large, an intra-Jewish conflict, since the owners of most of the garment factories were German Jews. It was clear in the end that, even in the *Goldene Medine*, all that glitters was not gold.

Even the heroine of Anzia Yezierska's story "How I Found America," with which we became acquainted at the beginning of this chapter, arrived at this realization. "Where is the golden country of my dreams?" But in spite of adversity, she does not give up, goes on searching for the America of her dreams, and ultimately finds it in the search itself: "We go forth all to seek America. And in the seeking we create her. In the quality of our search shall be the nature of the America that we create." It was surely this process of creating anew on one's own that enabled the immigrants to strike riches in their search for both spiritual and material benefits, for a new homeland, and above all for security for their children.

הגדה של הבית הלאומי

בפסח תר״ץ

ערוכה ומסודרת בידי אזרח וגר

יוצר הבית הלאומי בגן־העדן

ה ר צ ל (לבלפור, שהגיע זה עכשיו לגן־העדן): שלום עליך, רבי בלפור.
משום מה נחפזת כל־כך להסתלק מן העולם ? ומה שלום הכרזת־בלפור ?

ב ל פ ו ר (כשפניו מביעים עצבות): מתוך הפירוש החדש על הכרזת־
בלפור שהכינה ועדת־החקירה, ראיתי והנה עוד מעט ולא ישאר מהכרוזי כלום.
אמרתי: במקום שישאר בלפור בלי הכרזה, מוטב שתשאר ההכרזה בלי בלפור...

הוצאת "ים המלח" (בעריכת אפרכסת)

תל־אביב ═══════════════════ פסח תר״ץ

16. From Budapest to Tel Aviv
AN "OLD NEW LAND" IN ZION

AFTER THE AUSTRO-HUNGARIAN COMPROMISE of 1867, all of Hungary, Slovakia, and Croatia were ruled from Budapest, the capital of the smaller half of the empire run by the Habsburg monarchy. Theodor Herzl was only seven years old in that year. "Judapest" was what antisemites would later call his hometown, in which every fifth citizen was Jewish. Dori (as he was nicknamed) first experienced antisemitism as a child in Budapest, but it was after the family moved to Vienna, the capital of the Habsburg Empire's larger half, that Theodor, as a law student, would discover what this "birth stigma" of Judaism really meant. Although Herzl himself was admitted into "Albia," the Viennese student fraternity, shortly thereafter the fraternity closed its door to new Jewish members and openly acknowledged its antisemitism.

Modern Antisemitism

The term "antisemitism," a pseudo-scientific neologism referring to a new kind of Jew-hatred that was no longer religious but racial in nature, had only recently entered the modern vocabulary. The journalist Wilhelm Marr, author of an anti-Jewish tract entitled *Der Sieg des Judenthums über das Germanenthum. Vom nichtconfessionellen Standpunkt aus betrachtet* (The Victory of Judaism over Germandom: Regarded From a Non-Denominational Point of View), had coined the term in 1879. In the same year a debate raged that later came to be known as the *Berliner Antisemitismusstreit* (Berlin Antisemitism Dispute). In an essay in the prestigious scholarly journal *Preussische Jahrbücher*, the conservative historian Heinrich von Treitschke warned of a supposed flood "of assiduous pants-selling youths from the inexhaustible cradle of Poland." The same essay put into the mouths of the German people the words later taken up as a slogan by the Nazi smear sheet *Der Stürmer*: "The Jews are our misfortune." If Treitschke made antisemitism socially acceptable, it was the court chaplain of Kaiser Wilhelm I, Adolf Stoecker, who made it acceptable at court. In 1878 Stoecker founded his Christlich-Soziale Arbeiterpartei (Christian Social Workers' Party, after 1881 just Christlich-Soziale Partei), which attempted to pry the working class away from Social Democracy. When he failed to achieve this goal, he turned increasingly to the petty bourgeois strata in the hopes of convincing the lower middle class to take up the cause of excluding Jews from German society. Like Treitschke, Stoecker too was a deputy to the Reichstag, where toward the end of the nineteenth century antisemites of an even more radical stamp were represented by their own splinter parties.

It was in Herzl's domicile Vienna, however, and not in Berlin that political antisemitism would celebrate its greatest political triumphs during this period. Here Georg Ritter von Schönerer's nationalistic German brand of antisemitism competed with the Austrian Christian Social antisemitism of Karl Lueger, and it was the latter that would emerge the victor in this rivalry. After initial electoral successes in 1891, Lueger achieved his first absolute majority in the Viennese elections of May 1895 and finally became mayor in 1897, following a two-year interval during which Kaiser Franz Joseph had refused to appoint him to that post.

Herzl's great dream of becoming an author who would write dramas for the Burgtheater was only partly fulfilled. Some of his plays actually were produced, but with modest success. On the other hand, he proved to be an extremely successful feature writer for Vienna's *Neue Freie Presse*, for which he worked as Paris correspondent between 1891 and 1895. In Paris, Herzl's hopes for integrating Jews into European society were lost for good as he witnessed the scandal surrounding the Franco-Jewish officer Alfred Dreyfus. After he had been accused of high treason, Dreyfus was degraded in a public ceremony and exposed to the wrath of the masses. As Herzl reported in his dispatches from Paris, the mob did not stick to personal attacks on Dreyfus, but instead roared, *"Mort aux juifs"* (death to the Jews). After years of controversy that split French society into Dreyfusards and anti-Dreyfusards, Dreyfus's innocence was finally proven, and he was rehabilitated. By then, of course, Herzl realized that antisemitism had gained a foothold even in the motherland of emancipation.

In France, too, anti-Jewish sentiments had deep roots, which were certainly not limited to the reactionary political camp. Some of the early socialists, such as Charles Fourier, Alphonse Toussenel, or Pierre Joseph Proudhon, had equated Jews with capital, much as Karl Marx had done in one of his early writings from Germany, *On the Jewish Question*. Among the numerous antisemitic slogans, diatribes, and political pamphlets, none could rival Edouard Drumont's concoction *La France juive* (1886), published in 1887 in a popular edition, and in 1892 in an illustrated version. The anxieties fomented by German and French antisemites often paralleled each other. Wilhelm Marr painted the nightmare of a Germany dominated by Jews, just as Drumont conjured up the distorted image of a "jewified" France and Treitschke feared the corrosive influence of Jewish immigrants from the East. As early as 1850, in his pamphlet *Das Judenthum in der Musik* ("Jewry in Music"—which initially appeared anonymously in 1850, and then again in 1869 under his name), Richard Wagner warned about the damaging influence of Jews (including Jews baptized as Protestants like Felix Mendelssohn Bartholdy) on music.

How can one explain the emergence of all these irrational, fear-mongering scenarios? In the second half of the nineteenth century European society passed through a period of rapid transformation that entailed uncertainties and anxieties for many people. Often their traditional place in society was called into question, by the loss of a job or by relocating into a city. Large segments of the population became part of the proletariat. In the midst of this fundamental transformation of European society, Jews were among the upwardly mobile. They had traditionally been assigned the lowest place in a society defined as Christian; now they had become citizens with equal rights. The occupations into which they had been forced since the Middle Ages, such as trade and money-lending, now proved to be vehicles of economic ascension. Suddenly the Jewish neighbor was no longer someone on whom even a person from the lowest stratum of Christian society could look down. It did not matter that the Jewish community, less than one percent of the total population, hardly represented any kind of threat either in Germany or France, or even that the Jews in no way defined themselves as a closed society. No new scapegoat for the economic and social problems of the day was needed; the Jews were ready to hand. In fact old religious prejudices now could be given a new pseudoscientific foundation, for which the new nineteenth century phenomenon of racism supplied the necessary slogans. Not belief, but blood was what counted. No matter how much one assimilated to the German or French environment, or even if one changed one's religion—none of this mattered if the Jews were now declared to be a race.

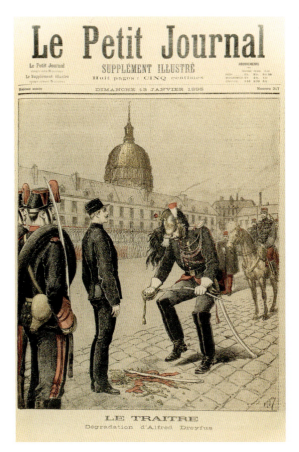

The public degradation of Alfred Dreyfus as depicted in the magazine *Le Petit Journal* of January 13, 1895.

This led to a far-reaching politicization of Jewish society. The only way to deal effectively with the collective accusation of the antisemites was to respond collectively. The first political organization to attempt this at the international level was the "Alliance Israélite Universelle," which had been founded in Paris in 1860 as a reaction to several antisemitic incidents but which, over the course of time, became increasingly devoted to the education of Jews in Oriental countries and the Balkans (see Chapter 17). The 1890s saw the creation of new Jewish organizations that committed themselves to Jewish self-defense against antisemitism and to comprehensive social integration.

The "Centralverein deutscher Staatsbürger jüdischen Glaubens" (Central Association of German Citizens of the Jewish Faith) conveyed the organization's mission in its title: German Jews were citizens like all other Germans, differing from their Protestant or Catholic neighbors only by virtue of their religious affiliation. The constitution of the German Empire had recognized their equal status. Antisemites now called this into question, and they had to be fought through journalistic and legal means. The Centralverein, known for short as the CV, provided the requisite tools for this battle. Its representatives went to court to charge antisemites with defamation, exposed the lies told by antisemitic politicians, and published brochures about the foundations of Judaism. On the whole, though, the success of these efforts was limited. The historian Theodor Mommsen, himself an active member in a solidarity group set up by non-Jews, the "Verein zur Abwehr des Antisemitismus" (Association for Defense against Antisemitism), explained it this way: "You are mistaken if you believe that anything at all could be achieved by reason. . . . It is useless, completely useless. Whatever I or anybody else could tell you are in the last analysis reasons, logical and ethical arguments which no antisemite will listen to. They listen only to their own envy and hatred, to the meanest instincts. Nothing else counts for them. They are deaf to reason, right, morals."

The Centralverein did not give up, however, and it became the largest German-Jewish organization. It is noteworthy that its membership increasingly consisted of Jews who continued to define Judaism as their religion even though they had themselves ceased to be religious. Only a small portion of German Jews (often the most prominent among them) were ready to take the step of formally converting and joining the Christian majority, a step that even a firm opponent of antisemitism like

Mommsen urged on the Jews. Most retained their affiliation with Judaism, even if they no longer practiced its rituals. Some found it dishonorable to turn their backs on a community still being persecuted, while others refused to break their ties with a thousand-year-old culture. The Centralverein offered them the opportunity to identify with Jewish concerns outside of the synagogue and traditional Jewish society, to view the struggle to complete emancipation as part of their Jewish identity. It was ironic that such an organization, which saw itself representing German citizens of the Jewish faith, became the forerunner of a secularized Jewish society.

In Eastern Europe, the politicization of Jewish society assumed different forms. Here the Jews were a long way from emancipation. They saw themselves not only as a religious, but also as a national community, and this is also how they were viewed from the outside. Secularization proceeded apace here as well, often in association with proletarianization, but the Jews still had their own language and associated forms of cultural expression. Thus, the historian Simon Dubnow could use his Jewish Folkspartey (People's Party) to demand rights of autonomy for a Jewish minority that, even though it did not possess any territory of its own, did have all the other trappings of a nation. More successful was the General Union of Jewish Workers, the Bund, which was Russia's oldest socialist party, founded in Riga in 1897, even earlier than the Russian Social-Democratic Workers' Party. For the Bundists, Yiddish as a language and culture was no end in itself, but rather simply a vehicle to a classless society. For them, the Jewish religion was just as much the opium of the people as the Orthodox Church was for their Christian comrades. For the sake of provocation, they publicly broke Jewish religious rules and cursed rabbis. Yet they remained Jews in the sense that they communicated with each other in Yiddish and attempted to secularize Judaism's social welfare values. In 1912, on the other side of the religious-political spectrum, Orthodox Jews founded *Agudath Israel* (the Israelite Union), a political movement and party with its own deputies represented in the Polish parliament, the Sejm.

Theodor Herzl and the Beginnings of Political Zionism

In 1896, in response to the new antisemitism, Theodor Herzl made a radical proposal in his book *Der Judenstaat. Versuch einer modernen Lösung der jüdischen Frage* (The Jewish State: An Attempt at a Modern Solution of the Jewish Question). Herzl had grown up in a secularized family. He did not have a bar mitzvah at age thirteen and did not have his son Hans circumcised. He was as poorly acquainted with the Hebrew language as he was with the liturgy of Jewish worship services. His parents' goal, and his own, was to merge into German-speaking society and culture. But the new antisemitism questioned the very possibility of admitting Jews into civil society. To comprehend fully Herzl's awakening from the dream of assimilation, one first needs to understand the profound pain he felt at its failure: "We have honestly endeavored everywhere to merge ourselves in the social life of surrounding communities, and to preserve only the faith of our fathers," he writes in *The Jewish State*. "It has not been permitted to us. In vain are we loyal patriots, our loyalty in some places running to extremes; in vain do we make the same sacrifices of the life and property of our fellow citizens; in vain do we strive to increase the fame of our native land in science and art, or her wealth by trade and commerce. In countries where we have lived for centuries we are still cried down as strangers. . . . If we could only be left in peace. . . . But I think we shall not be left in peace."

In *The Jewish State*, Herzl sketched out a pragmatic plan for a project he called a "Society of Jews," for which a "Jewish Company" would be founded in order to implement the project in economic terms. But where the Jewish state would be located, whether in Palestine or Argentina, remained open.

Before Herzl published his book, he entertained hopes
of persuading wealthy Jewish philanthropists to support his
ideas. Thus, he arranged a meeting with Maurice de Hirsch,
a millionaire from Munich who lived in Paris and ran a "Jewish Colonization Association" that had acquired agricultural
settlements in South America. Yet Hirsch could not warm to
Herzl's political plans for a Jewish state. Among Vienna's Jews,
too, there were few who showed any enthusiasm for Herzl's
ideas. The two Jewish publishers of his newspaper, the *Neue
Freie Presse*, refused to report on his plans, and Vienna's chief
rabbi, Max Güdemann, published a pamphlet against Herzl's
version of Zionism.

There were several reasons why so many Jews initially took
a negative view of Herzl's idea. For religious Jews it bordered
on blasphemy to anticipate the reestablishment of a Jewish
state. And it certainly did not make matters any better that
this was all supposed to happen under the aegis of an assimilated Jew like Herzl. Only when the messiah came, according
to the Orthodox belief, would Jews return to their historic
homeland. Assimilated Jews, such as Herzl himself had once
been, wanted to take root as loyal citizens of the countries in
which they lived. Zionism, they thought, would only provide
the antisemites with additional cannon fodder. Their loyalty to
another state would be interpreted as a sign of vacillation in
their loyalty to the homeland. And after all, they had defined
their Judaism, entirely in the spirit of the French Revolution,
purely as a religion. Herzl was calling this understanding into
question by talking about the existence of a Jewish people. He
knew that in the eyes of others—and often enough in Jewish
eyes as well—one remained a Jew even if one never attended a
synagogue. What united all Jews, according to Herzl, was their
common ancestry, their history, and their rejection by the society surrounding them.

That rejection was not always as drastic as the repudiation
articulated by the Viennese critic Karl Kraus, who accused the

The most famous photograph of Theodor Herzl shows him on the balcony of the Basel hotel "Drei Könige" ("Three Kings"). It was taken by Ephraim Moses Lilien during the Fifth Zionist Congress in 1901, and numerous versions of the photo have been used throughout the history of the Zionist movement.

Zionists of countering the antisemitic battle cry "Throw the Jews out!" with the taunt "Yes, throw us Jews out!" Yet even the organized Jewish community left Herzl in no doubt about its disapproval as he made preparations for the First Zionist Congress in Munich. Owing to severe opposition from the local Israelite Religious Community and the General German Rabbinical Association, he had to relocate the convention to Basel on short notice.

In August 1897, Herzl had the spotlight all to himself. Congress participants reported that he was celebrated like a king at Basel. He was a charismatic speaker and, above all, a brilliant organizer. The over two hundred attendees (including about twenty women) were not exactly the audience he had wished for: There were no Hirschs or Rothschilds, nobody of high standing, no distinguished names from Parisian, Viennese, or Berlin Jewish circles. Max Nordau was the only international celebrity. At the turn of the century Nordau was one of the most widely read cultural critics, whose book *The Conventional Lies of Our Civilization* (1883) had been translated into fifteen languages. Herzl, not without a certain kind of pride, spoke about the "army of *schnorrers*" he had assembled, even if the delegates were not beggars, but rather physicians, lawyers, journalists, writers, and eleven rabbis from twenty countries ranging from Algeria to the United States. Sixty-three delegates came from Russia alone, and there were also, in some of the Western delegations, Russian Jews who studied and worked in these other countries.

Herzl was not the first Zionist. The idea of a return to Zion, the hill in Jerusalem associated with messianic hopes and a symbol of the Jewish people's historic homeland, had been a constant throughout the millennia of exile. Jews all over the world prayed daily for their redemption and return to Zion. Medieval poets immortalized this longing in poetic form. Already in the generations prior to Herzl, there were writings that envisioned the establishment of a Jewish state as the natural response to modern nationalism. These included the 1862 book *Rome and Jerusalem* by Moses Hess, one of Karl Marx's comrades.

But only after the situation for Jews had worsened, especially in Eastern Europe with the wave of pogroms that followed the 1881 assassination of the Czar, did the idea of establishing a Jewish state acquire political momentum. Here, too, the outcry had come from a Jew who had originally been well-integrated: Leon

Pinsker, a respected physician from Odessa, wrote a pamphlet entitled *Auto-Emancipation* (1882) in which he described the path of assimilation as one that had failed and called instead for the self-emancipation of the Jews as a nation. The similarities between Pinsker's publication and Herzl's *The Jewish State* are astonishing, and Herzl later affirmed that he would not have written his *Judenstaat* had he been familiar with what Pinsker had written. Pinsker had also been a major participant in the attempt to combine the loose groups of those eager to emigrate to Palestine (the *Hovevei Zion* circles) into a political movement.

Among Odessa's intellectuals, though, there was one other colorful personality who could hold a candle to Theodor Herzl: Asher Ginsberg, better known by his pseudonym Ahad Ha'am (meaning "One of the People"), had been a Zionist long before Herzl had discovered Zion. Whereas Herzl wanted a "*State* for the Jews" (the more accurate, if less elegant, meaning of Herzl's *Judenstaat*), Ahad Ha'am was really pushing for a *Jewish* state. Both agreed that this should not be a religious state, but while Ahad Ha'am aimed at a revived Hebrew culture as the center of a new Jewish society, Herzl was concerned with saving Jews from physical danger. To Ahad Ha'am, Herzl's plan meant assimilation on a collective basis. He was afraid that the Jews would be establishing a state like all the others. To avoid that he championed the establishment of a spiritual and intellectual center in Palestine from which a renewal of Jewish culture would emanate. Ahad Ha'am also was among the first Zionists to warn about potential tensions with the Arab population.

The differences between Ahad Ha'am and Herzl reached a climax after the publication of Theodor Herzl's utopian novel *Altneuland* (Old New Land) in 1902. Here Herzl imagined an idealized society in which Jews and Arabs lived peacefully with each other and there were hardly any political conflicts—a society moreover that tapped the best of what every European country had to offer: English boarding schools, French opera houses, and (of course) Austrian coffee and pretzel sticks. Ahad Ha'am's reaction was scornful. Herzl's novel was "an ape-like mimicry devoid of any specifically national character."

There really was very little that was Jewish about Herzl's *Judenstaat*, aside from its inhabitants. It was to be a kind of modern welfare state, in which women would have equality, including the right to vote and run for office, a state of affairs still unknown in Europe at the time. The flag sketched by Herzl was adorned with seven stars, meant to symbolize a seven-hour workday. Hanging from the palm-trees would be another revolutionary innovation, "electric street lamps... like big glass fruits." It seemed self-evident to Herzl that the native Arab population would not want to deny itself access to this perfect political and social welfare system.

The Yishuv—The Jews in Palestine

At the beginning of the nineteenth century there were at most 10,000 Jews living in Palestine, where estimates of the total number of inhabitants ranged between 150,000 and 300,000. The largest Jewish community (4,000) was in Safed, where they were in fact a majority. Additional communities steeped in tradition existed in Tiberias and Hebron. Jerusalem gradually became the center of the *Yishuv* (the Jewish community that had settled in Palestine). By 1880, before the first wave of Zionist immigration (*aliyah*), Jerusalem's approximately 17,000 Jews once again, and for the first time in a long while, formed a majority in the city. Smaller communities had also formed in Haifa and Jaffa.

The Jewish population of Palestine prior to the Zionist waves of immigration was highly dependent on the money collected for them in the Jewish Diaspora, the *halukah*. Since living conditions in Palestine were hard but settling in the Holy Land was regarded as a religious commandment, the *halukah* was a kind of charity for the brothers and sisters who had taken this commitment upon themselves. But with the onset of Zionist immigration, the system of *halukah* was increasingly condemned as promoting an unproductive lifestyle. The first phase of agricultural settlements in Palestine began in 1870 with the founding of the agricultural school "Mikveh Israel" southeast of Jaffa. Additional settlements, founded with financial backing initiated by the Rothschilds and Baron Maurice de Hirsch, were to follow. They were managed out of Paris by institutions like the Alliance Israélite Universelle or the Jewish Colonization Association, and they served a similar purpose to comparable projects in North and South America. Their initiators were not interested at all in Herzl's political plans for a Jewish state.

According to the customary classification of different eras in Zionist history, the first wave of immigration or *aliyah* (literally, "ascent") to the land of Israel begins in 1881/82; in other words, long before Herzl appears on the scene. In contrast to the "Old Yishuv" who lived off charitable donations from the Diaspora, the Zionists of the "New Yishuv" were supposed to make of themselves a productive, primarily agricultural, people. The influence of Russian social revolutionaries and romantics could be seen at work here, and that is hardly surprising. The real foundations for Jewish society in Palestine were laid within the framework of the Second Aliyah (1905–1914), a movement that was much more firmly grounded in ideology.

In the years between 1904 and 1914 about 850,000 Jews emigrated from Eastern Europe to North America. In the same period Palestine's Jewish population grew from 50,000 to just about 80,000; nevertheless, it was in this decade that the course was set, both in terms of ideology and personnel, for the future development of the Jewish population in Palestine. The men who dominated Jewish politics in Palestine during the 1920s and 1930s and later formed the political elite of the young State of Israel had for the most part emigrated to Palestine before the

First World War and were socialized in much the same way: the prime ministers, David Ben Gurion and Levi Eshkol; the future presidents, Yitzhak Ben-Zvi and Zalman Shazar; as well as numerous other members of the socialist establishment, such as Berl Katznelson and Yitzhak Tabenkin. Although they were shaped by socialist traditions in Russia, they developed an understanding of democracy that promoted an open party system.

Along with the sanctification of agricultural work, one of the most important ideals for this generation of immigrants was the revival of the Hebrew language. During the Second Aliyah, Yosef Chaim Brenner, A. D. Gordon, Shmuel Yosef Agnon (who, however, would leave for Germany and stay there for over a decade), and other major Hebrew writers came to Palestine from Eastern Europe. Admittedly, pushing through Hebrew as the official language in Palestine's recently established institutions of Jewish learning was not uncontroversial. In 1912 a heated dispute broke out when the Hilfsverein der deutschen Juden (Aid Association of German Jews) created the Institute of Technology (first called the Technikum, later the Technion) in Haifa on condition that German be the language of instruction. In reaction a Hebrew-language school system was created that had over 3,000 students before the outbreak of the First World War.

The first kibbutz was founded in 1910 in Degania on the edge of Lake Kinneret when ten men and two women realized their dream of creating an economic collective that would manage its own affairs without any outside supervision or administration. The first kibbutzim were laid out as small units of twenty to fifty members who wanted to break with the traditional bourgeois mode of life: with private property, capitalist forms of employment, an urban lifestyle, and the nuclear family. But there were differences of opinion about what this agrarian socialist alternative meant in practice. Should children grow up with their

A three-dimensional greeting card for the Jewish New Year—printed in Germany in 1912 and with a Yiddish logo saying "Panorama of Tel Aviv"—idealizes the "first Jewish city." Between the ocean shore and the palm trees one can see the historical core of the city, founded only three years earlier.

parents or in a collective children's house on the kibbutz? Could women pursue the same agricultural work as men, and should they have equal rights in the administration? Did the kibbutz need to be autarchic and provide for everybody's essential needs? Since it was not always possible to reach consensus on these questions, several styles of kibbutzim soon emerged. Their numbers would multiply significantly after the First World War.

Cities, however, were the main sites of Jewish settlement. Tel Aviv's development is unique in this regard. Its name, which means "Spring Hill," goes back to Biblical sources, yet there is also a direct tie-in with Theodor Herzl, since this was the Hebrew title of his novel *Old New Land*. When the novel came out, the city did not yet exist. Only in 1909 was this "first Jewish city" founded north of Jaffa. Its origins gave rise to numerous legends: about how the first sixty properties were auctioned off by lottery to the city founders; how, from the beach on upwards, the first sandy pathways were laid out and the first urban institution, the "Kiosk," built; and how, within a few years, an infrastructure with shops and schools was in place. Theodor Herzl would not live to experience the founding of the city he had inspired. He had died in 1904 at the age of only forty-four. His diary entry of September 3, 1897, proved almost prophetic: "Were I to sum up the Basel Congress in a word . . . it would be this: *At Basel I founded the Jewish State.* If I said this out loud today, I would be answered by universal laughter. Perhaps in five years, and certainly in fifty, everyone will recognize this." Exactly fifty and half years would elapse before the founding of the State of Israel.

The first concrete diplomatic move in the direction of founding a state took place during the First World War, at the moment when Palestine came under British control. In a letter dated November 2, 1917, British Foreign Minister Lord Balfour asserted that his government would look with favor on the establishment of a homeland for the Jewish people in Palestine and endeavor to do whatever it could to achieve this goal. This was, to be sure, a rather vague formulation, but it was nonetheless the first time a major world power had given assent to the Jews' claim for a state of their own.

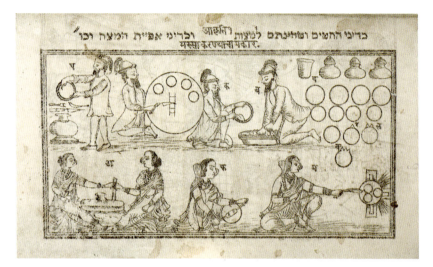

In the nineteenth century, some Iraqi Jews extended their trade ties and settled in India. There they encountered already existing communities in Bombay and other cities. This Haggadah was printed in Poona in 1874 and shows—by way of language, clothing, and customs—how closely Indian Jews were tied in with their surroundings. The lower half of the picture shows Indian-Jewish women baking matzah while wearing saris and seated in a typical Indian posture.

17. From Tétouan to Teheran
THE EUROPEANIZATION OF JEWS
IN THE ISLAMIC WORLD

IN 1892 MAÏR LÉVY, an employee of the Alliance Israélite Universelle, the most important aid organization for Jews in the Oriental world, wrote a comprehensive report about emigration from the northern Moroccan city of Tétouan: "At no time, has Tétouan been able to feed the 6000 Jewish souls that inhabit it. It is not a commercial town, nor an industrial one. At first, they [the Jews] did not go far from their native town. They would venture into the Moroccan interior, or go to Alcazar, Larache, Casablanca, and Tangier. Others, however, did not stop there. . . . Now the majority of the Jewish community of Gibraltar is composed of veteran émigrés or their descendants. All of the commerce is in their hands. . . ." Other Jews from Tétouan sought even more distant destinations. They went to Algeria, which was under French control, or to Rio de Janeiro, Buenos Aires, and Caracas, where opportunities for upward mobility and a Western education awaited them: "At fourteen, they dream of making a fortune. At sixteen or seventeen they are already making the voyage. . . . One sets sail for Caracas as easily as one went to Gibraltar or Oran twenty-five years ago." (Norman A. Stillman, *The Jews of Arab Lands in Modern Times* [Philadelphia: JPS, 2003] 203, 205.)

Stagnation and Change in the Islamic World

At the beginning of the eighteenth century around 370,000 Jews lived in northern Africa and the Middle East, about half as many as in Europe. One hundred years later, the half million Jewish inhabitants of the Islamic world made up only 20 percent of all the Jews in the world, and by the start of the twentieth century they constituted just 10 percent. But it was not just in terms of their numbers in comparison to Christian Europe but also in their everyday lives that the Jews of the Middle East and northern Africa had gone through major changes over these two hundred years. The growing political and cultural influence of the West affected the Jewish minority even more radically than it did the Muslim majority. Within a few generations, European colonialism changed their education and language, their cultural and religious values. The result was a Jewish community characterized by numerous contradictions. It remained a part of the Orient but was identified by those around it with the Occident; it underwent a series of thoroughgoing reforms, but was perceived as backward by Ashkenazic Jews; with Europe's help it liberated itself from anti-Jewish traditions that were part of Islam, but became the target of an antisemitism transplanted from the West.

Gibraltar, a favorite destination of the Jews from Tétouan, was one of the earliest Western enclaves in the region. The Treaty of Utrecht, which awarded the Rock in the south of Spain to England in 1713, actually stipulated that Jews be permanently banned from the crown colony. Yet as early as 1729 the Sultan of Morocco and the English government agreed to admit Jews temporarily for trade purposes. Permission for permanent settlement was not long in coming, and within two decades one third of the civilian population of Gibraltar was Jewish. While Jews continued to be prohibited from residing in Spain and Portugal, they could freely practice their religion in several synagogues in this English enclave on the Iberian peninsula.

On the whole, the lot of the *dhimmi* in the Islamic world had deteriorated since the Middle Ages. European travelers during the nineteenth century almost all agreed that their situation had become more oppressive than it was in the Christian world, even more dire than in the authoritarian Czarist Empire. Things were particularly wretched in those countries where Western influence was smallest. This was just as true of Iran as it was of Yemen and Morocco, where the Jews remained the only non-Muslim minority and were broadly dispersed throughout the country. On the streets of Iranian towns they were openly reviled and spat upon, and often physically assaulted. They were not allowed out on the street when it rained, because it was feared that their uncleanness would wash off and soil the Muslims. In deeply impoverished Yemen, the Jews belonged to the poorest segment of the population. They were forced to take on degrading jobs such as cleaning latrines, were not allowed to build any houses higher than two stories, had to walk to the left of a Muslim, and could only ride on donkeys—and even then they had to ride sidesaddle like women. Any criticism of Muslim authorities could lead to the death penalty. When the British conquered Aden in 1839, therefore, the colony attracted many Jews from the other parts of Yemen. Yemenite Jews also emigrated to Palestine. Approximately 2,500 lived in Jerusalem alone in 1908. Unlike Yemen, Morocco was entirely outside the control of the Sublime Porte. Here, out of reach of the Ottoman court, lived the largest Jewish community in the Arab world, under largely humiliating circumstances. They were allowed to wear only dark clothes, had to walk barefoot, and were forced into ghettos (*mellahs*). Hence the eagerness of Jews from Tétouan and other communities in Morocco to emigrate to the Western, or at least to the Western-influenced, world.

In a certain sense, the situation had reversed since the Middle Ages, when the Jews had lived under relatively tolerant circumstances in Muslim Spain and then later found refuge from Iberia in the Ottoman Empire. Now many Jews were returning to

A Jewish wedding in Morocco, depicted by the French painter Eugène Delacroix, who had traveled through northern Africa in 1832 and depicted life there from a European perspective.

the Christian from the Islamic world or trying to improve their fortunes by bringing themselves in line with Christian culture.

The majority of Jews under Islamic rule lived in the Ottoman Empire, which stretched from the Balkans to the Persian Gulf, and from the Maghrib to the Arabian Peninsula. Throughout the nineteenth century Western ideas increasingly penetrated the Empire, even influencing the life of the Jews there. The reforms introduced in 1839 by the reform-friendly minister Mustafa Rashid Pasha under the name "Tanzimat" (Turkish for "Reorganization") resulted in deep-seated changes in all areas of life. They ranged from the introduction of Western clothing, through new forms of architecture, to land reform. In addition, non-Muslim subjects of the empire were granted (at least in theory) the same civil rights previously enjoyed only by the

Muslim majority. At the same time, the different ethno-religious groups designated as *millets* (autonomous religious communities under Ottoman supervision)—such as Greeks, Armenians, and Jews—were able to maintain a larger measure of autonomy than was possible in the West. This was a way of accommodating the Western powers that were becoming increasingly influential in the region. Then, in 1856, equality for non-Muslims was sealed. All special taxes, especially the humiliating *jizya* (see Chapter 6), were abolished, and in their place a new tax was introduced that allowed Christians and Jews to be absolved from military service. Another important reform measure was the streamlining of internal Jewish structures. In 1837, for the first time, a chief rabbi—his title was Hakham Bashi (from a Hebrew-Turkish compound meaning "head sage")—was appointed for Istanbul, and later for other cities and provinces as well. He was regarded as the most important contact in the Jewish community for the Turkish authorities.

Colonization

The most crucial changes in Jewish life resulted from the Muslim world's progressive colonization by European powers. An example of this transformation at its most radical is provided by Algeria, where a French protectorate, which later became a département, was set up in 1830. This was followed in 1845 by far-reaching administrative reforms that, among other things, created three Jewish consistories with their own chief rabbis, who were not only charged with keeping watch over religious instruction, but also with encouraging their community members to take up "useful" occupations, for example agriculture. We are seeing now again in northern Africa the same debates about how to make Jews productive modern citizens as had accompanied emancipation in Europe before and after the French Revolution. The most momentous change in the legal status of

Algerian Jews took place in 1870, when the 30,000 Jews in the northern part of Algeria (but not those living in the Sahara) were turned into French citizens overnight. This declaration of citizenship was the first time that some Jews living on Islamic territory became citizens enjoying equal rights in a European state. With the beginning of the French protectorate in Tunisia in 1881 and in Morocco in 1912, the Europeanization of the Jewish population advanced in these places as well.

Tétouan, the city mentioned at the outset of this chapter, was pathbreaking in another respect. Here, in 1862, the Alliance Israélite Universelle founded its first school. The aid organization, established two years earlier and led for a long time by Justice Minister Adolphe Crémieux, had made it its goal to advocate for Jewish interests worldwide in the face of growing antisemitism. It was especially concerned with adapting the education of Jews under Muslim rule to Western standards. To the end of promoting this *mission civilisatrice*, it had established over a hundred schools by the turn of the century, and their number would continue to grow in the twentieth century. Here both religious and secular subjects were taught, and the language of instruction was usually French. They had a remarkably extensive system of schools for girls. These and other measures occasionally ran into heavy resistance from traditional religious authorities in the region. In France, by contrast, expanding the school system was granted the highest priority. In 1867 the Alliance set up its own teachers' seminar in Paris, where instructors for its school system were trained.

Hence, between Tangier and Baghdad, Tunis and Teheran, there emerged a modern Franco-Jewish educational system that decisively changed the lives of Jews in the Islamic world, as well as in the Balkans, within a generation. Together with the graduates of modern Christian schools, the schoolchildren brought up in the Alliance system became the carriers of a new middle class that was able to set itself up in trade and the free professions. For Jews this frequently meant a rapid ascent out of the lowest social stratum. In some respects, this swift upward mobility was analogous to developments that had taken place in Western and Central Europe one or two generations earlier. Yet here, too, social and economic success entailed some liabilities. Western education did not bring the Jews any closer to their Muslim neighbors; instead, it pushed them further apart. The Islamic world now saw the Jews as allies of European colonial power, itself regarded as an alien element out of place in their societies.

Secularization advanced with particular rapidity in the port cities of the Ottoman empire, such as Salonica, Izmir (Smyrna), Alexandria, and Beirut, which now became destinations for numerous immigrants from the rural hinterlands. The non-Muslim minorities, who frequently engaged in commerce and foreign trade, became major forces shaping these cities. In some regions, most Jews were concentrated in a few cities. In Tunis, for example, the city's nearly 20,000 Jews formed about a fifth of the population at the beginning of the 20th century, in Casablanca 6,000 Jews made up over a quarter of the city's residents, and in Baghdad at that time there were 50,000 Jews, one third of the inhabitants.

Salonica held a special place among the Jewish-influenced cities of the Ottoman empire. In 1882 its 48,000 Jews still made up over half the city's population, a much larger share than the Greek and Turkish population groups. Salonica's harbor, the city's most important source of income, was closed on the Sabbath—as were many shops in this "Jerusalem of the Balkans"—since most of the dock workers were Jewish. A flourishing cultural life, especially in Spanish (or else French and Hebrew) characterized this Jewish community. The Spanish spoken by the Jews of Salonica was so prevalent that even some non-Jews learned the language. With the incorporation of the city into the Greek state in 1912, the population transfers that ensued,

Apprentices at a school run by the Alliance Is-raélite in Tunis, 1901.

and finally the great fire of 1917 that made 50,000 Jews home-less, the florescence of this tradition-steeped community in the Ottoman empire came to an end. The city was abandoned by a large part of the Jewish population who preferred to live under Turkish control than under a Greek rule that embraced anti-Jewish measures.

The secularization process under Muslim rule was admittedly not as radical as in Europe, but to contemporary observers it did represent a rather drastic break with the past. The gap between an older generation steeped in tradition and their offspring now educated in the ways of the modern world would rapidly widen, especially in Algeria. Here, up through the turn of the century, most Jewish schoolchildren did not even attend Jewish schools, but went instead to regular French schools. Within Al-geria's Jewish community an often unbridgeable generation gap emerged, a chasm that rendered the younger generation literally speechless toward its own grandparents. Thus, at the beginning of the twentieth century the linguist Marcel Cohen has this to report: "[T]he grandparents speak Arabic between them-selves and with their children; they know little or no French; the parents, the middle generation, are truly bilingual; they use Arabic frequently, which was their home language, alongside

French which they learned at school; but the language of their household which they teach their children is only French, and frequently the children are, as a result, unable to converse with their grandparents." (Cited in Stillman, *Jews of Arab Lands in Modern Times*, 28.) The Arabic spoken by the grandparents was, as a rule, a Jewish-Arabic dialect that was very similar to the spoken Arabic of their surroundings but differed in pronunciation, contained Hebrew words, and was written using the Hebrew alphabet. The same was true of the Judeo-Persian used by Iranian Jews. Kurdish Jews developed different dialects based on the ancient Aramaic language used to write the Talmud. In some regions of Morocco, in turn, the Jews spoke Berber languages. The linguistic diversity of Jews in the Islamic world, therefore, nearly matched that of the region's Muslims.

In the Balkans and broad sections of Turkey and the Middle East, as well as in some communities in Morocco, the descendants of Jews from the Iberian peninsula continued to use the Judeo-Spanish language that is frequently, though incorrectly, designated as Ladino. Properly speaking, Ladino (derived from the medieval term for Spanish, *nuestro latín*) designates a form of Spanish adapted to sacral purposes and only used in writing. Judéo-Español, also known as *ǧudezmo*, changed its face at the end of the nineteenth century. The number of Hebrew loanwords (reserved almost exclusively for specialized religious terms) decreased, whereas more and more loanwords from Turkish and West European languages found their way in. Beginning in the 1840s, major newspapers appeared in Judeo-Spanish in Izmir, Istanbul, Salonica, and in the Balkans. Over the long run, however, French caught on among the educated classes. In Libya, where many Jews from Livorno had settled and had close trade ties with Italy, the dominant language of the educated class was Italian.

But new opportunities for social mobility and education were not the only changes that the growing influence of the European colonial powers wrought. Europe also exported Christian

Elphinstone College and the David Sassoon Library in the center of Bombay, today's Mumbai, were completed in 1870.

traditions of antisemitism, especially the ritual murder legends. Syria's Jews were made aware of this unfortunate development in a highly dramatic way in 1840. After a Capuchin monk of Sardinian origin had disappeared in Damascus, the authorities interrogated a Jewish barber, who confessed to the murder under heavy torture. Thereupon the monks accused the Jewish community of having killed the selfsame Father Tomaso for ritual purposes. Under the active influence of the French consul in Damascus, the most important leaders of the Jewish community were arrested. One of them died under torture, another converted to Islam, and others provided whatever testimony was demanded of them. Petitions to the French government from Damascene Jews, supported by England and (to a certain extent) Austria and Prussia, proved fruitless. A delegation of prominent European Jews, consisting of Adolphe Crémieux, the French Orientalist Salomon Munk, and the English philanthropist Sir Moses Montefiore, traveled to the region and succeeded in getting the Egyptian Pasha Muhammad Ali to release the Jews still under arrest. The Sultan in Istanbul later condemned the blood libel as a lie. It resurfaced again and again, however, in the Balkans and the Levant over the next several years. In the regions that lacked a Christian population, such as Morocco and Iran, the ritual murder legend remained unknown, even if anti-Judaism was no less scarce in those places.

This first international relief action on behalf of Jews can be regarded as a forerunner of the Alliance Israélite Universelle, as well as of other aid organizations: the Anglo-Jewish Association founded in 1871, the Israelite Alliance established in Vienna in 1873, the Aid Association of German Jews created in 1901, and the American Jewish Committee inaugurated in 1906.

Jews in the Islamic world were just as heterogeneous a group as they were in Christian-dominated Europe. There was a gigantic gap between the experiences of the relatively isolated Yemenite Jews and the Algerian Jews who adapted themselves to the world of French rule. In cities like Baghdad, Beirut, or Alexandria, small groups of Jews ascended into the social and economic elite. Most Egyptian Jews had first arrived there in the nineteenth century from other parts of northern Africa and the Middle East; some of them made enormous fortunes in the textile trade and banking, while others were respected lawyers and physicians. Western influence within the Jewish upper class manifested itself in altered forms of education, diet, and clothing. Thus, the upwardly mobile classes of Yemenite Jews wore the Turkish tarbush, while Iraqi Jews adopted first names borrowed from the English royal family, such as Edward or Victoria.

On the other side of the social spectrum, there were Jews in a number of Moroccan cities who lived in a secluded ghetto (*mellah*), cut off from the Western world. In Libya there were still Jewish cave dwellers who apparently lived untouched by modern civilization. Yet even in one and the same region there might be a world of difference between Jews who were rich and poor, religious and secular, those who had international experience and those who had never ventured outside their neighborhood. In Tunis the Arab-speaking and the Italian-speaking Jews each had their own synagogues and cemeteries and only married within their own group. The Jews on the Tunisian island of Djerba were far less affected by influences from the French colonial power than those in the capital city. In Morocco the line of demarcation ran between the descendants of those expelled from the Iberian peninsula (the *megorashim*) and the families who had already been living in Africa (the *toshavim*).

About half of the Jews in Baghdad lived under or at the poverty line, yet others built family empires that extended across the entire continent of Asia. No other family was as successful here as the Sassoons, a family of bankers and traders who, from their base in Iraq, founded branches in Bombay and Shanghai. Sheikh Sassoon Salah was finance minister to the pashas of Baghdad at the beginning of the nineteenth century. His flourishing textile business in south Asia earned the family the byname "Rothschilds of the East." His son David had a magnificent synagogue build for the growing Jewish community in Bombay and donated generously to orphanages and hospitals, schools, museums, and libraries in the city.

What the Sassoons were in the Far East, the Camondos were in the Middle East. Abraham Salomon Camondo, who had close ties to the sultan, founded, along with his brother Isaac, one of the most successful banks in Istanbul. The bank's loans financed a goodly portion of the Crimean War for the Ottoman Empire. Abraham Camondo also advised the governments of Austria and Italy, which elevated him to the nobility as a sign of gratitude. The Camondos were heavily involved in introducing a streetcar system and other technical innovations to Istanbul. Abraham's son Moïse settled in Paris and became one of the most important collectors of decorative art. It is one of the tragic ironies of Jewish and European history that the last descendants of the Camondos, the great promoters of the

Orient's Europeanization, ultimately became Europe's victims. Moïse de Camondo's son Nissim died as a French soldier in the First World War, while his daughter Béatrice and her husband and two children were murdered in Nazi concentration camps. Only stone memorials testify to the erstwhile fame of the Camondos: among them the Camondo Stairs in Istanbul and the Hôtel Camondo on the edge of the Parc Monceau in Paris, bequeathed to the city as the Museum of Decorative Arts.

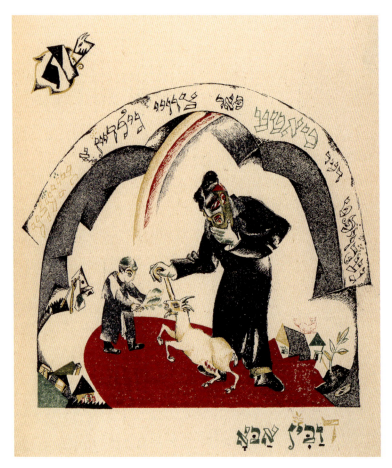

In 1919 the Russian avant-garde artist El Lissitzky, one of the cofounders of Constructivism, created illustrations for the song "Had Gadya," which is part of the Passover Haggadah. Lissitzky was one of the most important Soviet avant-garde artists, and he used his art to support the Russian Revolution. This example of Jewish book art offers a presentiment of the new possibilities that came out of the interplay between Jewish tradition and contemporary art.

18. From Czernowitz to Cernăuți
POLITICAL CRISIS AND CULTURAL FLORESCENCE BETWEEN THE WARS

From Multiethnic State to Nation-State

Rose Ausländer went to school in Austria-Hungary, published her first poems in Romania, found herself back in a ghetto set up under German surveillance, and experienced the end of the war in the Soviet Union. All this without ever leaving her hometown. It was the city itself that changed: It went from being called "Czernowitz" (sometimes spelled Tschernowitz in German) to "Cernăuți" (Romanian) in 1919, to "Chernovtsy" (Russian) in 1940, back to "Cernăuți" in 1941, to "Chernovtsy" once again in 1944, and since 1991, as part of Ukraine, it has been called "Chernivtsi." The interwar period, when almost half of the inhabitants of Czernowitz were Jews, was a period of uncertainty and change. "Lemberg" became "Lwów" (Polish, later the Ukrainian "Lviv"), "Posen" became "Poznań," and "Pozsony" (Hungarian), formerly "Pressburg," now became "Bratislava." Old empires fell, and new states emerged. They came and went for Ausländer as well. She left her homeland, emigrated to America, but then returned a few years later to Bukovina, where—according to Czernowitz's most famous poet, Paul Celan—"people and books lived."

The period of the First World War had crucially changed the entire Jewish world, in three ways. First, the enormous hopes that many Jews had placed in the project of integration were disappointed in the course of the war. Second, the war encouraged physical brutality and racist thinking of a previously unknown magnitude. Third, the decline and rise of states had a major impact on the political future of the Jews. At the start of the war, most of them had lived in the multiethnic states of the Romanovs, Habsburgs, and Ottomans. Now they found themselves living in new nation-states. In addition, the British had gained control over Palestine, and in the Balfour Declaration of 1917 they had promised the Jews the right to a "national home . . . in Palestine."

In those European countries where Jews had not felt fully integrated up until the outbreak of the First World War, the trenches were now supposed to enable what laws could not achieve; a common experience on the frontlines was supposed to help transcend the last remaining differences between Jews and other citizen-soldiers. Eighty-five thousand German Jews went to war for Kaiser and Fatherland, and 12,000 of them did not return. The situation was much the same elsewhere. Thus, the smaller Jewish community of France and Algeria mobilized 46,000 soldiers, of whom 6,400 fell in battle, and more than 2,000 of Britain's 40,000 Jewish soldiers lost their lives. In the Czarist army, which had not always treated Jews well, 600,000 Jews would serve in combat. Just as Catholics shot at Catholics, Jews also faced their co-religionists across enemy lines.

Yet it seemed to make little difference how patriotic Jews showed themselves to be; soon enough, in the very midst of war and even in the trenches, they became the target of antisemitic slurs. In France and England the Jewish communities largely consisted of East European immigrants. How could they, it was

Lovis Corinth: *Portrait of Maccabaeus—Hermann Struck* (1915). Hermann Struck was an Orthodox Jew and convinced Zionist. Yet he marched into Russia as a patriotic German in Prussian uniform. There he was inspired by his direct encounters with Lithuanian Jews to make the drawings for his book *The Face of East European Jewry*, to which the writer Arnold Zweig contributed a text that idealized the world of the east European Jews.

said in the Entente countries, fight on Russia's side when they themselves had fled from the Czarist regime? The accusation that Jews were cosmopolitans could be heard on all sides. No one believed that their patriotic enthusiasm could be genuine, even though the most important German-Jewish philosopher, Hermann Cohen, was promoting a symbiosis of "Deutschtum" and "Judentum" (Germanness and Jewishness), the German-Jewish writer Ernst Lissauer had penned a "Hymn of Hate against England," and even convinced Zionists went to war for their respective countries. For most Jews, social recognition was not achieved by the end of the war. In their recollections of life in the trenches, antisemitism weighed heavily.

On the other hand, and paradoxically, the war experience fostered a feeling of Jewish community that transcended borders. In particular, the encounter many German-Jewish soldiers from assimilated families had with East European Jews who seemed to behave more authentically led the former to reflect about returning to their own traditions. At first, this encounter had a material impact, resulting in the formation of relief committees for the destitute Jewish population of Eastern Europe. But among some German Jews it also left behind deep spiritual impressions. In their own surroundings they were no longer accustomed to seeing Jewish craftsmen and Talmud scholars, the Yiddish language had largely disappeared from Germany, and publicly living a Jewish life was something of a novelty.

Of all the European Jews, those in Eastern Europe were hit the hardest by the events of the war. In addition to hunger and epidemics, they were also victims of capricious officials. In April 1915 most Lithuanian Jews were evacuated by the Russian military authorities. A similar fate had been meted out to many Galician Jews after the invasion of the Czarist army. Their Yiddish language and admiration for German culture made the East European Jews look as if they might be potential allies of the German and Austrian troops. Only the overthrow of the czar in February 1917 brought a brief period of relief before revolutionary turmoil and civil war claimed new victims.

A European Jewry?

The revolutionary events of 1917 to 1920 catapulted individual Jews into the center of political activity as never before in European history. Antisemites did not care that Rosa Luxemburg had completely cut her ties to the Jewish community long ago, that the Jewish communities in Munich and Budapest had vehemently distanced themselves from such local revolutionary leaders as Eugen Leviné and Béla Kun, and that there was not the slightest feeling of belonging binding Lev Davidovich Bronstein, alias Leon Trotsky, to the Jewish community. Yet Jews knew all too well that though it might be Trotsky who was turning the world upside down, the price for this would have to be paid by the Bronsteins. What registered with the public in those days was the fact that Jews emerged as crucial political actors for the first time. On that 8th of November when the Berlin Jew Kurt Eisner was Bavarian premier for just one day, Thomas Mann wrote in his diary about "Jew rascals" who were leading a "Jew regiment."

Yet the Jewish masses (once again) were also at the center of events, specifically of postwar turmoil in Eastern Europe, and especially in the Ukraine. In the civil war raging there, Jews were caught between the frontlines no matter where they stood. Anti-Jewish violence under the government of Petliura claimed ten of thousands of Jewish casualties. In the Ukrainian town of Proskurov, Cossacks murdered 1,500 Jews on a Sabbath afternoon in February 1919. In Poland alone there were 106 pogroms in 1919. It is therefore entirely understandable that even anti-Communist Jews initially greeted the Red Army as their liberator. The Red Army, however, did not necessarily prove to be a friend of the Jewish population. Thus, the Russian-Jewish poet Isaac Babel noted in his diary on July 11, 1920: ". . . same old story, the Jews . . . expected the Soviet regime to liberate them, and suddenly here were shrieks, whips cracking, shouts of 'dirty Yid.'"

In Western Europe there were no such mass murders. But right-wing extremists in a Germany humiliated by defeat and all its consequences enjoyed a string of unprecedented triumphs. In France the antisemitic tract *The Protocols of the Elders of Zion* was making the rounds, and in Great Britain, where most Jews were immigrants, xenophobic noises were becoming more audible. Antisemitism, proving a more effective social adhesive than shared values had ever been, now bound the Jews of Europe together. Even the most assimilated Jews could no longer escape it. Some reacted to this hatred of Jews by finding their way back to Judaism. The Austrian composer Arnold

Schönberg, who had converted to Protestantism in 1898, began his road back after he was refused service at a hotel in an Austrian summer retreat because of his Jewish-sounding name, and it was completed with his official readmission to the faith in a Paris synagogue in 1933. In between lay a period of intensive rapprochement with Judaism, which culminated in two creative expressions, a Zionist play and the opera *Moses and Aaron*.

In fact, apart from antisemitism, there was little that held the Jews of Europe together. On the whole, the transformation of the European state system worked to the detriment of their unity. They were now split up in numerous states. In the three multiethnic empires where eight million out of the total of eleven million Jews had lived at the beginning of the century, they had been one of many different nations, religions, and cultures. In newly formed nation-states like Poland and Lithuania, but also in a significantly enlarged Romania, their status was less well defined than before the war. They were not members of the dominant nationality, but in contrast to the German, Hungarian, or Russian minorities, they also had no country that might protect their interests. In new artificial creations like Czechoslovakia and Yugoslavia, they were often seen as the only true representatives of the new political entity, whereas the others remained Czechs or Slovaks, Serbs, Croats, or Bosnians.

In the Balkans, Jews had already had their first taste of ethnic reorganization before the First World War. In the wake of the Balkan Wars, hundreds of thousands of Turks fled eastward, while entire Greek communities were driven out of western Anatolia and settled in Greece. Salonica, one of the largest Jewish communities of Europe, went from being under Turkish to Greek rule. The Jews living there had to choose whether to stay in their hometown, which had accommodated them for centuries, or remain loyal to the Ottoman rulers who had taken them in and protected them after their expulsion from Iberia. In a certain sense, the Balkan Wars and their aftermath constituted a prologue to the situation facing Jews throughout Eastern

Europe following the First World War. Who were the Jews, and how could they fit into the new state order? The Greeks of Salonica were Orthodox Christians, the Turks were Muslims, but the Jews were . . . just Jews. The situation was similar in Poland, where the Poles were Catholics, most Germans were Protestants, and the Ukrainians were Ukrainian-Orthodox or Greek-Catholic. But Jews in eastern and southeastern Europe were Jewish both in a religious and an ethnic sense. Their minority status therefore distinguished them from other minorities in multiple ways. This became quite apparent at the Paris Peace Conference of 1919, when East European Jews advocated for their rights as a national minority but West European Jews rejected any such minority status. In those countries where they had been granted emancipation, Jews viewed themselves as members of a religious community. Elsewhere they were regarded as a national minority that spoke either a Yiddish or Judeo-Spanish language different from that of their neighbors, was still often identifiable based on distinctive clothing, and had occupational structures that made them recognizable as a collective. These characteristics had begun to lessen, but they remained discernable in the postwar period.

The rift that split Jewish identity in Europe is most clearly seen in Czechoslovakia. Whereas Bohemian Jews had followed the Western model of acculturation and largely spoke German or Czech, the Jews in the far eastern part of the country were part of orthodox-style East European Jewry and mainly spoke Yiddish. In the census of 1921, only 15 percent of all Bohemian Jews who reported themselves as belonging to a Jewish denomination indicated that they also viewed themselves as members of a Jewish nation (almost all saw themselves either as Germans or Czechs), while 87 percent in the eastern part of Czechoslovakia gave their nationality as "Jewish." In the regions in between, Moravia and Slovakia, about half of all Jews gave their nationality as Jewish. In Romania, which had expanded considerably, major differences in the Jewish population were also discernible. The older Romanian communities in Regat had already largely acculturated to their surroundings. By contrast, Jewish congregations in the newly acquired provinces of Moldavia, Bessarabia, Bukovina, and Transylvania adhered to a more traditional way of life.

The largest Jewish community of the interwar period, Polish Jewry, was also extremely heterogeneous. When Poland regained its political unity after the First World War, it acquired territories that, for over a century, had belonged to three separate states in which the fortunes of Jews had been quite different. The Galician Hasidim had more in common with Hasidic Jews in Romanian Bessarabia than with the *Mitnagdim* in what was now Polish Vilna, and the German-speaking Jews of Posen (now Poznań) had more in common with Jews from Berlin than with their co-religionists in Bialystok. In Cracow the only Jewish daily paper came out in Polish, whereas in Warsaw both Jewish dailies continued to appear in Yiddish. In some big cities in Poland there were modern "temples" attended by the acculturated elite, while in the smaller cities the *shtibl*, the traditional prayer room, remained the principal place of worship.

The Jews of Europe were split in several respects. Where did they see their future—in Europe, America, or Palestine? Which language should they speak—the language of their neighbors or Yiddish or Hebrew? Should their political sympathies lie with liberalism, socialism, Communism, Zionism, or even the nationalism of their respective states? Should they practice their religion in a traditional, modern Orthodox, or Liberal style—or not at all? And what bound them to each other apart from the fight against their enemies?

City and Country

In the 1920s and 1930s, the majority of the Jewish population continued to be at home in Europe, but the centers of Jewish life had shifted conspicuously. Whereas 82 percent of all Jews had still lived in Europe in 1900 (69 percent in Eastern Europe alone), by 1925 their numbers were down to 62 percent (51 percent in Eastern Europe), and by 1939 they had been further reduced to 57 percent (46 percent in the East). North America and, to a lesser extent, Palestine were the new centers of Jewish life. By the mid-1930s the two cities with the largest Jewish populations were already in the United States: New York and Chicago.

An ongoing characteristic of Jewish population development was urbanization, which as we have seen began in the nineteenth century. In Łódź the Jewish community that numbered 2,700 in the middle of the nineteenth century grew to over 150,000 by the 1920s, and in Moscow the numbers went from 300 to 132,000 in the same period. Things looked much the same in the metropolitan centers of Central and Western Europe. Vienna registered an increase from 4,000 to 200,000, Berlin from 10,000 to 170,000, and London from 6,000 to 200,000. By the 1930s Jews were largely concentrated in big cities, and in some countries almost exclusively in the capitals, as in Denmark (92 percent), France (70 percent), Austria (67 percent), Great Britain (67 percent), and the Netherlands (60 percent). In Germany by 1933, over half of all Jews lived in ten large cities (a third in Berlin alone), and in the Soviet Union, where most Jews had been at home in smaller towns a generation before, 40 percent now lived in six cities—Moscow, Leningrad, Odessa, Kiev, Kharkov, and Dnipropetrovsk. In Poland a quarter of all Jews still lived in small towns and villages, in Lithuania over a third. In most countries, however, the once predominant rural Jews now seemed on the verge of disappearing.

The Jewish population of Eastern Europe was concentrated in certain regions and cities, where their presence was obvious to every visitor. In Polish Pinsk, for example, Jews made up 75 percent of the population, in Ukrainian Berdichev 65 percent, and in Romanian Kishinev and Iași 60 percent each. There were even some villages in Germany where Jews still formed about half the population, as in Hessian Rhina. Throughout Europe, the Jewish presence in major urban centers was also conspicuous. In Warsaw every third inhabitant was a Jew, in Salonica every fourth, in Budapest every fifth, and even in Amsterdam, Vienna, and Sofia Jews made up over 10 percent of the population. Germany was an exception: Frankfurt at 6 percent had the largest Jewish population of any major city. The Jews of Western Europe were concentrated for the most part in upper-middle-class neighborhoods, but high numbers could also be found in poor immigrant neighborhoods.

The structure of Jewish communities varied from country to country. In Germany Jewish communities, like Christian parishes, received financial contributions in the form of church taxes levied on their members. Although the Weimar Republic made it possible to withdraw from the local Jewish community without having to leave Judaism, anyone who registered a new address with the local authorities and designated his or her religion as Jewish was automatically enrolled as a member of the community. In France and Great Britain, by contrast, membership in a Jewish congregation was a purely voluntary act, and membership dues were paid in the same way as dues to other associations. Thus, there was the institution of the "Jewish Community in Berlin" (the very official-sounding "Jüdische Gemeinde zu Berlin"), but nothing really comparable in London or Paris, where numerous Jewish organizations existed side by side. Frequently, one of the larger Jewish communities in Germany or Eastern Europe might function more or less as a "city within the city," with its own welfare organizations, educational institutions, and sports clubs. In Salonica there were thirty synagogues, several Jewish hospitals and pharmacies, and a whole array of Jewish schools. Community representatives were designated through community elections, and in Eastern and Central Europe these were contested by different electoral slates, ranging from Zionists through the Orthodox to Liberals and Socialists, all running active campaigns against each other.

The occupations practiced by Jews also differed considerably from country to country. In Salonica there were Jewish dockworkers, in Antwerp and Amsterdam diamond cutters, in Alsace and southern Germany livestock dealers. Yet everywhere Jews were clearly over-represented in the commercial field and under-represented in agriculture. The long-term aftereffects of historical preconditions were at work here. In the Soviet Union Jews rapidly became proletarians, with the number of workers tripling between 1926 and 1935. In the big cities of Central Europe, the proportion of Jews among physicians and lawyers was especially high. At the beginning of the 1930s they formed the majority of physicians and lawyers in Budapest and Vienna, a statistic also reflected in the high percentage of Jewish students at these two cities' universities. Since de facto discrimination persisted when it came to hiring Jews for the civil service, the number of Jewish professors, lawyers, and teachers was significantly smaller. In Hungary, for example, where every second lawyer was Jewish, less than 4 percent of all judges were Jews. In mechanical trades the dividing line between Eastern and Western Europe was stark. Whereas only a few Jews worked as craftsmen in Western Europe, where the guilds had excluded them for centuries, in Eastern Europe there were numerous Jewish tailors and cobblers, bakers and goldsmiths.

All over Europe, laments about economic decline could be heard from within the ranks of the Jewish population. In Poland and Hungary antisemites organized boycotts that hit Jewish businesses especially hard; at the same time, quotas were placed on the number of Jewish students admitted to universities. One might ask then, why didn't more Jews leave Europe? Their reluctance was not always attributable to limited opportunities for emigration. Most Jews felt just as much at home in the countries where they lived as did their Christian neighbors, had emotional ties to their city or village, and viewed the increase in hostility as a temporary setback. They were also not the only population group under enormous pressure. Ukrainians in Poland, Hungarians in Romania, Germans in Czechoslovakia—they all lived as minorities in nation-states dominated by another ethnic majority. It was not always pleasant to live as a Protestant in a Catholic-dominated region, or vice versa. Socialists and nationalists fought each other on the street, and the economic crisis generated millions of unemployed. From this broad perspective, the special situation of the Jews was just part of a generally bleak situation. Everyday life for most Jews was not characterized by either physical violence or political persecution. Like their non-Jewish neighbors, they were preoccupied with earning a living and supporting a family as well as with being part of their religious congregation, local community, and homeland. For most, emigrating to another continent was a last resort.

Citizenship and Its Limits

On paper, the situation for European Jews improved in most countries after the First World War. The majority of postwar constitutions forbade discrimination on religious grounds. In practice, however, the promises embedded in the documents were rarely redeemed. Minority rights had often been included only in response to foreign—above all, American—pressure, and they met with little positive response in the general population. In the Soviet Union, the constitution's condemnation of antisemitism had little concrete impact on persistent anti-Jewish moods and political measures. For the first time, Jews could ascend to the highest political offices in both Russia and Germany. In 1917, five of the twenty-one members of the Central Committee of the Communist Party were of Jewish descent, but they often disappeared as quickly as they had risen. In Germany the best-known Jewish politician, Foreign Minister Walther Rathenau, became a favorite target of extremists and was assassinated after only a few months in office. In most states in the eastern part of Central Europe it remained inconceivable that a Jew might attain high political offices. In Western Europe there were no such obstacles. In England Jews were represented in some liberal cabinets as well as in Lloyd George's wartime cabinet, and in France Léon Blum served as premier in the 1930s. In Italy there were even Jews who belonged to the Fascist party, which only passed antisemitic legislation in 1938 under the influence of the National Socialists.

While the number of prominent Jewish politicians in Europe overall remained limited, the role Jews played in the continent's cultural life cannot be overlooked. What would German-language literature be without names like Franz Kafka, Franz Werfel, Stefan Zweig, Arnold Zweig, Alfred Döblin, Arthur Schnitzler, Jakob Wassermann, or Lion Feuchtwanger? Critics like Walter Benjamin and Siegfried Kracauer published in the *Frankfurter Zeitung* founded by Leopold Sonnemann or in the great Berlin newspapers that belonged to the Mosse and Ullstein families. Arnold Schönberg's music, Max Reinhardt's stage direction, Elisabeth Bergner's acting, Max Liebermann's painting, and Erich Mendelsohn's architecture left their mark on the culture of the Weimar Republic. Albert Einstein and Sigmund Freud opened up new perspectives in their respective fields. Outside the German-speaking world, the list of famous intellectuals and scholars, writers and artists grows longer still. One need only think of names like Osip Mandelstam in Russia, Henri Bergson in France, Italo Svevo in Italy, or Bruno Schulz in Poland. The Frankfurt School of critical theory was linked with Jewish names, as was the circle of art historians around Aby Warburg in Hamburg and much of psychoanalysis.

In 1919 modern Jewish studies—the *Wissenschaft des Judentums*—got its first significant secular research institute when the Academy for the Science of Judaism (*Akademie für die Wissenschaft des Judentums*) was established in Berlin under the leadership of the ancient history scholar Eugen Täubler. Yet the centers of Jewish research were increasingly shifting to other countries in the 1920s. The Yiddish Scientific Institute (YIVO) in Vilna and the Institute of Jewish Studies in Warsaw were among the new research centers in Poland. In Jerusalem the Institute of Jewish Studies formed the heart of the newly founded Hebrew University. It was, however, in North America where modern Jewish studies got its first chairs at some prestigious universities: at Harvard University for Jewish Philosophy and at Columbia University in New York for Jewish History.

In the United States, the interwar period was characterized above all by the Americanization of the immigrants' children. Yiddish culture, with newspapers, theaters, and film productions, was still lively in the 1920s and 1930s. The stars of the Yiddish stage and later of the Yiddish cinema—with Boris Tomashefsky and Molly Picon leading the way—became heroes to the immigrants. But the trend was clear: gradually the Yiddish language would yield completely to English. This was particularly obvious outside New York. In 1924 there were still two Yiddish newspapers in Chicago, and Cleveland and Philadelphia each had one. By the end of the 1940s only one Yiddish daily still existed in New York, and its circulation was dropping steadily. Yiddish theaters closed or became ever smaller with ever older audiences.

At the same time, more and more Jews found a place in American popular culture. George Gershwin and Benny Goodman represented a new direction in music; the *Jazz Singer* (1927), featuring Al Jolson as a Jewish cantor's son, was the first talkie; and Hank Greenberg became a baseball star. Gigantic film studios in Hollywood were founded by Jews like the Warner Brothers and Louis B. Mayer. But there were still obstacles on the way to the center of American society. American colleges restricted the admission of Jewish students. In his newspaper *The Dearborn Independent*, industrialist Henry Ford published the notorious *Protocols of the Elders of Zion* under the title *The International*

Jew: The World's Foremost Problem. In the South, Jews, along with blacks, were targets of the Ku Klux Klan, while in the 1935 Harlem riots blacks blamed Jews for the Depression. And around 30 million people listened to Father Charles Coughlin's antisemitic tirades on the radio.

In addition, there was the question of what posture one should adopt toward the acute threat emanating from Europe. The rise of the National Socialists sparked street protests by Jewish-American organizations. One of the chief initiators behind these demonstrations was the Reform rabbi and Zionist Stephen Wise, who had founded the Jewish Institute of Religion to train rabbis in New York and who headed the World Jewish Congress, which he helped create in 1936. Immigration from Europe persisted and, especially in the 1930s, brought important intellectuals and scholars to America. Albert Einstein was only the most famous name among this group. The New School for Social Research in New York (especially the graduate faculty associated with its University in Exile) was largely built on a staff of émigré scholars, and in rabbinical seminaries, such as the Hebrew Union College in Cincinnati, refugees made up a large share of the faculty.

During the interwar era reasons for emigrating could be found throughout Europe. In Eastern Europe the kind of autonomy promised by the new nation-states mostly proved to be an illusion. In Poland, for example, Jews were not allowed to keep their shops open on Sunday, which meant the loss of a sixth of their income for most shopkeepers, who also closed their businesses on Saturday for the Jewish Sabbath. Jews were allowed to maintain their own schools with Yiddish or Hebrew as the language of instruction, but these schools were not publicly subsidized, and often their school-leaving certificates were not officially recognized. In 1934 Poland officially declared its Minority Treaty (the "little Versailles" treaty concluded between Poland and the Allies in 1919) void. In Lithuania minority rights had already been dismantled in the 1920s. The only countries where Jews enjoyed protection of minority rights were Czechoslovakia and (with some small curtailments) Latvia.

East European Jews in west European metropolises—in London's Whitechapel, in the Marais in Paris, Vienna's Leopoldstadt, and the region around Berlin's Alexanderplatz—became more conspicuous after the First World War. The British-Jewish community, like the French-Jewish community, largely consisted of East European immigrants and their children. The second and especially the third generations, however, tried to flee these new ghettos. Many adhered to dietary laws only when they ate at home and attended synagogue only on the High Holy Days, changed their Jewish-sounding names, and attempted to assimilate to their English or French surroundings. Limited social acceptance was especially noticeable in the upper classes: Few golf clubs or elite boarding schools admitted Jews.

With respect to social integration, as in so many other areas, the Weimar Republic was situated somewhere between Eastern Europe and developments in the westernmost countries. Most German Jews, in spite of an antisemitism that was on the rise and becoming increasingly radical, felt integrated in Germany. There was a rapidly growing number of intermarriages, a clear indication that the boundaries between Jews and the larger society were slowly disappearing. Individual Jews were able to ascend to social positions that would have been inconceivable prior to the First World War. Thus, Max Liebermann became president of the Prussian Academy of Arts, and Ernst Cassirer was chosen as rector at the University of Hamburg. But both also faced antisemitic invective. Most Jews were members of sports clubs or other cultural associations open to the general public. Only a few small islands of Orthodox congregations remained in the big cities, and in the countryside the number of Jews still cultivating a traditional lifestyle was small. The majority were members of the metropolitan middle classes; they

The Lithuanian-born Ben Shahn, who immigrated to America as a child, was one of the most important painters of social realism. In 1936–38 he was commissioned to create a mural in the planned community of Jersey Homesteads (today known as Roosevelt) in New Jersey. For that commission he chose a three-panel sequence, reminiscent of the Haggadah, starting with slavery in Europe, continuing through liberation by way of emigration, and ending with redemption by way of Roosevelt's New Deal. The first panel reproduced here shows a group of immigrants (with the coffins containing the bodies of the anarchists Sacco and Vanzetti) led by Albert Einstein and Shahn's mother as they walk past immigration authorities on Ellis Island and sweatshops on the Lower East Side.

identified with the liberal traditions of the Enlightenment, read Goethe and Schiller, and enjoyed the brilliant cultural scene of the "Golden Twenties." German Jews were not blind to antisemitism—right-wing extremist parties were getting stronger and making themselves increasingly conspicuous in street violence against Jewish pedestrians or visitors to health spas—but the Jews could not imagine that this might lead to anti-Jewish measures decreed by the state.

The situation for Jews in the Soviet Union was no less complex. In the Czarist Empire they had, in spite of burdensome state restrictions and recurrent pogroms, been able to practice their religion freely. Under Bolshevik rule the fear of pogroms disappeared, but now they could no longer practice their religion undisturbed. Keeping the Sabbath, circumcising newborn boys, and providing kosher food were banished to the private sphere and frequently practiced in secret. The Jews were recognized as a nationality, to be sure, but in contrast to other national minorities they did not have any minority rights. Not only were Zionists and Diaspora nationalists banned; so too were other socialist Jewish parties like the "Bund." The Bolsheviks encouraged the dissolution of traditional Jewish community structures, by first establishing a Commissariat for Jewish National Affairs, and later a Jewish division within the Communist party (the *Yevsektsiya*). The long-term mission of both institutions was to dissolve autonomous Jewish culture and turn Jews into "useful citizens." During the first decade of Soviet rule, however, policies toward the Jews were somewhat contradictory. Yiddish culture was partly encouraged in order to exert political influence on the Jewish masses who still spoke Yiddish. Both the Yiddish State Theater and the Hebrew theater "Habima" were allowed to operate in Moscow. (The latter company left the Soviet Union at the beginning of the 1920s and, after a successful European tour, settled in Jerusalem, where it eventually became the National Theater of the newly established Jewish state.) In 1928, in an effort to counter the Zionist enterprise with a territorial Jewish project under Soviet auspices, Stalin proclaimed the underdeveloped region of Birobidzhan as an autonomous Jewish territory. This was an attempt to kill two birds with one stone: on the one hand to offer an alternative to Palestine, and on the other to transform a population-starved region into a flourishing Soviet province. But for the Jews this region bordering China exercised little attraction. Through 1933 only 8,000 Jews moved to Birobidzhan, where they never formed more than 20 percent of the total population.

In spite of all its shortcomings, the Soviet-Jewish experiment can be judged a success if assimilation is the criterion for success. Those Jews who wanted to become part of the new Soviet society and were prepared to abandon their Judaism were able to do so to an unprecedented extent. Even if most members of the new elite were not Jews, and most Jews did not identify with the new regime, Jews did constitute a relatively high proportion of the new state's ruling stratum. The reasons were obvious. They had been shut out of the old Czarist regime yet were among the social strata with the highest levels of education. In the Soviet Union, the way to move up was through education. In regions where Jews were a relatively high percentage of the population, they were also a large percentage of the academically trained professionals. In the Ukraine on the eve of the Second World War, for example, they made up 70 percent of all dentists, 59 percent of pharmacists, 45 percent of lawyers, and 33 percent of university professors. Almost all of the internationally renowned musicians and chess players from the Soviet Union had a Jewish family background. Most Jewish Communists made a point of leaving their Jewish background behind, but those around them constantly reminded them of it. After Stalin ruthlessly purged his ruling elite in the second half of the 1930s, only a few Jews remained in positions of political influence.

In different ways, Jews in the Weimar Republic and Soviet Union contributed to their own "burden of success," as the historian Fritz Stern once called it. The more they became part of their societies, the more forcefully they were opposed by the nationalist and antisemitic elements that were becoming increasingly radical. Doom and gloom scenarios, clothed in scholarly language or in the form of popular novels, started making the rounds. As early as the eve of World War I, the German Zionist and physician Felix Theilhaber had published a study entitled *The Decline of the German Jews*. For him it was

In this study for Marc Chagall's *Over Vitebsk*, the lot of the wandering Jews is vividly portrayed in the form of a Jewish shadow hovering over the town. Chagall was initially an enthusiastic supporter of the revolution, and in 1918 he founded an art school in his hometown, the Belarusian city Vitebsk, where El Lissitzky, Kazimir Malevich, Ivan Puni, and other avant-garde artists worked. Disillusioned with the revolution, Chagall left the Soviet Union in 1922.

not antisemitism but rather assimilation that was going to cause the dissolution of German Jewry within just a few generations. Two decades later the Communist Otto Heller encouraged precisely this kind of dissolution. His book *The Decline of Judaism* promoted a classless society as the ideal solution to the "Jewish question."

Jewish Renaissance and Zionist Politics

Some spoke of decline, others of rebirth. The notion of a Jewish renaissance was introduced by cultural Zionists like Martin Buber around the turn of the century, but it was during the

1920s that the catchword enjoyed wide popularity. What it signaled was a new awareness among many Jews from assimilated families of their Judaism. It was a reaction to antisemitism, but also as an expression of the quest for new certainties and community ties in an age of increasing anonymity and alienation. There was a growing trend for children to attend Jewish schools, for young people to form Jewish youth groups, and for adults to participate in different forms of Jewish adult education. The most successful undertaking of this kind in Germany was the "Freies Jüdisches Lehrhaus" (Free House of Jewish Learning), which opened in Frankfurt in 1919 and had its imitators in other cities as well. The Lehrhaus was closely tied to the personality of the philosopher Franz Rosenzweig who, on the verge of converting to Christianity, decided that he needed instead to come to terms with the religion he was about to abandon. Thereafter he co-authored, with Martin Buber, a translation of the Pentateuch, wrote (on his own) one of the most important philosophical works of modern Judaism, *The Star of Redemption*, and became the founder of modern Jewish adult education. No longer should "professional Jews" like rabbis and religion teachers be the ones providing instruction, but rather people like Rosenzweig who were themselves just beginning to draw closer to once Judaism again, this time "from the periphery back to the center." The program proved successful, but it came to an abrupt stop after just a few years owing to Rosenzweig's severe illness. His co-worker in translating the Bible, Martin Buber, was the second great intellectual figure in German-speaking Jewry. His writings on religious philosophy enjoyed something of a cult-like status, especially with the younger generation of German Jews.

In the West, engaging in Jewish culture meant adding another layer to multiple identities. Lion Feuchtwanger's novels on Jewish topics attracted non-Jewish readers and were just as much a part of German as of Jewish culture. This was noticeably different from Jewish culture in Eastern Europe, to which only Jews had access even when it was clearly influenced by contemporary trends like Expressionism.

In Poland there was a Jewish school system that ranged across the spectrum from Zionist-oriented Hebrew language schools, through different kinds of Orthodox religious schools, all the way to the radically secular schools of the socialist Bundists. But in the religious realm, too, there were important movements both in the West and East. Hasidic centers continued to exist in Poland and other East European countries, even if Russia was consigned to oblivion as a center of religious life and the United States was attracting more and more Hasidic rabbis and their followers. In Lublin the "Yeshivat Hakhmey Lublin" became an innovative center for Talmud study. In the Weimar Republic, some Orthodox thinkers made names for themselves, but the outstanding figure among German rabbis was clearly Leo Baeck. Baeck distinguished himself through his writings (*The Essence of Judaism*, 1905), and he became the spiritual leader of German Jewry in an unsettling time. He was a man of the center who, without being a Zionist, was favorably disposed toward Zionism and, without being Orthodox, showed respect for the Orthodox way of life. A ferocious struggle for political leadership raged in Germany's Jewish communities in the years prior to 1933. In the largest community, Berlin's, the Zionists campaigning on the Jewish People's Party (Jüdische Volkspartei) platform were able to join with the Orthodox to defeat the ruling (and for many years uncontested) party of the Liberals in the 1926 community election, but in 1930 they were sent back into the opposition. In Vienna the Zionists assumed control over community affairs in the 1930s.

After the Balfour Declaration of 1917, Zionism became a phenomenon that could no longer be overlooked within the Jewish world. In Germany and Austria its triumphs were measured less by the (extremely small) number of those emigrating to Palestine than by a change in the self-image of the Jewish population, the successful expansion of the Jewish educational system, and the partial reshaping of Jewish religious communities into broad-based *Volksgemeinden* (ethnic communities). An important pillar of Zionist "contemporary work" (*Gegenwartsarbeit*) was the establishment of Jewish sports clubs. Since the beginning of the century, going back to Max Nordau's call for the creation of a "muscular Judaism," clubs had been founded with heroic-sounding names like *Makkabi* (Maccabees), *Hakoa(c)h* (Strength), and *Hagibor* (The Hero). To the delight of many proud Jews, the Viennese Hakoah club became Austrian national soccer champion in 1925 and celebrated international triumphs. In addition to avowedly Zionist teams there were also Bundist teams in Poland, and even Liberal German Jews founded their own sport clubs. In addition, some clubs that would not define themselves as Jewish clubs were nonetheless called "Judenclubs" because they drew many of their fans from a bourgeois Jewish milieu. Among them were "Austria Wien" (Austria Vienna) and "MTK Budapest." Even "F. C. Bayern München" (Bavaria Munich), which became German soccer champion for the first time in 1932 under a Jewish president and Jewish trainer, was sometimes called a "Judenclub." Occasionally, muscular and spiritual power arrived at a symbiosis. Thus, after Friedrich Torberg (born Friedrich Ephraim Kantor) became Czechoslovakia's water polo champion along with his teammates from Hagibor Prague, he went on to author what must be the only water polo novel ever written (*The Team*, 1935).

Zionism in Central Europe was also successful in its outreach to non-Zionists, especially when it came to the project of building Palestine. To this end the Jewish Palestine Foundation Fund "Keren Hayesod" was founded in 1920, an organization that contributed to making Zionism "socially acceptable," even in circles that were skeptical to the point of rejection.

In the Soviet Union, after a brief initial period of openness toward the Hebrew language and Jewish cultural undertakings, the "Yevsektsiya" banned all Zionist activities. Most of eastern

Central Europe, by contrast, provided a nearly ideal breeding ground for the Zionist movement. The only exceptions were areas with a strictly Orthodox population, such as the extreme eastern part of Czechoslovakia or the Maramureş region of Romania, as well as areas with a relatively assimilated Jewish population, such as parts of Bohemia and Hungary. In general, however, Eastern Europe was the center not only of interwar Zionist activity, but also of emigration to Palestine. In addition, after the First World War Zionism was emboldened by the success of smaller national groups like the Estonians and Latvians, who had obtained states of their own, and even by the way that the old nation of the Poles had been restored. It seemed to many that Zionism's hour had arrived as well. In addition to fulfilling Herzl's goal of "conquering the communities," the Zionist movement also made it their highest priority to saturate the Diaspora with the Hebrew language and mobilize young people for emigration.

In Czechoslovakia, Zionism at times attained a special prominence because of the sympathy it garnered from President Tomáš Masaryk. Three interwar Zionist congresses took place on Czech soil (in Karlovy Vary [Karlsbad] and Prague), while in Hungary the Zionist Federation did not obtain legal status until 1927. The number of those who actually emigrated was relatively small in both of these countries, as in neighboring Romania, where Zionist representatives were also elected to parliament. The highest proportion of active Zionists and emigrants to Palestine came from tiny Lithuania, where only an infinitesimal part of the Jewish population identified with the dominant language and culture.

At the center of Zionist activities were Poland's roughly three million Jews. At times more than thirty delegates to the Polish parliament (the "Sejm") were Zionists. Many of the Jewish newspapers and magazines were pro-Zionist. The Zionist youth movement had over 100,000 members, and over 40,000 pupils studied in the Hebrew-language Tarbut school network. At around 140,000, the number of emigrants to Palestine between 1919 and 1942 was admittedly just a fraction of the Polish-Jewish population. At the same time, intra-Jewish differences in Poland were more pronounced than in Western Europe. Assimilationists, Orthodox Jews, socialist Bundists, and Autonomists took on the highly fragmented Zionist groups, many of which made common cause with the bourgeois Revisionist followers of Vladimir Jabotinsky in the 1920s. The only other place where the Revisionists were as important was South Africa, where Zionist commitment was especially intense among the country's relatively small Jewish population. During the 1920s the per capita revenue for Keren Hayesod from South Africa was the highest in the world. As early as 1930, 200 different organizations were affiliated with the Association of South African Zionists.

During the interwar era, the American branch of the organized Zionist movement rose to become its numerically strongest segment. Unlike Eastern European Jews, few American Jews were really interested in emigrating to Palestine. Most of them, after all, had only recently immigrated to the United States. One of the exceptions here was the future Israeli premier Golda Meir, who had been born in Kiev and grew up in Milwaukee before she settled on a kibbutz in Palestine in 1921. As a rule, however, American Zionists were more philanthropic than activist. Founded by East European Jewish immigrants against the express opposition of the German-Jewish establishment, Zionist organizations in the United States initially had to struggle for social recognition. It was, therefore, especially important when, at the very start of the twentieth century, the distinguished members of New York's Zionist Achavah Club were joined by Zionist groups established at Boston's respectable universities—Harvard, Tufts, and Boston University. But the ultimate breakthrough for American Zionism came in 1914, when the prominent lawyer Louis D. Brandeis was chosen to head the Federation of American Zionists; in 1916 Brandeis became the first Jew appointed to the Supreme Court. The Zionists were now a force to be reckoned with.

After the end of the war, the World Zionist Organization, whose headquarters during the war years had temporarily moved from Germany to neutral Copenhagen, got a new center in London and a new president in Chaim Weizmann. At a conference in 1920, a confrontation took place between the very different personalities of Weizmann and Brandeis. Brandeis was of the opinion that the main political demand of Zionism had been redeemed with the Balfour Declaration and that Zionists should now concentrate exclusively on building Palestine. But Brandeis's blueprint for the economic buildup in Palestine and a (preferably) decentralized administration (run out of Jerusalem rather than London) could not prevail against Weizmann and other European Zionists. In 1921 his followers also lost their leadership position in the Federation of American Zionists. The American Zionists, relatively small in numbers although the most important financial resource within the Zionist movement, were plagued by numerous internal disputes during the 1920s and 1930s. Only under the energetic leadership of Reform rabbis Stephen Wise and Abba Hillel Silver were they able to resume an active role at a time when the Jews of Europe were already in a state of acute crisis.

By now, in the immediate postwar period, Zionism was achieving some initial diplomatic success. In 1920 the San Remo conference passed a resolution entrusting Great Britain with the League of Nations mandate for Palestine on the basis of the Balfour Declaration. This established a basis in international law for the British Foreign Minister's promise to create a national homeland for the Jews. Zionists would spend the next few decades fighting to redeem this promise—and in so doing they would discover that the definition underlying Lord Balfour's formulation was highly malleable.

The beginnings were admittedly promising. After a transitional phase between 1917 and 1920, when Palestine was administered by the OETA (Occupied Enemy Territory Administration), Great Britain assigned Lord Herbert Samuel to the post of first High Commissioner for Palestine. That a Jew would be appointed High Commissioner was interpreted by many Zionists as at least a positive sign, if not as the dawn of a new age. And the fact that the Mandate provided for a "Jewish Agency" to cooperate with the administration in economic, political, and other matters was seen as clear evidence of a fresh start. But soon other tendencies in British policy became evident. In a white paper of 1922, Winston Churchill, who was then Colonial Secretary, made it clear that England did not intend that Palestine become "as Jewish as England is English." Jewish immigration should be allowed, but not to an extent greater than what the economy of the country could absorb. As a result Transjordan, until then linked to Palestine, was detached from the Mandate and became an independent state. When Lord Samuel reacted to the riots of 1921 with a temporary stop to immigration, he caused a fair amount of displeasure among the Zionists.

The Second Aliyah (immigration wave) had already brought the future political elite to Palestine on the eve of the First World War and laid the ideological foundations for Jewish society there. But it was the Third Aliyah after the end of the war that laid the foundations for statehood. In light of a Palestine now administered by the British, of terrible pogroms in the Ukraine in 1919/20, and of an increasingly aggressive political antisemitism that was also growing in Western Europe, the number of Jews leaving Europe rose appreciably. The roughly 35,000 immigrants of this third wave (1919–23) had been strongly influenced ideologically by the labor movement. Many of them, already prepared in Europe for agricultural work under the influence of the *Hehalutz* (Pioneer) movement, strengthened the kibbutz system in Palestine.

By contrast, the Fourth Aliyah that started in the mid-1920s took place under entirely different circumstances. New laws enacted in the United States between 1921 and 1924 had led to major restrictions on immigration to the country that had previously absorbed the bulk of Jewish refugees from Eastern Europe. Moreover, emigration from the Soviet Union, from which most of the socialist-inclined immigrants came, was down substantially. In the second half of the 1920s, Jewish Palestine welcomed a predominantly bourgeois class of immigrants, mostly from Poland, who helped to create an urban middle class. The middle classes were further fortified by the Fifth Aliyah in the 1930s, which brought numerous refugees escaping a Central Europe now dominated by the rise of the Nazi movement. In 1936 the Jewish population reached nearly 400,000, about a third of Palestine's total inhabitants. Over the course of time the Zionist labor movement had managed to reshape the rather passive, aid-dependent Jewish population of Palestine into an active force in charge of its own destiny. Agricultural settlements played an important part in implementing this ideological program, as they represented the physical regeneration of the Jews, something that had been repeatedly called for since the Enlightenment.

Nevertheless, over 90 percent of the Jewish inhabitants of interwar Palestine lived in cities, most of which had only recently been founded. Most important was Tel Aviv, whose development has been recorded in literary form by a number of writers. There is, for example, S. Y. Agnon's *Only Yesterday* and *Preliminaries* by S. Yizhar, which vividly describes the first streets in Tel Aviv, the transition from a communal-agricultural to an urban-bourgeois way of life, and also the terrible pogroms of 1921, in which the writer Yosef Chaim Brenner died. Within a matter of years, the Jewish town that had started out as a garden suburb of Jaffa became a lively Mediterranean metropolis with cafés and elegant shops, its population growing from 2,000 in 1914 to over 34,000 a decade later, and then to 120,000 by 1935. In 1925, two major cultural institutions emerged: *Davar*, the influential newspaper published by the trade unions, and the Ohel Theater.

Reuven Rubin, who immigrated to Palestine from Romania, embodied the new art style in Israel that emphasized the settlers' attachment to the countryside around them. *Orange Groves Near Jaffa* (1928) shows the blossoming landscape of the state being built by Jewish immigrants, with agricultural laborers and the tractor as a symbol of the "new Jew."

Leopold Pilichowski captures the opening of the Hebrew University in Jerusalem on April 1, 1925, at the very moment in which Lord Balfour delivers his address. Behind him, among others, the two Chief Rabbis of Palestine, the High Commissioner Sir Herbert Samuel, and Chaim Weizmann can be seen.

They were followed in the 1930s by the Philharmonic Orchestra and the Tel Aviv Museum of Art. The Habima Theater, founded in Moscow and renowned for its many touring engagements, would ultimately also find its home in Tel Aviv. In other cities as well, most notably perhaps in the northern port of Haifa, the 1920s and 1930s were a critical development phase. As for Jerusalem, the 1925 opening ceremony of Hebrew University made the city the centerpiece of a modern Jewish academic system.

The Hebrew University had been a vision of Chaim Weizmann, along with other Zionists, as early as the eve of World War I. Weizmann's other accomplishments included bringing prominent non-Zionists into the Jewish Agency, whose Jerusalem executive dealt with immigration to Palestine, land purchases, and building Zionist culture. The Agency's new recruits included Albert Einstein, future French premier Léon Blum, and the longstanding President of the American Jewish Committee, Louis Marshall. Enthusiasm about the establishment of the Jewish Agency in August 1929, however, evaporated within just a few weeks. Louis Marshall died, the stock market crash on Wall Street upset building efforts in Palestine, and in Palestine itself the most serious riots since the beginning of the Mandate erupted in August 1929. The riots were triggered by controversy over the Wailing Wall. Muslim authorities had already indicated some years earlier that they viewed setting up chairs for older people and a partition separating women from men as a violation of the status quo. When Arab construction work around the Wailing Wall aroused indignation among the Jewish population, this led to protest marches by several hundred young Jewish demonstrators. On August 23, the riots began to spill over into other cities, and within a week a total of 133 Jews were killed and several hundred wounded.

The events of August 1929 and the violence sanctioned by the Mufti of Jerusalem would overshadow every attempt at making political headway in Palestine during the 1930s. Even the British government, represented by a new High Commissioner, Sir John Chancellor, could make no progress at quelling the conflict. New commissions were constantly being sent from London to Palestine to work out solutions, usually in the form of partition plans, but ultimately they all came to naught. Immediately after the riots of August 1929, the British Colonial Secretary Lord Passfield appointed an investigative commission whose March 1930 report, the Shaw Report, held Arabs responsible for the massacre, but simultaneously highlighted the huge increase in Jewish immigration as the decisive factor contributing to instability in the region. The Shaw Report amounted to a de facto renunciation of the Balfour Declaration, and this had understandable repercussions within the Zionist movement. Increasingly, Weizmann came under fire as too pro-British. After he gave a press interview at the 1931 Zionist Congress in which he distanced himself from calling for a Jewish majority in Palestine, a majority of the delegates approved a vote of no confidence against him. But since Weizmann's opponents were seriously divided and his followers remained the largest faction, the outcome was merely the election of a new team favorably disposed toward Weizmann and headed by Nahum Sokolov. Weizmann himself was reelected to the leadership of the World Zionist Organization four years later. Zionism would now experience its most difficult phase. While millions of Jews in Europe were imperiled, the British were shutting the gates to Palestine ever tighter.

בן - בנימין

שֶׁפַּרְעֹה לֹא גָזַר אֶלָּא עַל הַזְּכָרִים
וְלָבָן בִּקֵּשׁ לַעֲקֹר אֶת הַכֹּל ‏"

Immediately after their liberation from the concentration camps, Jewish survivors started printing books again. Among the new publications was this 1948 Haggadah from Munich with woodcuts by Miklós Adler, which called to mind suffering while the wounds remained fresh. Here slavery in Egypt becomes a German concentration camp. Underneath a depiction of inmates being selected for the gas chambers, this saying from the Haggadah is written: "While Pharaoh decreed only against the males, Laban desired to uproot all."

19. From Everywhere to Auschwitz
ANNIHILATION

THE VIOLINISTS CAME FROM BELGIUM, Hungary, and Greece, the cellist from Germany, the singers from France and Czechoslovakia, and the accordion player from Holland. From every corner of Europe these young women had been shipped to the antechamber of death. They were members of the "Girls' Orchestra" at Auschwitz, which made music in the face of mass murder. They played as the work detachments marched in and out, gave Sunday concerts for the SS unit, performed before the notorious SS doctor Mengele, and once even for Heinrich Himmler. These young women, with their different backgrounds, were a microcosm of the entire camp. Esther Loewy (Bejarano), who played accordion in the orchestra, had grown up in Saarbrücken. Her father had been chief cantor of the Jewish congregation there before he and his wife were deported, in November 1941, to Kaunas in Lithuania, where they were presumably killed four days later. The singer Fania Fénelon (Goldstein) had attended the Paris Conservatory of Music and had performed as a chanteuse. The fact that her mother was French Catholic did not save her from being deported to

Auschwitz. The cellist Anita Lasker (Wallfisch) had grown up as the daughter of a lawyer and a violinist in a bourgeois family from Breslau. The conductor was Alma Rosé from Vienna, the niece of Gustav Mahler and daughter of the Vienna Philharmonic's concertmaster, Arnold Rosé. She conducted the "Girls' Orchestra" at Auschwitz until her death there in April 1944. Their music, like the threat of imminent death, united this group of young women, who communicated with each other in different languages and were members of different religious communities.

Revoking Emancipation

In the mid-1930s Oświęcim was a quiet Polish town that had been part of the Habsburg Empire until 1918 (the Austrian emperor had once graced himself with the title "Duke of Auschwitz"). Half of its inhabitants were Jews. No one could have suspected that, a decade later, the name of that town would be symbolic of the most lethal death machinery in human history. Nor could anyone have predicted the consequences that would follow on aging President Hindenburg's January 30, 1933, appointment of Adolf Hitler as Reich Chancellor. The Nazi party's platform of 1920 had vaguely pronounced Jews incapable of being *Volksgenossen* ("national comrades"; i.e., fellow ethnic Germans), and therefore not eligible for German citizenship. How this goal of disenfranchisement might be attained, or what the Jews might expect under National Socialist rule, was by no means clear. There was no doubt that the aim of National Socialists was to thoroughly exclude Jewish Germans from German society, but what did this ultimately mean? A status as second-class citizens? Expulsion? Physical annihilation? In 1933 no one could predict.

Germany was not the first European country to introduce antisemitic legislation in the interwar period. As early as 1924,

Romania had revoked the citizenship of numerous Jews who could not prove that they had lived in Bessarabia before 1918 or in Bukovina and Transylvania before the war. In Hungary, starting at the end of the 1920s, admission to universities was made dependent on the applicant's father's occupation, with the obvious aim of lowering the number of Jewish students. Polish officials saw to it that the number of Jews at Polish universities decreased by a third between 1923 and 1937, and in Hungary the Jewish student population fell from 32 to 10 percent between 1918 and 1932. In the mid-1930s, some Polish universities introduced into their lecture halls "ghetto benches" on which Jews were forced to sit. Although on paper Jews in eastern Central Europe were citizens with equal rights, they almost never became civil servants. In Hungarian, Romanian, Polish, and Baltic politics, anti-Jewish rhetoric played a role that should not be underestimated.

Nevertheless, January 30, 1933, marked a decisive turning point. For the first time, the representative of a radical party that prescribed militant action against Jews was entrusted with the affairs of state in a major European country. Fascism, which had already been in power in Italy for over a decade, was not yet firmly in the antisemitic camp. Some Jews were even active members of Mussolini's party. Hitler's victory, by contrast, gave all European antisemites a boost. In its wake, physical violence against Jews in Poland increased, and legal restrictions were placed on kosher butchering. The avowedly antisemitic politician Octavian Goga briefly took power in Romania in 1937, in May 1938 the Hungarian government introduced anti-Jewish laws that set quotas for the number of Jews in different occupational groups, and Italy enacted its own racial laws in 1938 under German pressure. At the end of the 1930s, fascist groups flourished: the Endeks in Poland, the Arrow Cross in Hungary, the Hlinka Guard in Slovakia, and the Iron Guard in Romania. In Spain and Portugal, where there had been almost no new

Jewish residents since the expulsion of the Jews at the end of the fifteenth century, Franco and Salazar came to power, two autocrats who rejected any overtures aimed at reviving Jewish life in their countries.

Although there were, to be sure, no anti-Jewish laws in the Soviet Union, it is striking how many high-ranking party comrades of Jewish background were banished from the political stage beginning in the mid-1930s. The only islands of relative calm that remained during the 1930s were in Western Europe, and even here there was cause for great concern. In France a Jewish premier, Léon Blum, briefly took office in 1936, but at the same time the Action Française was stepping up its right-wing nationalist campaigns. In Great Britain, talk of the perils of a worldwide Jewish conspiracy was increasingly heard. Synagogues in Leeds and Liverpool had already been damaged in 1932 and 1933, and a mob made up of members in the British Union of Fascists destroyed shops in the East End, London's Jewish neighborhood, yelling "Down with the Yids!" Even in the Benelux countries and Scandinavia, right-wing radicals were increasingly able to make themselves heard.

Although antisemitism was forging ahead all over Europe, nowhere did it assume such systematic forms as in Germany. The objective during the first years of Nazi rule was clear: exclusion and emigration for Jews. Accompanying the policy of *Gleichschaltung*—of forcing the political and social apparatus of Germany into line with National Socialism—was the removal of Jews from professional life. As soon as they were deprived of their economic foundation, it was assumed that they would take the next logical step and leave the country. The boycott of Jewish businesses organized by SA brownshirts on April 1, 1933, was followed, six days later, by the Law for the Restoration of the Professional Civil Service, which provided the legal foundation for excluding Jews and political opponents from

Germany's civil service apparatus, made up of over two million public officials from the national to the municipal level. "Civil servants who are not of Aryan descent are to be retired," stated Paragraph 3 of this law (and one "non-Aryan" grandparent was enough to meet the definition). From the beginning, therefore, Jews were defined according to a racial perspective, and not as members of a religious community. Also in April, quotas were established restricting the number of Jewish students in higher education.

Before too long there was a wave of dismissals at German universities that did not even stop short of firing prominent researchers, including Nobel Prize winners like the chemist Fritz Haber or the physicist James Franck. The former president of the Prussian Academy of Arts, Berlin painter Max Liebermann, died in 1934 shortly after realizing that his dream of assimilation was indeed but a dream. Seven years later his widow took her own life just as she was about to be deported. To Albert Einstein, around whom (as around Liebermann) numerous anecdotes grew up, has been attributed the quip (of which several versions have come down to us): "If my theory of relativity is proven correct, Germany will claim me as a German and France will declare that I am a citizen of the world. Should my theory prove untrue, France will say that I am a German and Germany will declare that I am a Jew." (Einstein in an address at the Sorbonne, possibly in early December 1929, reported in the *New York Times*, 16 February 1930, *Oxford Dictionary of Quotations*.) It hardly bothered the National Socialists that Einstein's theories proved valid and that he came to be regarded as the most important scientist of his generation. In May 1933 his writings were among those consigned to the flames, and a year later he was expatriated. In Freiburg, the new rector of the university, the philosopher Martin Heidegger, who in 1929 had already warned against a "Jewification" (*Verjudung*) of intellectual life in Germany, actively participated in the Aryanization process and refused to continue supervising the doctoral dissertations of Jewish students. He cut off all contact with his Jewish mentor, Edmund Husserl. Yet there were also attempts to stand by individual Jewish colleagues. The same Heidegger spoke out against the dismissal of the medical professor Siegfried Thannhauser, twelve colleagues of the philosopher Richard Hönigswald in Munich wrote a letter advocating his retention, and in Heidelberg there was a solidarity campaign by part of the medical faculty. These gestures, however, remained exceptions in a process that was either tacitly or actively supported by a large proportion of German academics. Among students the climate was considerably more radical. A majority of German students were already National Socialist by 1931, and Jewish lecturers at many universities were subjected to the harassment of the organized student body. The book burnings that took place on May 10, 1933, in all of Germany's major cities marked a temporary culmination in this process, rounding off the radicalization of a student body that was already right-wing and violence-prone.

It must have been especially disappointing to those affected by these anti-Jewish measures that there was no protest forthcoming from the very institutions that regarded themselves as independent or as moral authorities. This was especially disappointing in the case of the churches. The Protestant churches, in large part, quickly came under the control of the "German Christians," a movement that unreservedly backed National Socialist policy and endeavored to sever the Lutheran church from its Old Testament roots. The election of the National Socialist Ludwig Müller to the office of Reich Bishop in September 1933 underscored this line. Even the dissident Confessing Church was mostly equivocal in its opposition to National Socialism when it came to any kind of open protest against the persecution of the Jews. As a rule, it confined its support to helping so-called non-Aryan Christians, meaning Jews who had converted to Christianity and their offspring. The picture for Catholics was not much different. Most of them did reject Hitler, whom they viewed as anti-Christian, and his racist anti-semitism, but they made their peace with the new system and endorsed the Church's unbroken tradition of anti-Judaism. In September 1933 the Vatican concluded a concordat with Hitler's Germany.

Initially, German Jews reacted to their increasing isolation by consolidating their internal structures. For the first time in their history, they created an organization that represented them politically at the national level. This was the "Reich Representation of German Jews" (later: "Reich Association of the Jews in Germany"), headed by the Berlin rabbi Leo Baeck. At the outset of these agonizing years, German Jews also experienced a revival of Jewish cultural activity that was remarkably intense. In National Socialist Germany they expanded their adult education programs, restructured their publishing activities, and established a theater of their own. While the writings of Jewish authors were publicly banned and removed from public libraries in Germany, Jewish publishing houses were able to print Kafka, and the Jewish theater was the only place in National Socialist Germany where Lessing's *Nathan the Wise* could be performed.

This last burst of Jewish cultural activity in a time of persecution may appear paradoxical. It was, however, the logical result of the National Socialist policy of segregating Jews from non-Jews. National Socialist officials were prepared to tolerate Jewish culture, and even to support it up to a point, so long as this advanced the separation of Jewish from non-Jewish Germans. Numerous Jewish elementary and secondary schools were founded as a reaction to Jews being rejected and expelled

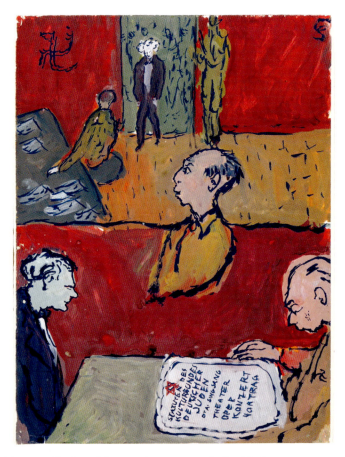

The artist Charlotte Salomon, who grew up in Berlin, left Germany in 1939 at the age of twenty-two and moved in with her grandparents in southern France. In October 1943, along with her husband, she was deported to Auschwitz, where (five months pregnant) she was presumably murdered right away. In 1325 gouaches painted in an Expressionist style, she traced her life between 1940 and 1942 under the title *Life? Or Theater?* This painting shows Kurt Singer, who later directed the Jewish Cultural Association, on one of his visits to propaganda minister Joseph Goebbels. The accompanying text reads: "I am the Minista for Propaganda, day and night must keep abreast and have no time at all to rest. Come in, come in. (Yes, this is a good project, he seems to be the right man. A pity he's a Jew—must see if I can't make him an honorary Aryan.)"

from public schools. And, with the establishment of the Central Agency for Jewish Adult Education, a matching network of continuing education was created.

Owing to the "Aryanization" of German theaters and orchestras, thousands of Jewish actors and musicians became unemployed in 1933. Many emigrated in search of a brighter future, but others were unable or disinclined to leave Germany. In July 1933 those who stayed behind founded the Cultural Association of German Jews (known after 1935 as the Jewish Cultural Association). The concerts, stage performances, and lectures of the Cultural Association were put on by Jews only and attended by an exclusively Jewish public (that is, of course, apart from the inevitable Nazi informers in the audience). Among Jews, there was a serious difference of opinion about whether to participate in this ghetto culture. Whereas most found in it some bittersweet comfort in a time of suffering, others—such as the writer Kurt Tucholsky, now living in Swedish exile—saw only self-deception that would ultimately distract the Jews from the life-saving goal of emigration.

The bulk of the German population did not take an active part in the anti-Jewish measures, but neither did they come to the aid of the Jews. Most adopted a passive stance and profited from the colleague whose job had to be filled, the neighbor whose furniture could be acquired for a song, and the shopowner forced to vacate his premises. There were, however, sporadic violent measures taken against Jews as early as the start of 1933. These included smearing businesses and private homes with graffiti, as well as harassing prospective emigrants and incarcerating individual Jews in concentration camps (at first usually reserved for political prisoners). Beginning in 1935, there was an appreciable increase in such physical attacks.

To the party leadership, worried (among other things) about how anti-Jewish measures were becoming increasingly arbitrary, it now became a matter of some concern to arrive at a more systematic regulation of the legal status of those Jews who had remained in Germany. In September 1935, during the Reich Party Congress that took place in Nuremberg, Hermann Goering publicly pronounced the measures known as the "Nuremberg Laws." These included the Reich Citizenship Law, which distinguished between "Reich citizens," who in the future would be the only ones granted full political and civil rights, and mere "nationals." Jews, again defined in racial terms, could not become Reich citizens. Now, entirely in the spirit of the original National Socialist party program, Jews were placed under a kind of alien law within their own country. The "Law for the Protection of German Blood and German Honor" banned marriages and extramarital relations between Jews and non-Jews. In addition, Jews were no longer allowed to hire Christian employees under the age of forty-five to work in their households.

The National Socialists created numerous categories of so-called mixed breeds (*Mischlinge*), first and second degree, privileged and non-privileged. The legal separation of Jews from "Aryan" society was now in full stride. How this would be implemented in practice, however, was a matter of controversy. Remarks made by some high-ranking party functionaries suggest that they were interested at this point in ghettoizing the Jews, not in their physical removal from society. Others pushed for an extra-German solution, either for expelling the Jews outright or so increasing pressure on them that they would flee the country voluntarily.

After an interlude at the time of the Olympic games in 1936, when the anti-Jewish mood was temporarily somewhat curbed, there was a rapid radicalization again in 1938. With the "Anschluss" (annexation) of Austria in March 1938, an additional 190,000 Jews came under National Socialist rule. The process of exclusion that had taken several years in the "Old Reich" was carried out here within a matter of months, a process

The painter Lea Grundig, born into an Orthodox family in Dresden, was active in the Communist Party at an early age. After a ban on exhibiting her work, imprisonment, and internment in a Slovakian refugee camp, she succeeded in emigrating to Palestine in 1941. After the war she first returned to Prague, then Dresden, and became a member of the Central Committee of the German Democratic Republic's ruling Socialist Unity Party. This picture from 1936 conveys the growing exclusion of Jews from German society.

that included Aryanization, incarceration, the confiscation of homes, and deportations.

By 1938, Jews in the new Greater German Reich increasingly saw their economic foundation pulled out from under them. Forced Aryanization accelerated. New professional bans pushed physicians and lawyers into the ranks of the unemployed or confined them to treating or representing only Jewish patients or clients. In August 1938, Jews were forced to adopt the middle names of Sara or Israel, and two months later, at the insistence of a Swiss government anxious about a wave of refugees, a large red "J" was stamped into their passports.

The violent climax of this wave of radicalization took place from the night of the 9th to the 10th of November, 1938. At the end of the previous month, 16,000 Polish Jews had been deported from Germany to Poland, initially to a no-man's-land near the Polish town of Zbąszyń. Herschel Grynszpan, whose own parents were among those expelled, hoped to call the attention of the world to the refugees' suffering by shooting Ernst vom Rath, Legation Secretary at the German embassy in Paris. The incident served as the pretext for a pogrom, planned well in advance, against Jews throughout Germany, a night of violence that came to be known colloquially by the belittling name of "Kristallnacht" (derived from all the broken window-glass that could be seen on every street with Jewish buildings). The main synagogues of Munich and Nuremberg had already been destroyed in the previous summer of 1938, but now, during the "Night of Broken Glass" (less euphemistically: the "Reich Pogrom Night") on November 9–10, synagogues went up in flames all over Germany and Austria. In addition, around 7,500 shops were pillaged, and several hundred Jews were killed. Over 30,000 Jewish men were put in concentration camps. A large proportion of the German people rejected this open brutality, but Joseph Goebbels noted in his diary: "As I am driven to the hotel, windowpanes shatter [they are being smashed]. Bravo! Bravo! The synagogues burn like big old cabins. German property is not endangered. At the moment nothing special remains to be done" (Friedländer 1997, 272). Goering decreed that the Jews had to provide compensation for the damages and imposed a fine of a billion Reichsmarks. With these events the persecution of the Jews entered a new and more violent phase, and it became all too clear to German Jews that they could not expect an end to the terror in their homeland.

Emigration

Only a minority of German Jews had opted for emigration in the years immediately after 1933. Most had seen in Hitler a passing spook or were willing to put up with their new status as second-class citizens so long as their lives were not in danger. They were Germans and had no intention of leaving their homeland. The *Reichsfluchtsteuer*—a tax that had to be paid before leaving the country—added an economic hurdle for anyone wanting to emigrate, quite apart from the linguistic and cultural obstacles they would face in a foreign country.

As a result of increasing disenfranchisement, the rate of Jewish emigration had already begun to skyrocket in the months prior to the November pogrom, and this was the case even though there were fewer and fewer places to which one could emigrate. An international conference summoned by President Roosevelt met in July 1938 in the French resort of Evian and disposed of any remaining illusions Jews might have had about other countries coming to their rescue. Representatives of thirty-two countries attended the Evian conference, but there was no place that wanted to take in the Jews. Only the dictator of the Dominican Republic, Rafael Trujillo, made a gesture that was generous, though unrealistic. In spite of the obvious suffering of the European Jews, not one major democratic state saw fit to open its gates. To the contrary: The British were preoccupied with placing more restrictions on Jewish immigration to Palestine; the Australians saw Jewish immigration as a peril to their "own race"; and although President Roosevelt had seized the initiative by convening the conference, the United States did not raise its immigration quotas. For Jews preparing to flee Europe, this often meant that only destinations like South America, east Africa, and (not least of all) Shanghai remained. After the annexation of Austria, emigration was accelerated by a "Central Office for Jewish Emigration" founded at the initiative of the Jewish community. Within a year over half of all Austrian Jews had left the country. No more than 130,000 Jews had left Germany in the years between 1933 and 1937, but almost the same number followed in the two years following, 1938 and 1939. Some of the emigrants who had fled to the neighboring countries of France, Holland, and Czechoslovakia were later hauled back by the Nazis. This also happened to some of the 900 passengers on the steamship "St. Louis" who had already set sail for Cuba with their dearly purchased entry visas before the Cuban government decided to declare their entry documents invalid. When the United States also refused to accept the refugees, they returned to a Europe on the verge of war. Together with about 13,000 other Jews from Germany (in its pre-1938 borders), some of them managed to get out in 1940 and 1941.

Shoah: Annihilation

The Jews in the areas conquered by Germany during the war would be given no such opportunities to emigrate. But what should be done with them? Among the Nazis different ideas made the rounds, including plans for deportation to Madagascar or to some kind of "Jewish reservation" in Eastern Europe. Soon after major portions of Poland had been conquered in the autumn of 1939, the Jews who lived there were concentrated in ghettos and made to perform forced labor. In February 1940 the first forced resettlements of German Jews into the Polish ghettos began, initially from Stettin, then from what had been Austria and from Czechoslovakia. Jews from the western German regions of Baden, the Palatinate, and the Saarland were deported to French camps. As of September 1941, all Jews in the Reich were forced to wear a yellow star with the label "Jude" on their clothing, and a few months later they also had to affix it to the doors of their homes. They were required to hand over warm clothing, were given food stamps for only a few essential products, and were no longer allowed to use public transportation.

In the countries occupied or controlled by Germany, too, the social exclusion of the Jews proceeded apace. Thus, the French government in Vichy enacted a series of laws in 1940/41 that, within a matter of months, caught up with the process of exclusion that had already taken place in Germany during the 1930s. In the Netherlands all Jews were removed from public service by November 1940, and the country's highest court unseated its own president, who was a Jew. Here, however, there were also cases of serious resistance by university teachers who demonstrated solidarity and workers who went on strike. In Belgium, where the removal of Jews from public life had also already begun in the autumn of 1940, pogrom-like assaults were staged in April 1941. Belgium's new racial antisemitism took on some of the trappings of the older religious antisemitism. On Easter Monday, mobs set fire to several synagogues and the house of the chief rabbi in Antwerp. Previously the inflammatory antisemitic film "Jud Süss" had been shown in the city. A coalescence of religiously motivated anti-Jewish prejudices with the new racial doctrines is also evident in the actions of Nazi allies in Eastern Europe. The Iron Guard in Romania, the Croatian Ustasha, and the Slovakian Hlinka Guards often undertook antisemitic actions that preempted the Germans' initiatives.

The Russian campaign in the summer of 1941 inaugurated a new phase of radicalization that made the physical annihilation of the Jews appear an increasingly possible alternative to ghettoization. In the occupied territories in the East, there were mass shootings of Jews. In September and October 1941, members of a mobile SS killing unit (*Einsatzgruppe*), with the active participation of the Wehrmacht, murdered over 50,000 Jews in the ravine Babi Yar near Kiev, 33,000 of them during

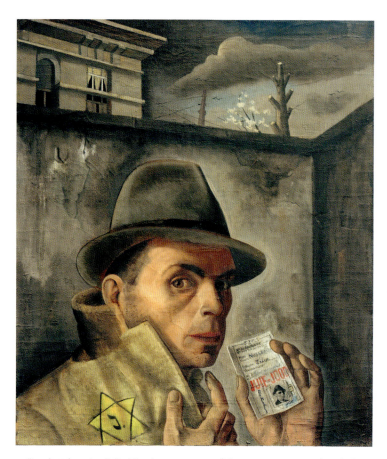

Osnabrück native Felix Nussbaum was one of the painters associated with the
"Neue Sachlichkeit" ("New Objectivity") movement. In 1937 he emigrated to
Belgium and was arrested there after the German invasion in 1940, but he managed to escape from a French internment camp and hide out in Brussels. In June
1944 he was arrested by the Wehrmacht and deported, along with his wife, to
Auschwitz, where both were murdered in August 1944. Many of his works from
his time on the run from Nazi persecution could be saved, including this self-
portrait that was probably painted at the end of 1943. The portrait shows him in
a walled-in street corner in front of a bare tree with the yellow star and with the
passport identifying him as a Jew.

the last two days of September alone. Up until December 1941, just as many Vilna Jews were murdered, most of them in the town of Ponary, just outside Vilna. In October 1941 the first trains rolled out of Vienna, Berlin, Prague, and Luxembourg, carrying 20,000 Jewish deportees to the ghetto of Łódź. They were followed in November by twenty-two transports with a total of 22,000 Jews heading for Riga, Kovno, and Minsk. The transports had been preceded by mass murders of the local Jewish population in these cities, in order to make room for the newcomers. Many of the deportees, however, did not even reach the ghettos; instead they were taken to the woods and immediately shot upon their arrival. Almost all Jews in the ghetto of Riga had been killed by the first week of December. In the final months of 1941, physical annihilation took precedence over all other options for getting rid of Jews. Hitler was making good on the warning he had already formulated in his January address of 1939, in which he had threatened the "annihilation of the Jewish race" in the event of a new world war. In public speeches as well as in confidential conversations in the autumn of 1941, he pushed for the extermination of the Jews in language radicalized almost to eschatological extremes: "By exterminating this pest, we shall do humanity a service of which our soldiers can have no idea," he said that October (Friedländer 2007, 273).

America's entry into the war after the Japanese attack on Pearl Harbor further accelerated measure against Jews. The mass murders of autumn 1941 were followed by increasingly systematic operations. Institutions ranging from the different branches of the national railway to the chemical industry were drawn into the machinery of killing. To this end, at the invitation of Reinhard Heydrich, chief of the Reich Security Main Office, fourteen high officials and SS officers arrived on January 20, 1942, at an idyllic lakeside villa in Berlin's Wannsee district. The "Final Solution of the Jewish Question" discussed here was the extermination of up to eleven million humans. They were to be "liquidated" in the most effective way possible. An unprecedented apparatus of destruction was to be mounted in mid-wartime. No one—no Jewish Nobel Prize winner, no Jewish woman, no Jewish child—was to be spared.

To ramp up the kill rate, gas chambers and additional crematoria were built. Mentally and physically handicapped people had already been killed with gas in 1939; in 1941 the SS began using mobile wagons outfitted for gassing. The first systematic gassings took place in the Chelmno concentration camp in December of 1941. Here 1,000 people were killed every day in the mobile wagons. In March 1942, the SS began for the first time to murder people in fixed gas chambers installed at the Belzec concentration camp. At the height of this systematic killing, up to 12,000 people a day were murdered in the gas chambers of the Auschwitz-Birkenau camp. But even after the killing process had been industrialized through the use of gas chambers, there continued to be mass executions by shooting.

Over the next several years a never-ending succession of trains deporting Jews from all over Europe rolled onward, after intermediate stops at collection points (such as Westerbork, Malines, and Drancy for Dutch, Belgian, and French Jews), to the extermination camps of Auschwitz, Majdanek, Treblinka, Belzec, Sobibor and Chelmno. In Belzec 434,000 Jews had been murdered by the end of 1942; only two survived the war. In Sobibor close to 100,000 Jews were killed during the first three months of the camp's operation. By October 1943 about 1.7 million Jews had been murdered in the three camps of Belzec, Sobibor, and Treblinka. In Auschwitz the gassings began in mid-February 1942. On March 26 the first transport from Slovakia departed for Auschwitz with 999 young women. On the following day there followed a transport with 1,000 Jews from the French town of Compiègne. Soon after, larger gas chambers were set up in nearby Birkenau. By the time the camp was liberated by the

Red Army, around 900,000 Jews had died there in gas chambers disguised as showers, poisoned by the insecticide Zyklon B. In contrast to the other extermination camps, Auschwitz was also a concentration camp, where some of the able-bodied were used as slave laborers or as subjects for gruesome medical experiments under the supervision of SS doctor Josef Mengele.

Even before people arrived at the camps, they had undergone harrowing journeys in overcrowded freight cars. There was no real ventilation and no way to dispose of excrement. Infants and the aged often died during transport. When the trains arrived under the glaring lights of Auschwitz's railway station, passengers were greeted by bellowing guards and barking German shepherds. Those picked for immediate death during an initial "selection" process were told that they were being sent for disinfection. The most gruesome work of all was forced on Jews commandeered into special units: they used pliers to remove gold teeth from the corpses, cut off their hair, and ripped out earrings. Soon afterwards, most of them would be on the way to the gas chambers themselves.

An effort was made to hide the details of the extermination process from the civilian population. But soldiers returning from the Eastern front and camp guards visiting their families told of conditions in the ghettoes and concentration camps and about the murder of the Jews. Even those who were unaware of the mass murders could not shut their eyes to other facts. The synagogues burned in November of 1938 were there for all to see. When, after September 1941, Jews throughout the Reich were forced to wear yellow stars on their clothing, those stars were visible to all. It was obvious that there was nothing voluntary about Jewish neighbors vanishing from the cities or about children and old people being commandeered into work details. By 1942 Hitler and other representatives of the state were talking with increasing openness about the eradication of the Jewish race—and there was no reason to doubt their words.

Some simply did not want to know what had happened to the Jews who disappeared, others justified the genocide as part of a necessary struggle for survival by the Aryan master race against menacing Jewish parasites. For years Nazi propaganda had denied Jews their humanity. The hate sheet *Der Stürmer* drew pictures of them with grotesque, animal-like faces, and propaganda films like *Der ewige Jude* (The Eternal Jew) linked them to vermin. On November 2, 1939, after driving through the Łódź ghetto, Propaganda Minister Joseph Goebbels noted in his diary: "We travel through the ghetto. We get out and observe everything in detail. It cannot be described. These are no longer human beings, these are animals. Therefore, it is no humanitarian task, but a surgical one. One must cut here, in a radical way. Otherwise Europe will perish of the Jewish disease" (Friedländer 2007, 21). Similar remarks were made by other leading government and Nazi party functionaries after the Wehrmacht invaded Poland. The inhibition threshold was lowered again and again. If these Jews were no longer human beings, they could be destroyed like vermin, and any kind of humanitarian feeling was out of place.

The moral perversion that had become widespread was perhaps most clearly expressed in the speech Heinrich Himmler delivered to SS generals in Posen on October 4, 1943, when he justified the murder of the Jewish people, including women and children, as a biological necessity. ". . . we don't want...to get sick and die from the same bacillus that we have exterminated," Himmler declared. It was his way of trying to assuage any moral scruples associated with the killings. One could, according to Himmler, kill thousands of people and remain "decent." On the other hand, he regarded personal enrichment "with even one fur, . . . with one cigarette, with one watch" taken from the dead as a wrong requiring harsh punishment.

The collaboration of large sections of the population in the areas controlled by the Germans was an essential part of the annihilation process. Like the Dutch police, the French police too moved vigorously to help the Germans arrest Jews in the occupied and unoccupied zones of France. In the countries of Eastern Europe, the SS often found local auxiliary troops willing to take an active part in the process of extermination. In some cases Poles, Ukrainians, and Lithuanians even murdered their Jewish neighbors without needing any encouragement from the Germans.

It is harder to evaluate the role of the councils of elders set up by the Nazis in European ghettoes and usually known as "Jewish Councils." Their representatives were intermediaries between the Jewish population and Nazi officials. They looked after the maintenance of everyday life in the ghetto and had to fill the numbered deportation lists they were given with names. In many cases, risking their own lives, they tried to bargain down the numbers or to postpone the deportations. They were, however, almost always powerless and were soon to become victims themselves. There is a telling farewell note from Adam Czerniaków, a former member of the Polish Senate and chair of the Council of Elders in the Warsaw Ghetto. When he was given the assignment on July 22, 1942, of preparing lists of 6,000 people, including children, for transport "to the East," he saw no choice but to take his own life the following day: "They are demanding that I kill the children of my people with my own hands. There is nothing for me to do but die. . . . Do not view this as an act of cowardice or an escape. I am powerless, my heart is breaking from sorrow and compassion, and I cannot bear this any longer. My deed will show the truth to everyone and maybe encourage the right way to act. I am aware that I am bequeathing to you a difficult legacy."

Resistance

Offering resistance to the persecution and murder of the Jews meant taking an incalculable chance. Yet in Germany and

German-occupied Europe, there were individuals willing to put their lives at risk time and again. Some hid Jews in their homes, others helped fabricate fake identity cards, yet others smuggled Jews across borders. It did not always require such extraordinarily heroic deeds to have an impact. For victims even the smallest sign that not everyone agreed with the official policy could be of comfort and encouragement. If a passer-by whispered "Chin up!" to a Jewish woman wearing a yellow star, if the baker packed a loaf of white bread into the shopping bag of a Jewish man who was only entitled to the cheapest rye bread, or if the air raid shelter guard went against official regulations and allowed Jews into the basement during a bomb attack, these were precious signals, understood and appreciated by the ostracized. They were, however, all too rare.

Organized resistance groups were often not devoid of their own antisemitism. The men around the 20th of July 1944 plot to kill Hitler represented a broad spectrum of opinion on the "Jewish question." Many of them, though they firmly opposed the murder of the Jews, were entirely in accord with their ostracism on the basis of the Nuremberg Laws. The most problematic position was undoubtedly that of the official churches, which repeatedly protested the social exclusion of "non-Aryan Christians" but, apart from some very isolated exceptions, were silent on the fate of the Jews themselves. This while the upper echelons of the church hierarchies in particular knew all too well how perilous the situation of the Jews had become.

Nor was the on-going annihilation of the Jews a secret outside Germany. The press reported on the concentration camps and mass shootings and extermination camps, though often only as an incidental story among many others. Indicative of this reportorial climate was what the *New York Times* did in 1942 with a comprehensive report on socialist resistance fighters from Poland that featured precise details of the extermination process and mentioned 700,000 as the number of Jews who had already been murdered. The June 27th edition of the *Times* devoted only a few lines to the story on page 5. The head of the World Jewish Congress office in Geneva, Gerhart Riegner, had indicated the extent of the tragedy in a telegram on August 8, 1942, in which he spoke about plans to extinguish European Jewry. Yet neither the British nor American government gave his report any credence. Even the account offered by Jan Karski, who had smuggled himself into the Warsaw Ghetto and reported on the situation to the Polish government-in-exile in London, did not result in any concrete actions. Focus was on winning the war; the annihilation of the Jews appeared as a kind of sideshow to that wholehearted effort. Even the International Red Cross let itself be duped into visiting a "model camp." A June 1944 delegation was taken to Theresienstadt in Bohemia, a relatively idyllic camp for older and more prominent prisoners. For most of those interned there it served merely as a brief intermediate stop on the way to Auschwitz or Treblinka.

In spite of other countries' lack of solidarity with Jews in distress, individual diplomats did manage to save several hundreds and even thousands of Jews by issuing letters of protection. The best-known such saviors are the Japanese vice-consul in Lithuanian Kaunas, Chiune Sugihara, and the first secretary of the Swedish legation in Budapest, Raoul Wallenberg. Both rescued a large number of Lithuanian or Hungarian Jews awaiting deportation, and both paid a high price for their benefactions. Sugihara was forced out of the diplomatic service after the end of the war, while Wallenberg was abducted to the Soviet Union and has been regarded ever since as a missing person.

Opportunities for Jews to offer resistance on their own were minimal. Nevertheless, there are many accounts of those in ghettoes and camps making contact with Polish or Baltic

A children's drawing by Helga Weissová created in Theresienstadt. Most of the children, who left behind thousands of drawings in Theresienstadt, were deported to Auschwitz and immediately murdered on arrival.

underground organizations, and Jewish resistance groups did emerge and undertake a variety of attempts at flight or armed struggle against the Germans. It must have seemed a hopeless struggle against an overwhelming enemy, but the most vital kind of resistance was the simple refusal to let oneself be dehumanized. Thus, to the extent that this was possible in the ghettoes under the most appalling conditions, people played music, held classes in secret, and prayed. The "Oyneg Shabes" (Sabbath celebration) group formed under the leadership of the historian Emanuel Ringelblum in the Warsaw ghetto compiled a secret archive that documented this time of terror for posterity.

The best-known chapter of armed Jewish resistance was undoubtedly the uprising in the Warsaw ghetto in April 1943. The situation in the ghetto had been escalating toward a crisis over a period of several years, ever since November 16, 1940, when the "Jewish residential district" was sealed off. The district consisted of two sections that were linked to each other by a wooden bridge that crossed over an "Aryan" street. Only Jews were now allowed to live here, and initially they numbered 380,000. The number had increased to 445,000 by May 1941, in spite of all the dead as a result of numerous deportations. On average, seven people lived to a room. Sometimes there were up to thirty. Hunger, cold, and despair were the lot of those (temporarily) spared deportation. The daily bread ration was fixed at under 100 grams, and the bread was often baked with sand or sawdust. In August 1941 the official calorie allotment dropped to 177 per person. The streets were full of beggars, many of them children. Some were too weak to pick up the occasional piece of bread thrown their way. The corpses of those who had starved and frozen to death became a customary part of the street scene.

The dissolution of the ghetto began on July 22, 1942. On that day deportation trains began leaving Warsaw heading for the newly built extermination camp of Treblinka. Every day thousands of ghetto inhabitants were rounded up at assembly points and sent in freight cars to their death. Small children and the elderly were among them, and hardly anyone harbored the illusion that these people might be assigned to work details. Within two months, 265,040 Jews from the Warsaw ghetto had been gassed in Treblinka, and an additional 10,380 killed in the ghetto itself. Some of the roughly 60,000 Jews who remained in the ghetto did not want to surrender without a fight. The actual struggle for the ghetto began on April 19, 1943, when deportations were scheduled to continue. Jewish partisans' organizations, using a few weapons captured from the Germans or dearly purchased from Polish underground organizations, took up their futile struggle mostly from bunkers and the sewage system underneath the ghetto. They were able to hold their own for a month, without receiving any appreciable assistance from the Polish population outside the ghetto. In the end the Germans burned down the entire ghetto and killed the majority of its inhabitants. On May 16, SS brigade commander Jürgen Stroop symbolically ended the uprising with the demolition of the Great Synagogue. The surviving Jews were deported to the Treblinka and Majdanek extermination camps. An uprising among the inmates of Treblinka on August 2, 1943, resulted in one section of the work camp going up in flames, which allowed about half of its 800 inmates to flee. Many of them, however, were recaptured within a few hours. In other camps, too, as in Sobibor in October 1943, there were uprisings by inmates that made escape to freedom possible for a few individuals. The unrest was always quickly subdued.

The last ghetto in Poland was in Łódź. Here, in the summer of 1944, there were still about 77,000 Jews who hoped to be liberated by the approaching Soviet troops. Yet at the end of August their fate was sealed. Most were deported to Auschwitz. When the city of Łódź was finally liberated in January 1945, only 877 Jews were left in the ghetto. Of the 3.3 million Jews who had lived in Poland before the war, at most 40,000 survived inside the country.

The End

In many other European countries the situation was not much better. In the last years of the war, trains carrying those marked for death rolled out of every corner of the continent headed for the extermination camps. Some governments, though allied with the Germans, recoiled from abandoning "their" Jews to the Nazi death machinery. The Italian Fascists, for example, even attempted abroad (as in Salonica) to shield Jews from deportation. Only after the German occupation of Italy were

Italian Jews deported to Auschwitz. Hungarian Jews were also initially spared at the insistence of the Hungarian government, though this only lasted until the Wehrmacht invaded in March 1944. Through July 9 of that year, 438,000 Hungarian Jews were deported to Auschwitz, of whom 90 percent were immediately gassed. Only in Budapest itself did a considerable number of Jews stay on. The Bulgarians delivered Jews in the newly occupied regions of Thrace and Macedonia to the Germans without much of a fuss, but they did not hand over Jews from the Bulgarian heartland. Public protests and, especially, resistance from parliament and the Bulgarian-Orthodox Church prevented handovers there. The only country where practically all the Jews were saved was Denmark. Popular resistance was widespread and deportation plans were leaked, with the result that practically all of Denmark's 7,000 Jews were put on boats and brought to neutral Sweden in a nighttime operation on October 2, 1943, before their scheduled transport to the concentration camps. Most of the roughly 700 Danish Jews who were deported to Theresienstadt also managed to survive.

A perfectionist mania dictating that the Jews of Europe had to be killed to the last man can be seen at work in the case of Finland. About 150–200 Jews had fled there from other European countries, and during a visit to Helsinki in July 1942 Himmler was insistent that they be deported to Germany. There was no economic or political benefit to be gained from this demand; it was motivated solely by an ideological obsession to annihilate the Jews as thoroughly as possible. After public protests, the Finnish government made a small group available for deportation. On November 6, 1942, eight Jews from Finland were deported to Estonia; and seven of them did not survive the war.

In the German-occupied territories, deportations could be carried out without any need to consult allied governments. In Salonica the centuries-old Jewish community was dissolved within a matter of weeks. In the spring of 1943, with almost no impediments in their way, the Germans deported 45,000 of the city's 50,000 Jews to Auschwitz. When Athens was slated to follow a year later, the move encountered more resistance. But even Jews living on the smallest of Greek islands were deported to Auschwitz.

Hitler and his minions were not only responsible for the most cold-blooded genocide in the history of humankind. They had also turned Europe into one great ruin, removed Germany from the map as a single political entity, and sacrificed millions of human beings to a megalomaniacal idea. Far from admitting his crimes, Hitler insisted on the absolute priority of Jewish annihilation down to the very end. Before he took his own life along with Eva Braun, he reminded the prostrate German people of their most important future duty: "Above all I charge the leaders of the nation and those under them to scrupulous observance of the laws of race and to merciless opposition to the universal poisoner of all peoples, international Jewry."

What the Allies had discovered in the meantime exceeded their most horrific wartime experiences. The first liberated extermination camp was Majdanek, which the Red Army reached at the end of July 1944. Auschwitz was liberated on January 27, 1945. The traces of mass murder were still fresh everywhere. In the weeks immediately preceding liberation, many of the inmates had been sent on so-called death marches. Undernourished and scantily clothed, they were forced to trudge hundreds of kilometers through the cold winter into areas still under German control. The concentration camps in Bergen-Belsen, Buchenwald, Flossenbürg, Dachau and Mauthausen, along with their branch camps, swelled with thousands of Jewish prisoners from Eastern Europe. Many died in the camps, if they had not already died on the death marches. Some succumbed to malnourishment and diseases immediately after their long sought-after liberation. Frequently, all that the British and American liberators were able to do was remove the mountains of corpses. The number of Jews murdered by the National Socialists during the war is somewhere between 5.6 and 6.3 million. In the perception of most of the Jews who survived, Europe had become a giant graveyard from which no Jewish life could ever sprout again.

This Jerusalem Haggadah from 1968 expresses the Messianic hopes associated with Israel's victory in the Six-Day War and the reunification of Jerusalem. The sentence "Next year in Jerusalem," which is spoken at the end of the evening Seder service, appears to have been fulfilled here.

20. From Julius Streicher's Farm to the Kibbutz
THE JEWISH WORLD AFTER THE HOLOCAUST

IN 1946 JULIUS STREICHER, the former Gauleiter of Franconia and editor of the antisemitic hate sheet *Der Stürmer*, was awaiting his execution in Nuremberg. Meanwhile his confiscated estate in nearby Pleikershof had become a place of refuge for about 150 Jewish Holocaust survivors. Here they set up an agricultural collective, which they named Kibbutz Nili (after a Zionist spy ring active during the First World War), and prepared for emigration to Palestine. It is one of the ironies of history that the predominant language spoken was Yiddish, that the Star of David replaced flags with swastikas, and that the birth of Jewish children was celebrated—all on Streicher's property. Esther Barkai lived at Pleikershof from May 1946 until the late autumn of 1947. Her story could stand in for that of many of the farm's inhabitants. Born in Warsaw in 1919, she had survived the ghetto uprising and the Majdanek concentration camp. At the end of the war she found herself in the American-occupied zone awaiting the establishment of the State of Israel. She emigrated as early as possible, in May of 1948, and settled on a kibbutz: "One thing was clear to me," she later recalled. "After what we went through, now I'm going to a country of my own, my homeland. . . . Kibbutz Nili was a training camp for us." (Jim G. Tobias, *Der Kibbuz auf dem Streicher-Hof. Die vergessene Geschichte der jüdischen Kollektiv-farmen 1945–48* [Nuremberg: Dahlinger und Fuchs, 1997] 61.)

The Wandering Goes On

Esther Barkai was one of around a quarter million Jewish "displaced persons" in postwar Europe. "DPs" was the collective name given to these refugees who found themselves on the territory of the vanquished powers after the end of the war. During the second half of the 1940s in Germany, Austria, and Italy, they created an extensive infrastructure of Jewish life with self-governing institutions, Yiddish newspapers, religious study, stage productions, and sports. Their renewed lust for life is all the more astonishing in light of the fact that most had lost their entire families and needed to reorient themselves completely after being liberated. They did not want to return to their East European homelands, where only new animosities awaited them. Their property had been taken over by others, who were now fearful of having to return these spoils of war. In several localities in Poland there were violent attacks on Jews who had ventured to return. They culminated on July 4, 1946 in the Kielce pogrom, a local massacre to which forty of some 200 Jews returning to that city fell victim. As in the prewar period, religious and political motives were intertwined here. A ritual murder legend was making the rounds. At the same time, the local population identified Jews, a few of whom were in prominent positions, with the new Communist rulers and spoke derisively of "Judeocommunism" (Żydokomuna).

Although the term "displaced persons" was only applied to designated people within the territory of Europe's vanquished countries, a great many of the Jews who remained in their East

European homelands also felt like refugees. Their communities had been destroyed, their families murdered, and Jewish
religious life could not develop under Communism. But where
should the Jews of Eastern Europe, more than a quarter million
in number, go? The State of Israel did not yet exist, and restrictive immigration laws limited access to the United States. For
the survivors it was sobering to see that, even after the genocide, part of the world still opposed the establishment of a Jewish state. The British in charge of the Mandate refused, even
after the Conservative government of Churchill was replaced in
1945 by a Labour government, to concede a part of Palestine to
the Jews, as the Balfour Declaration of 1917 had promised. The
Jews detained in German camps now proved useful as a moral
weapon in the struggle for an independent state, a process symbolized most clearly by the odyssey of the 4,500 passengers on
the Haganah (Zionist armed forces) ship "Exodus 1947." The
British refused to let the ship land in Haifa in July 1947 and,
after a four-hour battle that cost the lives of three crew members, forced the passengers to return to Europe. Most ended
up as inmates in camps near Lübeck, behind barbed wire and
watchtowers. Thousands of other Jewish refugees from Europe
had already been interned in Cyprus by the British. Those who
had survived the genocide had been liberated, to be sure, but
by no means were they free. The moral outcry following the
Exodus tragedy did not fade away unheard. This episode—and
in fact the general hopelessness of the Jews two years after the
end of the war—would not remain without consequences for
coming decisions on Palestine's future.

So long as the fight against Hitler's Germany lasted, even
the Jews of Palestine were, out of necessity, allied with the British. Their fate depended on an Allied victory against Rom-
mel's troops in North Africa. In addition, the political leader
of Palestinian Arabs, the Grand Mufti Muhammad Amin al-
Husseini, openly supported Nazi policy. He had chosen Berlin

שוין גענוג!
בוויל א היים!

ער האט שוין פארגעסן,
און גייט אין א נייעם
גלות!
געדינק ייד, יעדער
גלות פירט צום
אונטערגאנג.

This poster from a Zionist association of Holocaust survivors in Germany and a Zionist youth federation shows Jewish displaced persons the way to their future. Above the dark, menacing skyline of New York and a hesitant immigrant on the left, there is this Yiddish text: "He has already forgotten and is heading into a new exile. Know, Jew, that every exile leads to downfall!" On the right-hand side of the poster, by contrast, above the sunlit coast of Israel and a more determined immigrant, it says: "Enough already! I want to go home." The background was the large number of Holocaust survivors who, uninterested in leaving for a conflict-ridden Palestine, applied instead for visas to the United States.

as his domicile, and was given a reception by Hitler in November 1941. Among the Jews of Palestine, these sympathies did not go unnoticed. In the last months of the war a Jewish brigade from Palestine even fought as part of the British army. But after the war was over, armed struggle against the British Mandate began. While the larger, more moderate section of the Jewish underground army, the Haganah, spoke out against terrorist

The first Israeli premier David Ben Gurion reads the Israeli declaration of independence on May 14, 1948, underneath a portrait of Theodor Herzl.

tactics, the smaller and more radical Irgun under the command of Menachem Begin carried out attacks on the British. These culminated on July 22, 1946, in the bombing of the King David Hotel, which was used by the British administration. The attack cost ninety-one lives.

In the end the British decided to leave the future of Palestine in the hands of the newly founded United Nations. On November 29, 1947, its General Assembly voted to accept a partition plan that would divide Palestine into a Jewish state, an Arab state, and an international zone around the holy sites in Jerusalem and Bethlehem. The Zionist leadership under David Ben Gurion accepted the plan, even though it did not fully meet their expectations. The Arab world, by contrast, categorically rejected any partition of Palestine. The region's five Arab states declared war on Israel on its Independence Day, May 14, 1948. By the time this war was over, Israel was able to add more territory to those areas already assigned to it in the partition plan. The holy sites around the Temple Mount, however, were conquered by Transjordan, which forbade Jews access to the Wailing Wall and to the Old City of Jerusalem. A Palestinian Arab state was not founded; instead, Transjordan (soon renamed Jordan) annexed the West Bank, while Egypt administered the Gaza Strip.

Nearly three quarters of a million Palestinians fled their homeland in the course of the war. They fled partly as a result of violence by Jewish underground organizations, as in the Arab village Deir Yassin, and of deliberate evictions by Israeli troops, and partly as a response to Arab leaders' calls for them to flee. For the Palestinian Arabs, Israel's independence was recollected as the *Nakba* (catastrophe). Although the Israeli declaration of independence talked about the Jewish character of the new state, it left no doubt that it would "ensure complete equality of social and political rights to all its inhabitants irrespective of religion, race, or sex." This theoretical pledge and its practical implementation, however, have repeatedly clashed, as for example when it comes to the confiscation of Arab land and the exclusion of Israeli Arabs from military service.

In 1950 the Knesset, Israel's parliament, passed a special "Law of Return" that granted all Jews the right to Israeli citizenship. In the following decades Israel became a new home to millions of Jewish refugees, especially refugees from Eastern Europe and the Arab world. Within the first five years of its existence, about 700,000 Jews immigrated, thereby doubling Israel's Jewish population. By 1956 the figure had risen to 2.1 million.

In the first half of the 1950s, major remnants of Jewish communities still existed in Eastern Europe. 220,000 Jews lived in Romania, for example, where they were organized into 126 communities with 32 Talmud Torah schools. Figures on the Jewish community in Poland vary between 45,000 and 75,000.

In 1955 there were seven Jewish elementary schools in the country and three high schools with Yiddish as the language of instruction, though without any religious content in their curriculum. About thirty Yiddish books were published annually. There were Yiddish theater groups and a Yiddish press. Under more favorable conditions, Jewish life might have continued to develop in countries like Romania, Hungary, and Poland even after the Holocaust, and even if these communities were mere shadows of their prewar selves. But political circumstances did not allow for this. Under the pretext of anti-Zionism, the final phase of Stalinist rule in the Communist world witnessed antisemitic "purges" that culminated in show trials in the Soviet Union and Czechoslovakia in 1952/53. At the birth of the State of Israel, Czechoslovakia had supported its Israeli allies by delivering weapons to them; now, as dictated by Soviet policy, it stood by the Arab countries in their fight against Israel. "Zionists" and "cosmopolitans" became anti-Jewish code words. In 1951 fourteen high-ranking party functionaries, including General Secretary Rudolf Slansky, were arrested on suspicion of harboring sympathy for Israel (among other charges). Eleven of the fourteen, including Slansky, were Jews. The Slansky trial, which was permeated with antisemitism, ended with eleven hangings, carried out on December 3, 1952. Jews were removed from the party apparatus and other important positions. The same thing happened in a parallel campaign in the German Democratic Republic. These events unleashed a wave of Jewish emigration to the West.

In the Soviet Union itself, the anti-Jewish movement, which had already assumed menacing proportions with the state-ordered murder of the popular Yiddish actor Solomon Mikhoels and the removal of other Jewish intellectuals, reached its climax in the months just prior to Stalin's death in March 1953. True to the antisemitic tradition that saw a Jewish conspiracy behind every misfortune, Stalin attributed the death of some of his closest confidants to a plot by Jewish doctors and had a number of them arrested. More far-reaching measures were only prevented by Stalin's death. In Romania, where the largest Jewish community in Eastern Europe (outside of the Soviet Union) had managed to survive, there were several trials of Zionist activists in 1953 and 1954, frequently leading to lengthy prison terms. In the following years the regime allowed Jews to emigrate to Israel—albeit only in exchange for lucrative payments. Starting in the mid-1950s, almost all of the few remaining Jewish communities in Eastern Europe of any significance dissolved, falling victim to the Communist world's increasingly anti-Israeli and often also antisemitic policies. Of the 420,000 surviving Jews in Romania, 273,000 went to Israel. The figures were 170,000 out of 215,000 for Poland, and for Bulgaria 42,000 out of 49,000. Only in Hungary did a majority of the 145,000 surviving Jews remain, yet even there about 25,000 Jews had chosen Israel as their new homeland by 1967.

Parallel to this East European emigration, the Arab world's still important Jewish communities emptied out during the 1950s and 1960s. Many of them had been deeply integrated into the culture and politics of their countries, especially in Iraq. The country's Communist Party had been closely affiliated with Iraqi Jews, and Jewish singers like Salima Mourad and Nazem El Ghazali were among the country's most popular musicians. With one exception, all the musicians who represented Iraq at the first Arab Music Festival in Cairo in 1932 were Jews, and the major founders of Iraqi Radio were Jews as well. In Baghdad at the beginning of 1950, every fourth inhabitant was still Jewish. But Arab nationalism's vehement rejection of the State of Israel, measures taken against Zionist leaders during a wave of arrests in October 1949, and the assumption that all Jews were sympathetic to the enemy State of Israel led to violent riots and government measures against Jewish communities in Arab countries. In March 1950 Iraq allowed its Jewish population to emigrate. By the end of 1951 over 90 percent of Iraq's 115,000 Jews had left for Israel, and their property was, for the most part, confiscated. Only about 6,000 Jews remained in Iraq.

In Syria in 1947 there were anti-Jewish pogroms, in the wake of which two thirds of the Jewish population left the country. Palestinian refugees were given accommodations in the Jewish quarters of Damascus and Aleppo. A series of anti-Jewish laws and trials against relatives of emigrants to Israel further exacerbated the situation. The only Arab country in which the number of Jews temporarily increased after 1948 was Lebanon, whose tiny Jewish community grew to 9,000 with the arrival of refugees from Syria and Iraq. The outbreak of Lebanon's first civil war in 1958 resulted in emigration to Israel from Lebanon as well. Thus, just as in Syria and Iraq, there was no longer any organized Jewish life in Lebanon by the end of the century. In 1949/50, in a spectacular airlift, about 49,000 Jews were brought to Israel from Yemen.

The Jews of Egypt, among whom there were numerous immigrants from other Arab countries, and also from Europe, were relatively well integrated during the first half of the twentieth century. They made important contributions to the early development of Egyptian cinema, and in the field of music there were also prominent Jewish names. Egypt's most celebrated female singer on the eve of Nasser's rule was Leila Mourad, the daughter of Iraqi and Polish Jews who had converted to Islam. But here, too, the establishment of Israel gave rise to anti-Jewish feelings that erupted with particular ferocity after Gamal Abdel Nasser came to power in 1954. Even Leila Mourad, who in 1953 had been declared the official singer of the Egyptian revolution, ended her career a year later.

In Morocco on June 7, 1948, shortly after the State of Israel was founded, there was anti-Jewish violence in Jérada (Djérada) und Oujda, where forty-three Jews were killed. Initially, however, a majority of the country's Jews remained, in part

"Operation Flying Carpet" brought Jews from Yemen to Israel in 1949/50. In this photo, a group of Yemenite Jews in Lod, east of Tel Aviv, looks at a map of their new homeland.

because hurdles were put in the way of prospective emigrants who were old, infirm, and poor, and in part because official policy was by no means anti-Jewish until Morocco became independent in 1956. A leading Jewish personality, Leon Ben Saken, became a minister in the first Moroccan cabinet, and other Jews also held important positions in public administration and the legal system. When emigration to Israel was declared illegal under pressure from other Arab states, however, the situation worsened. About 25,000 Jews emigrated illegally to Israel between 1956 and 1961, and once emigration was legalized in 1961, the number rose to include an additional 90,000 over the following three years. This meant that a majority of Morocco's former Jews now called Israel home. In Turkey, too, where Jews suffered little from persecution, most nonetheless emigrated to Israel. Yet, except for those immigrants who lacked alternatives, Israel was not the sole destination. Of Algeria's 135,000 Jews, a majority of whom were French citizens, most chose France as their new home, as did most of Tunisia's Jews, whereas some of Libya's Jews went to Italy. After the Islamic Revolution, many Jews fled Iran for the United States.

By no means did the establishment of the State of Israel mean an end to Jewish life in the Diaspora. In the Soviet Union there were still over two million Jews, whose Jewish affiliation was noted in their identity papers under the category of "nationality," even though they were not allowed to practice their religion freely. After Stalin's death, the immediate physical threat to Jews disappeared, but discrimination in the workplace and in everyday life remained, and Jews were not permitted to travel abroad. In the 1967 Six-Day War, the Soviet Union and its satellite states supported the Arab countries against Israel, and afterwards (with the exception of Romania) they broke off diplomatic relations with the Jewish state. In 1968, after an official campaign that held the Jews responsible for unrest in Poland, practically the last Jews remaining there fled the country, including numerous Communist activists. Soviet Jewish intellectuals, in the face of official discrimination and drawing an analogy to the "homecoming" of Poles, Volga Germans, and Koreans, called for the right to emigrate to Israel. When several hundred exit requests were unexpectedly granted, the authorities were suddenly swamped with applications, especially in the Baltic Soviet republics. In the course of the diplomatic thaw during the détente years in the 1970s, the Soviet leadership temporarily relented and allowed about 250,000 Jews to leave in hopes that this relaxation would lead to improved trade relations with the United States. But in the second half of the 1970s, the Soviets again restricted emigration.

Western Europe experienced an unexpected revival of Jewish life in the decades following the Second World War. London and Paris took the place of Berlin, Vienna, Budapest, and Warsaw as centers of Jewish life, even though the Jewish presence in those cities was far less apparent than it had been in the prewar centers. Both in France and Great Britain, a strong pull toward assimilation was apparent. Admittedly, three Yiddish daily newspapers were published in Paris a decade after the end of the war, and the Yiddish language was still used among the older generation of immigrants, but for the younger generation the picture looked much different. Among France's roughly 300,000 Jews in 1955, there were about 40,000 school-age children, but only 400 of them attended Jewish schools, with an additional 1,300 having religious instruction once or twice a week. Only with the massive immigration of North African Jews in the 1960s did the picture change substantially. In the decades to follow, new Jewish schools were created, new communities were founded (especially in southern France), new synagogues were built, and kosher restaurants opened. Intellectuals (who enjoy widespread recognition in France) like Alain Finkielkraut, André Glucksman, Bernard-Henri Lévy, and Albert Memmi openly acknowledge their Jewishness.

In Britain's Jewish communities, assimilation had not advanced quite so far by the beginning of the 1970s. To be sure, the second and third generation of English Jews had largely moved away both from the religious and the secular legacies of their East European immigrant ancestors. But in 1963 there were still nearly 9,000 Jewish children attending 48 Jewish day schools, and 57 percent of all Jewish children received some kind of formal Jewish education. At the beginning of the 1960s there were 400 synagogues and eight Talmud schools (yeshivas) in England and Wales. But the trend in Great Britain began moving in the opposite direction to France's. By the 1970s, a large proportion of Jewish students and academics were no longer members of any Jewish organization. Jewish boarding schools steeped in tradition closed their doors. There was no wave of immigration comparable to the influx of Algerian and Moroccan Jews to France; in fact within just three decades the Jewish community lost a quarter of its 400,000 members, most of whom (as in France) had lived in the capital.

In Germany and Austria, Greece and the Netherlands, small Jewish communities were able to form, but in cities like Berlin, Vienna, Salonica, and Amsterdam there was no longer anything like the diverse Jewish life they once enjoyed. The only exception was Belgian Antwerp, where a lively Hasidic community formed around the diamond cutting business. The most prominent Jewish politician in postwar Europe was the longtime (1970–83) Chancellor of Austria, Bruno Kreisky. He maintained a critical distance from his Jewish background, however, and his relations with the State of Israel were extremely strained. Austrian politics again became the focus of Jewish organizations in 1986 when Kurt Waldheim was elected Federal President even though, as a young officer during World War II in Salonica, he had known about the deportation of Jews there and then had assiduously denied this knowledge for years afterward. Discussions surrounding the Waldheim affair led to a more thoroughgoing debate about the self-image long cultivated by Austrians that they were the "first victims of the National Socialists."

In Germany in the 1960s, the Jewish community had about 25,000 members, over 90 percent of them living in West Germany. There were some prominent returnees, such as the writers Arnold Zweig, Anna Seghers, Stefan Heym and Stephan Hermlin, who settled in East Germany, but they remained outside organized Jewish life. Some intellectuals—among them Ernst Bloch, Alfred Kantorowicz, and Hans Mayer—left their newly acquired academic positions in the East and resettled in the West, where a number of prominent intellectuals, such as

Theodor W. Adorno and Max Horkheimer, as well as actors like Fritz Kortner and Therese Giehse, had already taken up residence. Apart from these and a few other notables, the country's once rich and highly creative German-Jewish culture had almost completely disappeared. This was also true of the Jewish community's internal life. Germany's postwar Jewry no longer produced Jewish philosophers and theologians of the stature of a Martin Buber, Franz Rosenzweig, or Leo Baeck. Most of the Jews now living in Germany were barely familiar with these names. A majority of the postwar Jews were displaced persons who could not make up their minds about whether they should travel on to Israel or America, or else they were immigrants who arrived later from Eastern Europe, Iran, or Israel. They had highly ambivalent feelings about residing in the "land of the perpetrators," and for several decades they were often ostracized by the rest of the Jewish world. At its first postwar convention, the World Jewish Congress questioned the very idea of Jewish life in Germany, and the State of Israel shared the Congress's misgivings. The association founded in 1950 as an umbrella organization for all of Germany's Jewish communities, the "Central Council of Jews in Germany," clearly signaled this break with the past in its name. The new self-image was no longer that of "German citizens of the Jewish faith," but rather of Jews living in Germany. Although new synagogues were dedicated in the 1950s and 1960s, a sense of impermanence persisted. Only the breakup of the Soviet Union with all its ramifications brought about a major change. In the years following 1990, over 100,000 Jewish immigrants came with their families to Germany from Eastern Europe and the (former) Soviet Union. Today they form a clear majority in the Jewish communities. As in most other European countries, most synagogues in Germany now follow an Orthodox rite, though a majority of their members live a broadly secular life. Since the 1980s there are also a few Liberal congregations, and the first female rabbis.

To train rabbis, cantors, and religious teachers, the College of Jewish Studies was founded in Heidelberg in 1979 (sponsored by the Central Council of Jews in Germany), as was the Abraham Geiger College in Potsdam in 1999 (in association with the World Union of Progressive Judaism). There are other small rabbinical seminaries elsewhere in Europe, notably in London, Paris, Budapest, Rome, and Amsterdam.

Sweden and Switzerland, which remained neutral during the Second World War, enlarged their Jewish communities somewhat by taking in refugees, but major centers of Jewish life could never develop there. Both countries have regulations that prevent a Jewish butcher (*shohet*) from slaughtering animals according to the prescriptions of *kashrut* (the Orthodox Jewish dietary laws). Two countries once under German occupation yet evincing a relatively continuous Jewish history were Denmark and Italy. In Denmark almost the entire community was saved and sent to Sweden in October 1943, and it returned unscathed after the end of the war. In Italy the majority of Jews survived the period of persecution; many of them were hidden in churches and monasteries, where some were baptized. Not all of them returned to Judaism after the war. The most spectacular case of conversion was that of the chief rabbi of Rome, the Galician-born Israel Zolli (Zoller). After the German invasion of 1943 he left his community and took refuge in the Vatican. Following the liberation of Rome his community refused to reinstate him as chief rabbi, whereupon he adopted the Catholic faith. There was also the sensational case of a reverse conversion, when twenty-three peasant families in the Apulian village of San Nicandro converted to Judaism; most of them emigrated to Israel in 1949. Italy's Jewish survivors were joined in 1945 by some displaced persons from Eastern Europe who decided to remain in Italy. By the mid-1970s over 40 percent of Italian Jews lived in Rome, with the rest spread across twenty other communities. Although the Jews in Italy comprised an infinitesimal 0.05 percent of the total population, there were a number of important intellectuals among them, such as the writers Alberto Moravia, Giorgio Bassani, Italo Svevo, Carlo Levi, and Primo Levi. Italian Jewry was also filled out by immigration, especially from Libya and Iran, so that the community was able to maintain a constant size of about 35,000 people.

New Continents

After the Second World War, an especially intense kind of Jewish life developed in relatively new communities in such far-flung places as Australia, South Africa, Canada, and Latin America. Most Jews came to these countries from Eastern Europe and were either part of the immigrant generation or of their first-generation offspring. Pockets of Yiddish speakers flourished longer in these outposts than elsewhere, and a large share of Jewish schoolchildren attended Jewish schools.

There had been organized Jewish communities in Australia since the 1840s. From out of their ranks came General John Monash, supreme commander of the Australian armed forces in the First World War. During this period Australia's approximately 20,000 Jews made up about 0.4 percent of the population. Only after the end of the Second World War did the community experience significant immigration, especially the immigration of Holocaust survivors. By the beginning of the 1960s its numbers had reached 60,000, a majority of whom lived in the two centers of Melbourne and Sydney. In contrast to Western Europe and the United States, the Australian Jewish community was little threatened by advancing assimilation. Australia had one of the highest shares of Jewish day school attendance (with 60 percent of all Jewish children attending fifteen of these schools in 2004) and one of the lowest rates of interfaith marriage.

The situation was similar in South Africa, where the first Jews had already arrived with the Dutch East India Company in the seventeenth century. Organized Jewish life did not begin, however, until Russian Jews began to immigrate in the 1880s. The roughly 4,000 Jews who arrived in 1880 were followed by 40,000 more over the following three decades. German-Jewish immigrants fortified the community in the 1930s. By 1936 the Jewish community had doubled in size to 90,000; it reached 115,000 by 1960. In the apartheid state, Jews were treated like all other privileged whites, but antisemitism also developed under the influence of racist thinking in nationalist circles, especially around the National Party. Among the civil rights activists who rejected the apartheid state there was a relatively large proportion of Jews, such as the Nobel Prize-winning author Nadine Gordimer, the politician Helen Suzman, who was the only representative of the Progressive Party in the South African parliament between 1961 and 1974, and Joe Slovo, a Communist who lived in exile for more than twenty years and upon his return became the first white person elected to the executive council of the African National Congress. Among the political leaders of South Africa's Jews, however, there were also those who advocated and accommodated the policy of apartheid. A distinguishing feature of the Jewish community in South Africa was its close ties to Zionism and the State of Israel. There was in fact a higher percentage of Jews with Zionist sympathies in South Africa than in any other country. Relations between South Africa and the State of Israel, in spite of Israeli politicians' official condemnations of apartheid, were also largely positive. With the end of white rule, numerous South African Jews left the country.

In Canada, where the first Jewish community had been founded in the middle of the eighteenth century, the big turning point came in the 1880s, when tens of thousands of Russian-Jewish immigrants found refuge there. Between 1880 and 1900 the Jewish community increased from 2,500 to nearly 20,000. Although antisemitism was part of everyday life, especially in the French-speaking part of Canada, the community grew rapidly and reached 170,000 by 1941. During the first few post-war decades, about 35,000 Jewish Holocaust survivors found a new home in Canada. By the beginning of the 1970s, 250,000 Jews lived in the country. The older center of Jewish Canada was Montreal, which also attracted Jewish immigrants from Francophone parts of northern Africa, but Toronto slowly caught up with and eventually overtook Quebec's largest city as the new Jewish center. In both cities most Jews lived in pre-dominantly Jewish neighborhoods, where there were Jewish day schools and synagogues representing a variety of denomi-nations and movements. In 1990 about 90 percent of all Jewish children in Toronto had received some kind of Jewish educa-tion. Canada remained one of the few Jewish Diaspora com-munities that continued to grow even beyond the turn of the millennium.

The situation in Latin America differs from that of that of English-speaking countries. The origins of Jewish life here also go back to the Russian-Jewish wave of emigration at the end of the 19th century, which was characterized by diverse agricul-tural projects, especially in Argentina. The Spanish-speaking elite often tried to attract Jewish immigrants because of what was, at least subliminally, a racist-motivated policy of "lighten-ing" the population, even though this was inconsistent with the Catholic religious monopoly in these societies. The larg-est Latin American Jewish community by far emerged in the European-dominated countries, here primarily in Argentina, and most especially in its capital of Buenos Aires, where one of the world's most active Jewish communities worldwide (nearly 200,000 strong) sprang up, as well as one of the last enclaves of Yiddish cultural activity. On the other shore of the Rio de la Plata, in neighboring Montevideo, the capital of Uruguay, an-other important Jewish community emerged in the twentieth century. Uruguay's 50,000 Jews constituted the third-largest

Jewish community in Latin America and formed the largest
Jewish percentage of any Latin American country's population.
Most Latin American countries took in a proportionally high
share of German-Jewish emigrants, especially Chile, where
about 18,000 Central European Jews comprised the majority
of the Jewish community. Within a single generation, a Jewish
community arose in Brazil as well, drawing refugees from various regions threatened by antisemitism. It grew from 6,000 in
1928 to 42,000 six years later and reached 110,000 by the end of
the 1940s, with São Paulo and Rio de Janeiro as its most important centers. By 1958 about 35,000 additional Jews had immigrated to Brazil, especially from Arab countries.

The diversity of Jewish life is exemplified in Mexico City, where
most of Mexico's approximately 40,000 Jews lived during the
postwar decades. They were organized into seven different communities: an Arab-speaking community of Jews from Aleppo,
another Arab-speaking congregation from Damascus, one for
Ladino-speaking Jews from the Balkans, German-speaking
and Hungarian-speaking communities, one English-speaking
community from the United States, and Yiddish-speaking congregations from Eastern Europe. For a long time these communities remained apart from one another, married within
their own groups, and maintained their own rituals. Eighty-five
percent of all Jewish children in Mexico City attended Jewish
schools, and Jewish community centers were often sites of social
interaction and sports. The cohesion of the entire Jewish community in Latin America is relatively strong. Support for Israel
is especially pronounced and has been expressed in a relatively
high level of emigration, especially from those countries under
military dictatorship or experiencing major economic problems.

An additional factor that kept all the different strains of
Judaism together was their common struggle against the ac-
ceptance and integration of former National Socialists. The
Israeli secret service's 1960 kidnapping of Nazi criminal Adolf

Eichmann, who had been hiding in Argentina, drew worldwide attention to this chapter in Latin American history. Antisemitism played a significant role in the right-wing circles close to the military dictatorships. An especially dark chapter was the rule of General Ongania, who removed Jews from civil service positions in Argentina shortly after coming to power in 1966 and had Jewish businessmen arrested, along with professors and students at the University of Buenos Aires.

At Home in America

Almost at the same time as Stalin's Doctor's Plot, the Slansky trial in Czechoslovakia, and the campaign against Zionist leaders in Romania, a dramatic trial was taking place in the United States. Later observers might characterize it as an American Dreyfus affair, but the prosecution for treason of the Jewish couple Julius and Ethel Rosenberg (now known to have been spies for the Soviet Union) was not comparable to any of those antisemitic show trials. In what was perhaps the most sensational courtroom drama of the McCarthy era, these two Communist activists were sentenced to death for passing on details of the American atomic weapons program to the Soviet Union and executed on June 19, 1953. Not only the accused, but also the judge and the prosecuting attorney were Jews. The trials of the McCarthy era were not part of any deliberate antisemitic campaign, and yet there was a palpable fear that the entire Jewish community might somehow be implicated. Jewish-American organizations like the American Jewish Committee favored the execution of the Rosenbergs and distanced themselves from any possible association with the accused.

The Rosenberg trial took place at a time when American Jews had not yet made their way into the center of American society. There were still elite clubs that excluded Jews and leading universities that restricted the enrollment of Jewish students.

As a reaction to this, Brandeis University, named after the first Jewish Supreme Court justice, was founded in 1948 just outside Boston. It was open to all denominations and was meant, above all, to serve as a home for Jewish students not admitted to other colleges. Beginning in the 1960s Jews were again guaranteed unrestricted access to all of the country's universities. By the end of the twentieth century there were Jewish presidents at some of the very universities that, only a few decades earlier, had limited the enrollment of Jewish students. Especially striking was a surge in Jewish studies. Today many young American Jews get their first real introduction to their own religion and culture in a university setting. In addition, the growth of Jewish day schools has allowed a larger group of schoolchildren to acquire basic knowledge about Judaism and its sources, accompanied by what is often an excellent familiarity with the Hebrew language.

Since the 1970s Jewish politicians have increasingly occupied prominent positions in national politics. The best known of these figures are Henry Kissinger, a German-Jewish émigré who rose to become Secretary of State in Richard Nixon's Republican administration, and Senator Joseph Lieberman, who belonged to the moderate wing of modern Orthodoxy and was nominated as the Democrats' vice presidential candidate in 2004. Secretary of State Madeleine Albright came from a Czech-Jewish family that converted to Catholicism in order to escape National Socialist persecution. In 2009 there were fourteen Senators and thirty-one Members of Congress in the House of Representatives counted as Jewish, all but one of them Democrats (or independent Senators affiliated with the Democratic caucus). This reflects an unbroken tradition of support for the Democratic Party among most American Jews, even though their socioeconomic profile would seem to better fit a typical Republican constituency.

The Jewish presence in U.S. politics may be a relatively recent development, but Jewish impact in other areas of the American

The actor Leonard Nimoy as Mr. Spock, showing the Vulcan salute based on the Jewish priestly blessing.

scene has a longer history. Jewish writers, actors, and musicians have helped shape American culture over the last fifty years to an extent only equaled by the German-speaking intellectuals and artists in the early twentieth century. Along with writers like Saul Bellow, Bernard Malamud, and Chaim Potok, Philip Roth is especially noteworthy for the wide variety of Jewish themes developed in his novels—ranging from subject matter drawn from his own childhood in Newark, through relations between Israel and the Diaspora, to the world of Jewish retirees in Florida.

The concentration of Jews in the American film industry was quite strong from the beginning, and even today at the start of the twenty-first century it has hardly abated. Hollywood would never have become what it is today without its Jewish producers, not to mention Jewish actors and directors, including a number of émigrés. Woody Allen is unequaled as the filmmaker responsible for the image of the neurotic New York Jew. It may be just a coincidence that the figure of Superman was created by two Jewish artists from Cleveland. That Superman embodied the ideals of many Jews fighting for the weak against the poor could just as easily be given a universalistic interpretation,

Bob Dylan during the bar mitzvah of his son Jesse at the Wailing Wall in Jerusalem, 1983.

but the fact that his name on the planet Krypton was originally Kal-El can only be accounted for by the Hebrew meaning of the name ("the God who is light") and explained by the background of the superhero's creators. It is much the same with the Vulcan salute of Mr. Spock, which mirrors the Jewish priestly blessing remembered from synagogue by Spock's portrayer, Leonard Nimoy, the child of East European immigrants.

In the immediate postwar decades, hardly anyone influenced the music scene more profoundly than the longtime principal conductor of the New York Philharmonic, Leonard Bernstein, who also had a close association with the Israel Philharmonic Orchestra and composed a number of pieces on his own with Jewish themes. Jewish subjects also showed up in the work of such popular American singers and actors as Barbra Streisand and Neil Diamond. Streisand got closest to her Jewish background in the movie *Yentl*, based on a story by Isaac Bashevis Singer. In this portrait of an East European shtetl, projected through a strong American lens, she not only played the title role of the Talmud student disguised as a boy, but also wrote the screenplay, directed, and produced the film. Neil Diamond also found his way back into a Jewish milieu when he appeared in a remake (1980) of the first talking picture, *The Jazz Singer* (1927), playing the lead role of the son who breaks out of his Jewish background to become a Broadway star.

Like Diamond and Streisand, the folk and rock musician Bob Dylan was born in the early 1940s. He grew up as Robert Allen Zimmerman in the small town of Duluth, Minnesota, where there was no Jewish community. A year before his bar mitzvah, his parents arranged for a rabbi to come to Duluth from Brooklyn to instruct him in the Jewish religion. Bob Dylan wrote and performed love and protest songs that, in the eyes of his fans and of the media, turned him into a prophet and spokesman for his generation—titles he vehemently rejected. He had a close involvement with Christianity in the late 1970s, writing songs inspired by religious themes, but a few years later returned to Judaism. Dylan was influenced by the Lubavitcher Hasidim, whose spirituality resonated with his generation's search for meaning.

The leader of this messianic movement (also called *Chabad* Hasidism) was Rabbi Menachem Mendel Schneerson, who was the Lubavitcher rebbe for forty-four years until he died, childless, in 1994 at the age of ninety-two. Some of his adherents took this as a sign that he must be the messiah, and so they did not choose a successor. The Messianic Age had now dawned, they effusively proclaimed. At the same time, the Lubavitcher movement continued its active missionary work (the only Hasidic group to do this) among secular Jews, not only in Israel and the United States, but also and increasingly in regions lacking a solid Jewish infrastructure. Thus, at the start of the twenty-first century, numerous Jewish communities in Eastern and Central Europe, as well as new congregations in the Far East, are dominated by Chabad. The movement provides these communities with a Jewish infrastructure and dispatches rabbis from its headquarters in Brooklyn to locations all over the world. In 2007 there were 3,300 Chabad centers in seventy countries.

Schneerson had grown up in the Ukraine and studied mathematics in Paris prior to 1941, when he boarded one of the last ships to cross the Atlantic during the Second World War and settled in the Hasidic neighborhood of Crown Heights in Brooklyn. A large percentage of American Jewry's postwar religious leadership shared Schneerson's European roots. Rabbis Aaron Kotler, Joseph Soloveitchik, and Moshe Feinstein were among the pillars of Eastern European-style Orthodox Judaism, while Rabbi Joseph Breuer founded an Orthodox congregation in the German-Jewish tradition of his grandfather, Samson Raphael Hirsch, in Manhattan's Washington Heights. In contrast to Israel, where only Orthodox Judaism is officially recognized, the United States is the undisputed center of Jewish religious pluralism. In the Reform movement, too, some of the most important spiritual leaders (such as Rabbis Joachim Prinz and Alexander Schindler) came from Germany. In addition to the Reform movement's and Conservative Judaism's ongoing development, a fourth current within American Judaism crystallized in 1968 when the movement known as Reconstructionism established its own rabbinical seminary following the teachings of the religious philosopher Mordecai Kaplan. Kaplan, who had taught for over half a century at the Jewish Theological Seminary in New York, defined Judaism as a religious civilization, ascribed a purely abstract role to God, and questioned some of the theological principles underlying both Conservative and Reform Judaism.

A longtime colleague and, at the same time, spiritual antipode of Kaplan was the Polish-born and Berlin-educated religious philosopher Abraham Joshua Heschel. He was one of the most important advocates of Christian-Jewish dialogue and was among the most prominent of those Jewish theologians who vehemently opposed the Vietnam War and supported the American civil rights movement.

Like Heschel, many American Jews were outspoken proponents of racial integration. Most came from families whose European forebears had themselves felt the full force of discrimination and racism. But the relationship between Jews and blacks was not untroubled. Democratic presidential aspirant Jessie Jackson called New York "Hymietown" in 1984, and the leader of the Nation of Islam, Louis Farrakhan, spoke abusively of the Jewish religion. Tensions climaxed in 1991 when an African-American child was run over by a Hasidic driver and violence erupted against Orthodox Jews in the streets of Brooklyn, in the course of which a Yeshiva student was stabbed. The deeper sources of these tensions may lie in the unequal development of these two once-persecuted communities. While Jews have climbed high on the social scale within a few generations, especially along the path of education, a large part of the African-American population remains stuck on the lower socioeconomic rungs.

The most important intra-Jewish development in the religious realm concerns the place of women in the synagogue. In contrast to the prevailing practice of Liberal congregations in Germany, in many American synagogues women had been sitting together with men as early as the nineteenth century. Now, however, they could also take on active roles, be counted in a *minyan* (the ten adults required for congregational prayer), and called to bless or read from the Torah. In 1968 the first female rabbinical student was admitted to the Reform movement's rabbinical seminary, and in 1985 the first female Conservative rabbi was ordained. Both had forerunners in Germany, where Fräulein ("Miss") Rabbi Regina Jonas was the first woman ordained (in 1935). Jonas never had a congregation and fell victim to the Nazi genocide against the Jews a few years later. In contrast to such halting steps towards women's integration in

Rabbi Abraham Joshua Heschel (second from right) on the legendary march from Selma to Montgomery on March 21, 1965, along with Martin Luther King Jr. (fourth from right).

interwar Europe, interrupted by the Holocaust, the inclusion of women as rabbis and later as cantors made rapid progress in postwar America. By 1994 there were four hundred women rabbis. The ordination of women was not on the table in Orthodox Judaism, but a stronger effort was made to incorporate women in religious services by letting them deliver sermons in the synagogue and by upgrading the bat mitzvah ceremony for girls who had come of age religiously.

Another turning point in the religious development of American Judaism was the decision of the Reform movement, against established custom, to accept the children of Jewish fathers and non-Jewish mothers into the Jewish community. This has created two different criteria for Jewish affiliation. The question "Who is a Jew?" is complicated today by the fact that Orthodox Judaism does not automatically recognize as Jews those converted by non-Orthodox rabbis. The number of annual conversions in the United States rose from around 3,000 in 1954 to 10,000 twenty years later. The converts included some prominent Americans: Sammy Davis Jr., Marilyn Monroe (after her marriage to the playwright Arthur Miller), and Elizabeth Taylor (after her marriage to the singer Eddie Fisher). A situation arose where the definition of a Jew was fluid, depending on whose criteria were applied. Finally, at the beginning of the twenty-first century, the question of whether homosexuals could exercise the same functions in Judaism as heterosexuals landed on the agenda. On this question, too, Conservative Judaism eventually followed the lead of the Reform and Reconstructionist movements by allowing gays and lesbians to train and hold office as rabbis. Another development is the greater effort made to integrate non-Jewish partners from interfaith marriages, along with the children from these marriages, and to socialize them within the Jewish community.

The dominant demographic trends in American Judaism during the first postwar decades were migration from the city to the suburbs and from the East coast to the West and South. The Lower East Side and other traditionally Jewish big city neighborhoods now became home to generations of non-Jewish immigrants from East Asia and Latin America. Most Jews had risen into the middle class and exchanged cramped city apartments for houses of their own in the suburbs. About a third of the Jewish metropolitan population moved during the first two postwar decades to suburbs like Teaneck and Englewood across the Hudson River from New York, or Highland Park and Skokie outside Chicago, towns where they often remained in a predominantly Jewish setting. Religious practice might be on the decline, but Jews still felt the need to join a synagogue, just as their Christian neighbors became members of churches. Synagogues now became community centers, meeting places, and settings for social occasions and family celebrations. Beginning in the late 1960s, and inspired in part by the student rebellion, a countermovement outside the organized religious denominations became widespread. This so-called *havurah* movement (from a Hebrew word meaning "fellowship" or "circle of friends") promoted the decentralization of large synagogues into smaller, more intimate prayer and study groups. Not all havurah activities would be controlled by rabbis, cantors, or by the congregational executive; instead responsibility would be shared among the members of the group.

In the late 1940s two thirds of American Jews had lived on the northeast coast of the United States, between Boston und Washington. A half century later the percentage was only half. Los Angeles and Miami had become new centers of American Jewish life, alongside New York and Chicago, Philadelphia and Boston. Whereas religious life in California had been unusually lax and institutionally unstructured in the past, by the 1970s all the major rabbinical seminaries from New York and Cincinnati had opened branches in Los Angeles. Among California's "new" were not only Jews who had come from the East coast, but also many immigrants from other countries: a large Iranian-Jewish community, Jews from the former Soviet Union, and an increasing number of Israelis who, in search of material prosperity and a more peaceful everyday life, emigrated from the Jewish state to the "Golden Land."

Israel—An Embattled Homeland

Long after its War of Independence was over, Israel remained at the center of Middle Eastern discord. Over the next several decades, its conflict with neighboring Arab states erupted in a number of additional wars: the Suez War in 1956, the Six-Day

War in 1967, the Yom Kippur War in 1973, and the Lebanon War in 1982. Over the long run, the most important of these was the war of 1967, in which the Israeli army took the Golan Heights from Syria, the West Bank from Jordan, and the Gaza Strip and Sinai peninsula from Egypt. Jerusalem was reunited and declared the capital of Israel. At the same time, the Arab population now under Israeli control skyrocketed. Israel did not annex these territories, but its deliberate settlement policy became an obstacle to the subsequent handover of these territories to a Palestinian state.

Beginning in the mid-1980s, the Palestinians fighting for their independence stepped up their resistance, which coalesced in two uprisings (*intifadas* in Arabic), one between 1987 and 1993 and a second between 2000 and 2005. The Arab world's originally categorical refusal to recognize Israel was relaxed in 1977 with the first visit of an Arab head of state (Egyptian President Anwar al-Sadat) to Israel. Peace treaties signed with Egypt in 1978 and Jordan in 1994, along with an interim agreement reached with the Palestinians in 1995, opened up prospects for peaceful coexistence. The Israeli army's withdrawal from southern Lebanon and the Gaza Strip also raised hopes. Regrettably, growing violence on both sides, the continuation of the settlement policy in the occupied territories, and the Palestinian leadership's radicalization via the Islamist Hamas movement, have continued to block a final peaceful resolution.

In a history of the Jews, the Middle East conflict can only be given marginal treatment. It requires a book of its own. Yet Israel as a Jewish state had an impact on the course of Jewish history in the second half of the twentieth century that extended well beyond the Middle East conflict. For the first time in two millennia, a Jewish state had reemerged, and this happened immediately after the annihilation of what had been the center of Jewish life in Europe. Israel was (and has remained) a country of immigrants during the first six decades of its existence. As late as 2006, one third of all its inhabitants were born elsewhere, and a majority of the rest were the children of immigrants. In a society that brings together people from such different countries as Yemen and Germany, Morocco and Russia, cultural conflict is unavoidable. Even if the different immigrants had a certain Jewish consciousness in the old environments from which they came, each group was still part of its own unique Diaspora society, spoke its own language, and had developed a distinct style for worship in Hebrew. Some of the immigrant groups gained a measure of dominance, leaving others feeling oppressed. Polish Jews long dominated the political institutions of Israel, and German Jews its legal system and academic life. Immigrants from Arab countries, by contrast, were acutely conscious of discrimination. In the 1970s, a social protest movement of "Black Panthers" emerged among Sephardic Israelis, modeled on the militant African-American group in the United States. The dominance of Ashkenazic Jews in the political arena and within the influential trade union federation Histadrut was one of the causes of the political earthquake of 1977, when the nationalist Menachem Begin ousted the social democrats who had governed the country without interruption since independence. It was, paradoxically, Israel's first right-wing government that made the first territorial concessions, returning the Sinai to Egypt after Anwar al-Sadat's surprise visit to Jerusalem and the peace treaty concluded following the 1978 Camp David Accords.

While ethnic tensions between European and Oriental Jews leveled off over the years, the rift between the political camps persisted. A clear sign of how intense the polarization had become was the hostility to which Premier Yitzhak Rabin was subjected as a result of his peace initiative, and which led to his assassination on November 4, 1995, by a nationalist extremist. The most serious point of contention was over concessions to the Palestinians and the related issue of returning the West Bank territories (which many Israelis call by their Hebrew names Yehuda and Shomron, or Judea and Samaria). Again it was a hardliner—Defense Minister Ariel Sharon, who had been held responsible for the massacre committed by Lebanese Christian militias in the refugee camps Sabra and Shatila in 1982—who as Premier carried out the withdrawal from the Gaza Strip, against vehement resistance from within his own political camp. Political polarization has grown steadily. On one side is the settlers' movement, which became increasingly influential after the 1967 war, and on the other the "Peace Now" movement, which reached its zenith during mass protests against the 1982 Lebanon war.

Another area of conflict in Israeli society is in the religious arena. A growing and increasingly militant religious minority confronts the country's secular majority. Israel sees itself as a Western-style secular democracy in which several facets of life are controlled by religious authorities, including marriage and divorce. Israeli law does not provide for civil marriage, so only members of the same religious community can marry one another—although marriages concluded abroad are recognized. There are also restrictions on the use of public transportation on Saturdays, the Jewish day of rest. Most buses do not operate on this day, nor does the official Israeli airline El Al. Here, as in many other areas, people find ways to get around these restrictions, as when private buses travel through Tel Aviv or a charter airline affiliated with El Al takes care of air traffic on Saturday. On the whole, as with ethnicity and politics, it is hard to overlook a certain polarization in the religious sphere that has impacted Israel's first six decades as a modern nation-state. Whereas most Israelis at first kept certain religious traditions, today an increasingly strict Orthodoxy confronts a secular public that is, in part, either openly anti-religious or else completely uninterested in religion.

Despite all these conflicts, which have erupted on top of the Arab-Israeli conflict, Israel's achievements are considerable.

These include the formation of a society that is diverse yet has a sense of unity, the modernization of a country that was before barely developed, and economic prosperity. At the beginning of the twenty-first century, only 3 percent of Israel's population is still working in the agricultural economy once envisioned as the modern Zionist ideal; instead Israel has become a leader in the high-tech industry. Today microchips, not oranges, are the major export item. In the cultural sphere, too, Israel can count a number of impressive achievements: it modernized the Hebrew language, has a Nobel Prize winner in literature (S. Y. Agnon, 1966), and has produced such important writers as Amos Oz, A. B. Yehoshua, and David Grossman. In their works, these authors repeatedly pose the question of Israel's Jewish identity.

Even at the end of the twentieth century, Israel remained the most important country of immigration for Jews escaping persecution. Since the 1980s nearly 100,000 Ethiopian Jews, also called *Beta Israel* or *Falashas* (actually a derogatory term for foreigners), were brought to Israel in several airlifts. According to their own tradition, they belonged to Jewish tribes based in Ethiopia since ancient times. The Ethiopians were, however, unacquainted with the rabbinic traditions that had developed in other parts of the Jewish world, and a great controversy broke out when the Chief Rabbinate demanded that they undergo a formal conversion. There have been similar discussions about the significantly larger wave of immigrants from the Soviet Union. The breakup of the Soviet Union had led to the emigration of over a million Jews, of whom about three quarters of a million settled in Israel—the largest influx since the beginning of the state. It was not always possible to unambiguously ascertain the Jewish affiliation of these Russian, Baltic, Ukrainian, and Georgian Jews who began arriving in large numbers in the 1990s. They knew little about Judaism as a religion, had not been socialized as Zionists, and did not understand any

Hebrew. In Israel they set up their own Russian-speaking culture that has conspicuously shaped the country's media, music, art, and everyday life.

Zionism in its classical form had assumed that the Jews could only have a future in the Jewish state itself. As it became evident after several decades that the Diaspora remained viable, that persecuted Jews in some countries preferred emigrating to France or America over Israel, and even that an increasing number of Israelis were leaving the country, new concepts for the relationship between Jews in Israel and the Diaspora had to be developed. An especially radical argument came from the "Canaanites," a movement that was numerically small but hard to ignore in the Israel of the 1950s and 1960s. This movement, led by the poet Jonathan Ratosh, drew a sharp dividing line between Israelis on the one hand and Jews (outside Israel) on the other. Their adherents traced Israel back to pre-Biblical traditions (in "the land of Canaan") and stressed the Israelis' closeness to their Arab neighbors in the Orient as opposed to their distance from Westernized Jews remaining in exile. Although this mindset quickly declined as an organized movement, among non-religious Israelis the difference between Jews and Israelis became increasingly salient. Religious Israelis (with the exception of some circles in the settler movement) could just as easily practice their religion in New York or London as in Tel Aviv or Jerusalem, and they were therefore more receptive to Diaspora life in the "pre-Messianic era." To many secular Israelis, by contrast, being Jewish means especially, if not exclusively, being an Israeli. For this group, the notion of Jewish existence outside the Jewish state casts doubt on the path they have chosen. Other Israelis see in the Jewish Diaspora, especially in North America, a source of better ties to the world of states outside Israel. Proposals for more intensive Diaspora involvement in Israeli reality range from the utopian idea of founding a second, advisory chamber representing

Jews from the Diaspora to the already implemented "Birth-right" program that invites young Jews from all over the world to travel through Israel.

As the largest Diaspora community and as citizens of the country with the closest ties to Israel, American Jews undoubt-edly assume a special role when it comes to supporting the Israeli state. It is often forgotten that American Jews were not always so committed to a Jewish state, and that the stance of the United States towards Israel was initially quite ambivalent. During the 1950s and 1960s most American Jews defined themselves as a religious denomination and were mostly concerned with in-dividual integration and recognition. Identification with Israel was not conducive to this kind of self-definition. The intensifica-tion of ethnic pluralism in the United States since the 1960s—as expressed in slogans like "Black is beautiful" or policies such as the acceptance of Spanish-language schooling—encouraged the ethnic self-definition of Jews as well. This new ethnic pride be-came a driving force, strengthening links to Israel.

The decisive event that assured intense U.S. support for Is-rael, both material and spiritual, was the 1967 Six-Day War. Anxieties about the very survival of the Jewish state triggered by the aggressive rhetoric of Egyptian President Nasser pre-cipitated spontaneous relief actions of unforeseen dimensions. Over the following decade these anxieties would receive addi-tional sustenance from the PLO's numerous terrorist attacks, the Yom Kippur War of 1973, the UN resolution of 1975 equat-ing Zionism with racism, and by the sensational liberation of Israeli hostages at Entebbe airport in 1976. The late 1960s and the 1970s, when Israel was under extreme political and military pressure, constituted the period of Diaspora Jewry's strongest solidarity with Israel. What may also have played a special role in the United States was a desire to avoid being reproached once more for having done too little, as in the period of the Ho-locaust, for imperiled Jews in other countries.

This surge of support for Israel seemed to ebb somewhat at the beginning of the 1980s. Significant among the factors contributing to the abatement of solidarity were the electoral victory and ultraconservative policies of Menachem Begin and his right-wing Likud bloc, the bad press Israel got after a brief glimmer of hope in the wake of the Camp David Accords with Egypt, the Lebanon War (which was controversial inside Israel itself), the election of the racist (Brooklyn-born) Meir Kahane to the Knesset in 1984, and a growing divisiveness within Israeli society. Over the long run, however, American Jews have a record of unbroken solidarity with Israel, which shows up in spontaneous relief actions during crisis periods. One of the most important American lobbying organizations is the American Israel Public Affairs Committee (AIPAC), which was founded during a period of difficult relations between the United States and Israel under the Eisenhower administration and continues to be an advocate for Israeli concerns.

The deep fissure within Israeli society, especially on questions of politics and religion, has also left its traces among the Jews of the Diaspora. Only a few became such radical critics of the State of Israel as the linguist Noam Chomsky. But America's non-Orthodox Jews have increasingly expressed their concerns about the dominant influence of Orthodoxy, not only in Israel itself but also on questions of conversions to Judaism and marriages concluded outside Israel. Representatives of the Reform movement have often gone beyond strictly religious concerns and spoken out bluntly on political issues of the day. Thus, since the 1980s, critical remarks about whatever Israeli government happens to be in power have become increasingly audible. At the same time, unconditional solidarity with Israel by fundamentalist and often missionary Christian groups in the United States has disturbed many liberal Jews, who would prefer different allies. The magazine *Tikkun*, founded in 1986 by Rabbi Michael Lerner, an activist veteran of the Berkeley student revolt, has emerged as a Jewish forum frequently critical of Israel and an antipode to *Commentary*, the established periodical of conservative Jewish intellectuals and a training ground for some of America's leading neoconservatives.

Outside Orthodox islands in Jerusalem, Brooklyn, and a few other places, religious practice and religious knowledge have sharply declined among today's Jews. But Jewish identity is defined more strongly than ever by external threats. Trials of Holocaust perpetrators, documentary and feature films, and the construction of memorials and museums like Yad Vashem in Jerusalem, the United States Holocaust Memorial Museum in Washington, and the monumental Shoah memorial in Berlin keep the horrors of the past before the broader public's consciousness. They also serve as a cautionary history lesson pointing to possible dangers, both present and future, that face the Jews in their state. At the same time, there has been a universalization of Holocaust memory, especially apparent when Nobel Prizes were awarded to Holocaust survivors and authors Elie Wiesel in 1986 (Peace) and Imre Kertész in 2002 (Literature), when an International Holocaust Conference was convened in Stockholm in 2000 and attended by representatives of forty-four states, or when Holocaust memorial days were introduced in several countries on January 27, the day Auschwitz was liberated. Nevertheless, there are still Holocaust deniers, in whose ranks one may even find a head of state like Iran's President Ahmadinejad.

Present threats also shape Jewish identity in the twenty-first century. Jewish community centers have frequently become high-security zones that can be recognized from a distance by the presence of police. Terror attacks on Jewish community centers happen from Vienna to Djerba, and from Istanbul to Buenos Aires, where the bloodiest attack on a Jewish community center took the lives of eighty-five victims in 1995. Terror at the beginning of the twenty-first century emanates both from right-wing nationalists and fundamentalist Islamists and cannot be separated from the Middle East conflict. It is one of the ironies of history that Israel is regarded as a safe refuge for Jews all over the world, while at the same time its existence is viewed by some Jewish intellectuals as a source of danger for Diaspora Jews.

The Jewish community has lost much of the diversity and internationality that characterized it for so long. There are, admittedly, still Jewish communities in nearly one hundred countries, but many of them number no more than a few hundred members and are on the verge of dissolving. Of the once flourishing Jewish community in the Arab world, only a remnant of about 5,000, mostly elderly Jews is left, almost all of them living in Morocco and Tunisia. Two somewhat larger Jewish communities exist in the Islamic-dominated countries of Turkey (nearly 20,000 members) and Iran (over 10,000 Jews). The Jewish population in the states of the former Soviet Union has been reduced to a mere fraction of its former size. Communities in Eastern Europe, with the exception of Hungary's, are tiny. In all of Europe, including Russia and Turkey, there are only 1.5 million Jews left. Over 80 percent of all Jews worldwide live in Israel and the United States, over a third of them in the two metropolitan areas of Tel Aviv and New York.

According to some official statistics from 2006, for the first time the number of Jews in Israel (5.3 million) has surpassed that of Jews in the United States (5.2 million). Only about 5 percent of all Jews lived in the Jewish state in 1948, sixty years later it was over 40 percent. These statistics expose what is a fundamental challenge for Jewry in the twenty-first century: It has become impossible to give a universally valid answer to the question: Who is a Jew? Do only children of Jewish mothers count, or should one also include the descendants of Jewish fathers? Is a profession of belief in Judaism what counts, or should ancestry suffice? What kind of conversion is legitimate? These are all questions to which there is no clear-cut answer.

Thus, some statisticians speak of 5.2 million American Jews, others of 6.4 million.

In Europe a phenomenon has become widespread that one might describe as Jewish culture without Jews, or as "virtual" Jewish culture. In centers with a rich Jewish past but no significant Jewish present, klezmer music is celebrated, Jewish museums are built, restaurants are named after historic Jewish figures, Jewish Studies programs are created at universities, and Jewish bookstores are established. In this fashion Europe attempts to fill a void in its history of which it is increasingly conscious. But it does so while contributing little to real Jewish life.

At the beginning of the twenty-first century, thirteen million Jews form just a tiny share of the world's population of over 6.5 billion people. Yet fascination with Judaism in its different manifestations endures. In the field of religion, Christianity and Islam continue to grapple with their Jewish roots. In political discourse, the State of Israel receives more international attention than almost any other country. The awarding of four out of six Nobel Prizes in literature between 2002 and 2007 to persons of Jewish ancestry underscores the continuing vigor of Jewish cultural creativity. Yet anti-Jewish myths have not faded away, and an antisemitic concoction like *The Protocols of the Elders of Zion* continues to be published in numerous countries and languages. We cannot know what the future holds for the Jews of the twenty-first century, but it is certain that their history will continue to fascinate humankind for generations to come.

Appendix
JEWISH HISTORY IN NUMBERS

Countries with the largest Jewish communities around 1898	
Russia	5 700 000
Austria-Hungary	1 860 000
USA	1 000 000
Germany	568 000
Ottoman Empire	466 000
Romania	300 000
Morocco	150 000
Ethiopia (Falashas)	120 000
Great Britain	100 000
Netherlands	97 000
France	72 000
(plus Fr. Morocco & Tunisia	(93 000)

Countries with the largest Jewish communities around 1930	
USA	4 228 000
Poland	2 980 000
USSR	2 673 000
Romania	900 000
Germany	564 000
Hungary	476 000
Czechoslovakia	400 000
Great Britain	300 000
Austria	250 000
France	220 000
Argentina	200 000
Palestine	175 000
Lithuania	155 000
Netherlands	150 000
Morocco	143 000
Canada	126 000

Countries with the largest Jewish communities 1948		Countries with the largest Jewish communities 2006 (together over 97 % of all Jews)	
USA	5 000 000	Israel	5 315 000
USSR	2 000 000	USA	5 275 000
Israel	750 000	France	492 000
Romania	380 000	Canada	373 000
Argentina	360 000	Great Britain	297 000
Great Britain	345 000	Russia	228 000
Morocco	286 000	Argentina	185 000
France	235 000	Germany	118 000
Canada	180 000	Australia	103 000
Hungary	174 000	Brazil	97 000
Algeria	130 000	Ukraine	80 000
Brazil	110 000	South Africa	72 000
South Africa	100 000	Hungary	50 000
		Mexico	40 000
		Belgium	31 000

Jewish population in Israel and the USA

	Israel	USA
1945	565 000	4.3 million
1970	2.6 million	5.4 million
2006	5.3 million	5.2 million

Cities with the largest Jewish population around 1930		Cities with the largest Jewish population 1948	
New York	1 765 000	New York	2 000 000
Warsaw	309 000	Chicago	300 000
Chicago	305 000	Tel Aviv	250 000
Philadelphia	270 000	Philadelphia	245 000
Budapest	218 000	London	234 000
London	210 000	Los Angeles	225 000
Vienna	202 000	Buenos Aires	165 000
Berlin	173 000	Bucharest	160 000
Łódź	156 000	Boston	137 000
Odessa	153 000	Paris	125 000
Paris	150 000	Budapest	110 000
Kiev	140 000	Casablanca	100 000
Moscow	132 000		
Buenos Aires	110 000		

Cities with the largest Jewish population 2006	
Tel Aviv	2 751 000
New York	1 750 000
Jerusalem	670 000
Los Angeles	668 000
Haifa	657 000
Miami	498 000
Beersheva	349 000
Philadelphia	285 000
Paris	284 000
Chicago	265 000
Boston	235 000
San Francisco	218 000
London	195 000
Toronto	180 000
Washington	166 000
Buenos Aires	165 000

Source: American Jewish Yearbook

Further Reading

THERE HAS BEEN SUCH ENORMOUS GROWTH in publications on Jewish history that it would be presumptuous to offer a systematic overview in just a few pages. The following list of references makes no claim to be exhaustive. It is intended to facilitate further reading. Only English-language works are included.

Surveys

A Jewish-American perspective may be found in Louis Finkelstein, ed., *The Jews: Their History, Culture, and Religion*, 2nd ed. (New York: Harper, 1960). A classically Zionist historical interpretation is expressed in the work of Haim Hillel Ben-Sasson, ed., *A History of the Jewish People* (Cambridge, MA: Harvard University Press, 1976). Post-modern influences are incorporated in David Biale, ed., *Cultures of the Jews: A New History* (New York: Schocken, 2002). An introduction written mostly from the perspective of intellectual history is provided by Robert M. Seltzer, *Jewish People, Jewish Thought* (New York: Macmillan, 1980). The most recent and up-to-date comprehensive Jewish history is John Efron et al., *The Jews: A History* (Upper Saddle River, NJ: Pearson Prentice Hall, 2009). On modern history, see also Lloyd Gartner, *History of the Jews in Modern Times* (Oxford: Oxford University Press, 2001), and Howard M. Sachar, *The Course of Modern Jewish History*, new rev. ed. (New York: Vintage, 1990).

Works on Jewish Historiography

Baron, Salo Wittmayer. *History and Jewish Historians: Essays and Addresses.* Philadelphia: Jewish Publication Society of America, 1964.

Brenner, Michael. *Prophets of the Past: Jewish Historiography in the Nineteenth and Twentieth Centuries*. Princeton, NJ: Princeton University Press, 2010.

Funkenstein, Amos. *Perceptions of Jewish History*. Berkeley, CA: University of California Press, 1993.

Meyer, Michael A. *Ideas of Jewish History*, 2nd ed. Detroit: Wayne State University Press, 1987.

Myers, David N. and David B. Ruderman, eds. *The Jewish Past Revisited: Reflections on Modern Jewish Historians*. New Haven: Yale University Press, 1998.

Rosman, Murray Jay (Moshe). *How Jewish Is Jewish History?* Oxford: Littman Library of Jewish Civilization, 2007.

Schorsch, Ismar. *From Text to Context: The Turn to History in Modern Judaism*. Hanover, NH: University Press of New England, 1994.

Yerushalmi, Yosef Hayim. *Zakhor: Jewish History and Jewish Memory*. Seattle: University of Washington Press, 1982.

Biblical and Ancient History

Avi-Yonah, Michael. *The Jews of Palestine: A Political History from the Bar Kokhba War to the Arab Conquest*. Oxford: Blackwell, 1976.

Cohen, Shaye J. D. *From the Maccabees to the Mishnah*. Philadelphia: Westminster Press, 1987.

Collins, John J. *Between Athens and Jerusalem. Jewish Identity in the Hellenistic Diaspora*. New York: Crossroad, 1983.

Feldman, Louis H. *Jew and Gentile in the Ancient World. Attitudes and Interactions from Alexander to Justinian*. Princeton, NJ: Princeton University Press, 1993.

Finkelstein, Israel and Neal A. Silberman. *The Bible Unearthed: Archaeology's New Vision of Ancient Israel and the Origin of its Sacred Texts*. New York: Free Press, 2001.

Gager, John E. *The Origins of Anti-Semitism: Attitudes Toward Judaism in Pagan and Christian Antiquity*. New York: Oxford University Press, 1983.

Gruen, Erich S. *Diaspora: Jews amidst Greeks and Romans*. Cambridge, MA: Harvard University Press, 2002.

Miller, J. Maxwell and John H. Hayes. *A History of Ancient Israel and Judah*. Philadelphia: Westminster Press, 1986.

Schäfer, Peter. *Judeophobia: Attitudes toward the Jews in the Ancient World*. Cambridge, MA: Harvard University Press, 1997.

Shanks, Hershel, ed. *Ancient Israel: From Abraham to the Roman Destruction of the Temple*. Washington DC: Biblical Archaeology Society, 1999.

Christian Middle Ages and Early Modern Europe

Baer, Yitzhak Fritz. *A History of the Jews in Christian Spain*, 2 vols. Philadelphia: Jewish Publication Society of America, 1971.

Bonfil, Robert. *Jewish Life in Renaissance Italy*. Berkeley, CA: University of California Press, 1994.

Chazan, Robert, ed. *Church, State and Jew in the Middle Ages*. New York: Behrman House, 1980.

Cohen, Jeremy. *The Friars and the Jews: The Evolution of Medieval Anti-Judaism*. Ithaca: Cornell University Press, 1982.

Cohen, Mark R. *Under Crescent and Cross: The Jews in the Middle Ages*. Princeton, NJ: Princeton University Press, 1994.

Gerber, Jane S. *The Jews of Spain: A History of the Sephardic Experience*. New York: Free Press, 1992.

Idel, Moshe. *Kabbalah. New Perspectives*. New Haven, CT: Yale University Press, 1988.

Israel, Jonathan. *European Jewry in the Age of Mercantilism, 1550–1750*. Oxford: Oxford University Press, 1985.

Katz, Jacob. *Exclusiveness and Tolerance: Jewish-Gentile Relations in Medieval and Modern Times*. New York: Behrman House, 1961.

———. *Tradition and Crisis: Jewish Society at the End of the Middle Ages*. New York: New York University Press, 1993.

Marcus, Ivan G. *Rituals of Childhood: Jewish Acculturation in Medieval Europe*. New Haven, CT: Yale University Press, 1996.

Oberman, Heiko A. *The Roots of Anti-Semitism in the Age of Renaissance and Reformation*. Philadelphia: Fortress Press, 1984.

Roth, Cecil. *The Jews in the Renaissance*. Philadelphia: Jewish Publication Society of America, 1959.

Scholem, Gershom. *Major Trends in Jewish Mysticism*, 3rd rev. ed. New York: Schocken, 1954.

———. *Sabbatai Sevi: The Mystical Messiah*. Princeton, NJ: Princeton University Press, 1973.

Yuval, Israel. *Two Nations in Your Womb: Perceptions of Jews and Christians in Late Antiquity and the Middle Ages*. Berkeley, CA: University of California Press, 2006.

Jews under Islamic Rule

Ashtor, Eliyahu. *The Jews of Moslem Spain*, 3 vols. Philadelphia: Jewish Publication Society of America, 1973–84.

Benbassa, Esther and Aron Rodrigue. *Sephardi Jewry*. Berkeley, CA: University of California Press, 1999.

Cohen, Mark R. *Under Crescent and Cross: The Jews in the Middle Ages*. Princeton, NJ: Princeton University Press, 1994.

Goitein, S. D. *A Mediterranean Society*, 6 vols. Berkeley, CA: University of California Press, 1967–1993.

———. *Jews and Arabs*. 3rd rev. ed. New York: Schocken, 1974.

Lewis, Bernard. *The Jews of Islam*. Princeton, NJ: Princeton University Press, 1984.

Rodrigue, Aron. *French Jews, Turkish Jews*. Bloomington, IN: University of Indiana Press, 1990.

Stillman, Norman A. *The Jews of Arab Lands*. Philadelphia: Jewish Publication Society of America, 1979.

———. *The Jews of Arab Lands in Modern Times*. Philadelphia: Jewish Publication Society, 1991.

Central European Jewry in Modern Times

Brenner, Michael. *The Renaissance of Jewish Culture in Weimar Germany*. New Haven, CT: Yale University Press, 1996.

Elon, Amos. *The Pity of It All: A History of Jews in Germany, 1743–1933*. New York: Metropolitan Books/Henry Holt, 2002.

Feiner, Shmuel. *The Jewish Enlightenment*. Philadelphia: University of Pennsylvania Press, 2004.

Kaplan, Marion. *The Making of the Jewish Middle Class: Women, Family, and Identity in Imperial Germany*. New York: Oxford University Press, 1991.

Katz, Jacob. *Out of the Ghetto: The Social Background of Jewish Emancipation, 1770–1870*. Cambridge, MA: Harvard University Press, 1973.

———. *Tradition and Crisis: Jewish Society at the End of the Middle Ages*. New York: New York University Press, 1993.

Kieval, Hillel J. *The Making of Czech Jewry*. New York: Oxford University Press, 1988.

Meyer, Michael A., ed. *German-Jewish History in Modern Times*, 4 vols. New York: Columbia University Press, 1996–98.

———. *The Origins of the Modern Jew: Jewish Identity and European Culture in Germany, 1749–1824*. Detroit: Wayne State University Press, 1979.

Reinharz, Jehuda. *Fatherland or Promised Land: The Dilemma of the German Jew, 1893–1914*. Ann Arbor, MI: University of Michigan Press, 1975.

Sorkin, David. *The Transformation of German Jewry, 1780–1840*. New York: Oxford University Press, 1987.

Wistrich, Robert S. *The Jews of Vienna in the Age of Franz Joseph*. New York: Oxford University Press (Littman Library), 1989.

East European Jewry in Modern Times

Dawidowicz, Lucy S., ed. *The Golden Tradition: Jewish Life and Thought in Eastern Europe*. New York: Holt, Rinehart and Winston, 1967.

Frankel, Jonathan. *Prophecy and Politics: Socialism, Nationalism, and the Russian Jews, 1862–1917*. Cambridge: Cambridge University Press, 1981.

Gitelman, Zvi Y. *A Century of Ambivalence. The Jews of Russia and the Soviet Union, 1881 to the Present*. New York: Schocken, 1988.

Klier, John D. *Russia Gathers Her Jews: The Origins of the "Jewish Question" in Russia, 1772–1825*. Dekalb, IL: Northern Illinois University Press, 1986.

Mendelsohn, Ezra. *The Jews of East Central Europe between the World Wars*. Bloomington, IN: Indiana University Press, 1983.

Pinkus, Benjamin. *The Jews of the Soviet Union*. Cambridge: Cambridge University Press, 1988.

Slezkine, Yuri. *The Jewish Century*. Princeton, NJ: Princeton University Press, 2004.

Stanislawski, Michael. *Tsar Nicholas I and the Jews*. Philadelphia: Jewish Publication Society of America, 1983.

West European Jewry in Modern Times

Benbassa, Esther. *The Jews of France: A History from Antiquity to the Present*. Princeton, NJ: Princeton University Press, 1999.

Endelman, Todd M. *The Jews of Britain, 1656–2000*. Berkeley, CA: University of California Press, 2002.

Hertzberg, Arthur. *The French Enlightenment and the Jews*. New York: Columbia University Press, 1968.

Hyman, Paula. *From Dreyfus to Vichy. The Remaking of French Jewry, 1906–1939*. New York: Columbia University Press, 1979.

———. *The Jews of Modern France*. Berkeley, CA: University of California Press, 1998.

Katz, David S. *The Jews in the History of England*. Oxford: Clarendon Press, 1994.

Marrus, Michael Robert. *Politics of Assimilation. A Study of the French Jewish Community at the Time of the Dreyfus Affair*. Oxford: Clarendon Press, 1971.

Marrus, Michael R. and Robert O. Paxton. *Vichy France and the Jews*. New York: Basic Books, 1981.

Wasserstein, Bernard. *Vanishing Diaspora: The Jews in Europe since 1945*. Cambridge, MA: Harvard University Press, 1996.

American Jewry

Diner, Hasia R. *The Jews of the United States, 1654 to 2000*. Berkeley, CA: University of California Press, 2004.

Elkin, Judith Laikin. *Jews of the Latin American Republics*. Chapel Hill, NC: University of North Carolina Press, 1980.

Feingold, Henry L., ed. *The Jewish People in America*, 5 vols. Baltimore: Johns Hopkins University Press, 1992.

Howe, Irving. *World of Our Fathers*. New York: Harcourt Brace Jovanovich, 1976.

Meyer, Michael A. *Response to Modernity: A History of the Reform Movement in Judaism*. New York: Oxford University Press, 1988.

Sarna, Jonathan. *American Judaism*. New Haven, CT: Yale University Press, 2004.

Whitfield, Stephen J. *In Search of American Jewish Culture*. Hanover, NH: University Press of New England [for] Brandeis University Press, 1999.

Antisemitism and the Holocaust

Dawidowicz, Lucy S. *The War Against the Jews, 1933–1945*. New York: Holt, Rinehart and Winston, 1975.

Friedländer, Saul. *Nazi Germany and the Jews*, 2 vols. New York: HarperCollins, 1997–2007.

Gilbert, Martin. *Kristallnacht*. London: HarperPress, 2006.

Hilberg, Raul. *The Destruction of the European Jews*, rev. and definitive ed. New York: Holmes and Meier, 1985.

Katz, Jacob. *From Prejudice to Destruction: Anti-Semitism, 1700–1933*. Cambridge, MA: Harvard University Press, 1980.

Longerich, Peter. *Holocaust: The Nazi Persecution and the Murder of the Jews*. New York: Oxford University Press, 2009.

Poliakov, Léon. *The History of Anti-Semitism*. 4 vols. Philadelphia: University of Pennsylvania Press, 2003.

Pulzer, Peter. *The Rise of Political Anti-Semitism in Germany & Austria*, rev. ed. Cambridge, MA: Harvard University Press, 1988.

Segev, Tom. *The Seventh Million: The Israelis and the Holocaust*. New York: Hill and Wang, 1993.

Yahil, Lena. *The Holocaust: The Fate of European Jewry, 1932–1945*. New York: Oxford University Press, 1990.

Zionism and the State of Israel

Avineri, Shlomo. *The Making of Modern Zionism: Intellectual Origins of the Jewish State*. New York: Basic Books, 1981.

Eisenstadt, Shmuel N. *The Transformation of Israeli Society*. Boulder, CO: Westview Press, 1985.

Elon, Amos. *Herzl*. New York: Holt, Rinehart and Winston, 1975.

Harshav, Benjamin. *Language in a Time of Revolution*. Berkeley, CA: University of California Press, 1993.

Laqueur, Walter. *A History of Zionism*. New York: Schocken, 2003.

Mendelsohn, Ezra. *On Modern Jewish Politics*. New York: Oxford University Press, 1993.

Myers, David. *Re-inventing the Jewish Past. European Jewish Intellectuals and the Zionist Return to History*. New York: Oxford University Press, 1995.

Sachar, Howard M. *A History of Israel*, 3rd ed., rev. and updated. New York: Knopf, 2007.

Segev, Tom. *One Palestine, Complete: Jews and Arabs under the British Mandate*. London: Little Brown, 2000.

Shimoni, Gideon. *The Zionist Ideology*. Hanover, NH: University Press of New England [for] Brandeis University Press, 1995.

Vital, David. *The Origins of Zionism*. Oxford: Clarendon Press, 1975.

———. *Zionism. The Formative Years*. Oxford: Clarendon Press, 1982.

Wasserstein, Bernard. *Divided Jerusalem: The Struggle for the Holy City*. New Haven, CT: Yale University Press, 2001.

Zerubavel, Yael. *Recovered Roots. Collective Memory and the Making of Israeli National Tradition*. Chicago: University of Chicago Press, 1995.

Zipperstein, Steven. *Elusive Prophet. Ahad Ha-Am and the Origins of Zionism*. Berkeley, CA: University of California Press, 1993.

Picture Credits

Page xvi, courtesy of the Library of the Jewish Theological Seminary of America, New York. Page 4, akg-images / Erich Lessing. Page 5, akg-images. Page 12, Victory stela of Merenptah (c. 1236–1217 BC) known as the Israel Stela, from the Mortuary Temple of Merenptah, Thebes, New Kingdom, 1213–1203 BC (granite) by Egyptian 19th Dynasty (c. 1297–1185 BC). Egyptian National Museum, Cairo, Egypt / Giraudon / The Bridgeman Art Library. Page 12, akg-images / Erich Lessing. Page 13 (upper and lower), akg-images / Erich Lessing. Page 14, the British Library, Sloane MS 3173, f. 27r. Page 18, the National Museum of Bosnia and Herzegovina, Sarajevo. Page 23, Israel Department of Antiquities and Museums. Page 26, dpa-Bildarchiv. Page 28, akg-images / Suzanne Held. Page 30, Klau Library, Cincinnati. Hebrew Union College–Jewish Institute of Religion. Page 35, courtesy of the Library of the Jewish Theological Seminary of America, Mic. 8270. Page 37, Israel Antiquities Authority, Jerusalem. Page 38, akg-images. Page 41, Peter Palm. Page 45, akg-images / Erich Lessing. Page 52, akg-images / Erich Lessing. Page 54, akg-images / British Library. Page 61, akg-images. Page 66, akg-images. Page 67, Nationalmuseum Damaskus/ Art Resource, NY. Page 68, MS. Hunt 448, fol. 100a. Bodleian Library, University of Oxford. Page 73, akg-images / British Library. Page 75, akg-images / Erich Lessing. Page 82, akg-images / British Library. Page 87, Staatsbibliothek Preussischer Kulturbesitz, Orientabteilung. Page 89, akg-images. Page 91, © Nour Foundation. Courtesy Khalili Family Trust. JLZ 270 12/17, The Nasser D. Khalili Collection of Islamic Art, London. Photo: Ch. Phillips, Sci. 158. Page 94, the Israel Museum, Jerusalem. Pages 102 and 103, Groeningemusuem Brügge. Page 105, akg-images. Page 108, Staats- und Universitätsbiblioth ek

Hamburg Cod. Hebr. 37. Page 109, Peter Palm. Page 112, Hessisches Landesmuseum, Darmstadt / bpk. Page 113, British Library/Art Archive. Page 116, akg-images / British Library. Page 121, akg-images / Bildarchiv Steffens. Page 125, Peter Palm. Page 127, akg-images. Page 136, courtesy of the Library of the Jewish Theological Seminary of America, New York. Page 141, Bibliothèque Nationale de France. Page 146, courtesy of the Library of the Jewish Theological Seminary of America, New York. Page 150, Harvard College Library. Page 156, Nationalmuseum Warschau, Collections of the Department of Scientific Documentation and the Department of Ancient Graphics. Page 163, collection of Mrs. Maurice Sternberg. Page 166, Emilie G. L. Schrijver / Falk Wiesemann (Hg.): Die Van-Geldern-Haggadah and Heinrich Heines "Der Rabbi von Bacherach," Verlag Brandstätter, Wien 1997. Page 170, Universitätsbibliothek Johann Christian Senckenberg Frankfurt am Main. Page 175, from terracotta group Bockhandel, Stadtmuseum Stockach. © Stadt Stockach. Page 180, Jüdisches Museum, Prague; Photo: Dana Cabanová. Page 184, akg-images. Page 188, Harvard College Library. Page 192, Musées de la ville de Paris © SPADEM. Page 195, The Jewish Museum, New York, gift of Mr. and Mrs. Richard D. Levy /bpk. Page 197, akg-images. Page 205, bpk. Page 208, Heb 4905.93*, Houghton Library, Harvard University. Page 213, Peter Palm. Page 218, Montana Historical Society, Research Center Photograph Archives, Helena. Page 219, Levi Strauss & Co. Archives, San Francisco. Page 222, Harvard College Library. Page 226, Peter Palm. Page 231, Tel Aviv Museum of Art. Page 241, The Jewish Museum, New York, gift of Lester S. Klein / Scala, Florenz. Page 246, Zev Radovan, Jerusalem (Zev Radovan's Bible Land Pictures). Page 250, Colver Pictures, Inc., New York. Page 251, Brown Brothers, Sterling, PA. Page 254, Library of Congress. Page 259, akg-images. Page 264, picture-alliance © Delius / Leemage. Page 270, the Gross Family Collection, Tel Aviv. Page 272, courtesy of the Library of the Jewish Theological Seminary of America, New York. Page 276, akg-images / Erich Lessing. Page 282, Images of Asia. Page 286, The Jewish Museum, New York, gift of Leonard and Phyllis Greenberg. Photo: John Parnell. © The Jewish Museum / Art Resource / Scala Florenz. Page 289, Städtische Galerie im Lenbachhaus, Munich. Page 303, Scala, Florenz. Page 306, akg-images © VG Bild-Kunst, Bonn 2008. Page 315 (upper), Rubin Museum, Israel. Page 315 (lower), The Hebrew Univeristy of Jerusalem. Page 326, Charlotte Salomon Foundation, Joods Historisch Museum, Amsterdam. Page 329, Staatliche Galerie Moritzburg Halle, Landeskunstmuseum Sachsen-Anhalt. Photo: Reinhard Hentz, Halle © VG Bild-Kunst, Bonn 2008. Page 334, akg-images, © VG Bild-Kunst, Bonn 2008. Page 342, Helga Weissová. Page 348, Harvard College Library. Page 352, The Ghetto Fighters' House in Memory of Itzhak Ketznelson, Kibbutz Lohamei Haghetaot. Page 353, akg-images. Page 358, © Bettmann/CORBIS. Page 370, Paramount Pictures. Page 371, Associated Press / Zavi Cohen. Page 375, akg-images. Endpapers courtesy of the Library of the Jewish Theological Seminary of America, New York.

Index of Names

This index contains the names of people, Biblical figures, dynasties, ethnic and religious groups, and organizations. Italicized page numbers refer to captions for illustrations.

Index of Place Names

This index contains the names of cities, countries, and regions.
Italicized page numbers refer to captions for illustrations.

A Hebrew map was published for the first time in a Haggadah printed in Amsterdam in 1698. The above illustration is taken from the reprint of 1712. The map of the Holy Land is oriented toward the east. The Nile delta can be seen at the bottom right. The Jordan runs horizontally from left to right. The map mentions events and symbols from the history of the people of Israel, like a table listing 41 stations of the exodus from Egypt and the ship on which the prophet Jonah tried to flee. The eagle refers to Exodus, Chapter 19, Verse 4: "Ye have seen . . . how I bore you on eagles' wings." Cows and beehives, way to the left on the veranda of the house, symbolize milk and honey—and thereby the Promised Land.